D0554265

NOTHING
BUT THE
TRUTH

CRITICAL AMERICA

Richard Delgado and Jean Stefancic
GENERAL EDITORS

STEVEN LUBET

NOTHING
BUT THE
TRUTH

Why Trial Lawyers Don't, Can't, and
Shouldn't Have to Tell the Whole Truth

NEW YORK UNIVERSITY PRESS
New York and London

NEW YORK UNIVERSITY PRESS
New York and London

Library of Congress Cataloging-in-Publication Data
Lubet, Steven.
Nothing but the truth : why trial lawyers don't, can't, and shouldn't
have to tell the whole truth / Steven Lubet.
p.   cm. — (Critical America)
Includes index.
ISBN 0-8147-5173-3 (cloth : alk. paper)
1. Law—United States. 2. Trial practice—United States.
3. Truthfulness and falsehood.   I. Title. II. Series.
KF384.Z9 L83 2001
347.73'75—dc21   00-011952

To Natan Isaac and Sarah Nomi

CONTENTS

ACKNOWLEDGMENTS

I am grateful to the following people for their comments, advice, and other input:

Kathy Abrams, Frank Adams, Ann Althouse, Adnan Arain, Mary Becker, Bruce Boyer, Christopher Bracey, Robert Burns, Paul Carrington, Louis DeCaro, Richard Delgado, Kathryn Doi, Paul Finkelman, Nabil Foster, Monroe Freedman, Despina Papazoglou Gimbel, Alan Gless, Philip Hamburger, Alicia Hawley, Timothy Hoff, Wythe Holt, David Kertzer, Jane Larson, Niko Pfund, Jeffrey Rice, Dorothy Roberts, Alex Rose, James Simeri, Rayman Solomon, William Springer, Jean Stefancic, Piper Taggert, Timothy Terrell, Paulette Van Zant, Marianne Wesson, David Winters, faculty workshop participants at Northwestern University, the University of Alabama, the University of Iowa, and the University of Colorado, and the students in my Lawyer-Storyteller seminar at the Northwestern University School of Law.

I am particularly indebted to Morgan Cloud (who told me why I should write this book), Linda Lipton (who showed me how to make it all fit together), and Fred Lubet (who ensured that it would all make sense).

And of course, the habitues of the Unicorn Roundtable left their own indelible stamp on this endeavor, whether they admit it or not.

This project received generous support from the Northwestern University School of Law Class of 1962 Reunion Gift Fund, which also resulted in the publication of the following articles: "The Forgotten Trial of Wyatt Earp," 72 *Colorado Law Review* ___ (2001); "John Brown's Trial," 52 *Alabama Law Review* ___ (2001); "The Man Who Shot Liberty Valance: Truth or Justice in the Old West," 48 *UCLA Law Review* ___ (2000); "Murder in the Streets of Tombstone: A Legendary Theory of the

Case," 27 *Litigation* 35 (2000); "Rumpled Truth on Trial," 94 *Northwestern University Law Review* 627 (2000); "Conflict of Interest at the O.K. Corral," 3 *The Green Bag* 2d 141 (2000); "Reconstructing Atticus Finch," 97 *Michigan Law Review* 1339 (1999); "Judicial Kidnaping, Then and Now: The Case of Edgardo Mortara," 93 *Northwestern University Law Review* 961 (1999); "Moral Adventures in Narrative Lawyering," 2 *The Green Bag* 2d 145 (1999).

STORYTELLING LAWYERS

The best trial lawyers are storytellers. They take the raw and disjointed observations of witnesses and transform them into coherent and persuasive narratives. They develop compelling theories and artful themes, all the better to advance a client's cause, whatever it might happen to be. "Give me the facts," says the attorney, "and I will turn them into the best possible case."

The popular image is that lawyers, and trial lawyers in particular, are cunning deceivers and misleaders, flimflam artists who use sly rhetorical skills to bamboozle witnesses, turning night into day. In this conception, lawyers tell stories only in order to seduce and beguile the hapless jurors who fall prey to the advocate's tricks. Critics believe that the system would be better and more honest if the witnesses were simply asked to speak, without the distorting impact of lawyers' involvement.

But that view is wrong. As the following chapters—each one describing the events of a trial—will show, lawyers often use the techniques of narrative construction to enhance the truth, not to hide it. A fully developed and well-conceived "trial story" may result in an account that is actually "truer" in many respects than the client's uncounseled version of events, even though the narrative was adroitly structured with courtroom victory in mind.

Trial lawyers, the legal profession's ultimate positivists, tell stories because that is what works. There is nothing intrinsically valuable about storytelling at trial, other than the fact that a logical, interesting, linear narrative has proven to be the most successful way to persuade the fact finder. If some other method worked better—opera singing, gymnastic floor exercise, emotive grunting—lawyers would adopt that approach instead.

Storytelling, however, cannot be defended merely because it is an effective device. That would justify the uncharitable, though extremely popular and certainly not irrational, view that attorneys are literary mercenaries, paid to concoct whatever tale a gullible jury is most likely to accept.

In fact, the lawyer's art—shaping disparate statements into a single meaningful account—is not an unprincipled act of creating useful fiction. It is just the opposite. A conscientious attorney fashions a story not to hide or distort the truth, but rather to enable a client to come closer to the truth. Language is an inherently awkward and indefinite instrument for conveying exact meaning, but precision is required in courts of law. The lawyer's storytelling seeks to employ language in the way that best communicates the client's case, making sure that the client actually gets to say what she really means. Without the lawyer's storytelling a client would be nearly incapable of accurately informing the judge or jury, cast adrift in a sea of ambiguity, approximation, and imprecision.

Any tool can be misused. Some lawyers spin clever fictions to assist in client fraud, just as other practitioners might devote their particular talents—computer programming, feats of strength, diplomacy, poetry—to either honorable or evil purposes. But as a baseline for lawyers, and excepting the out-and-out swindlers and thieves, storytelling is a noble pursuit.

There are three structural devices that add great power to the stories of trial lawyers: theory, theme, and frame.

A "theory of the case" explains what happened. It is a concise account of the facts and law, leading directly and rationally to the conclusion that the lawyer's client should win the case. In essence, a theory completes the sentence, "We win because. . . ." In the impeachment trial of President Clinton, for example, one aspect of the defense theory was that the president's words, even though misleading, had been "legally accurate."

A theory of the case provides the necessary bridge between the potential drama of the story and the requirements of the law. A winning case theory has internal logical force, explaining why the discrete facts, however interesting (or boring) they may be, actually add up to "proof" that the attorney's client is right. Popular imagination notwithstanding, a trial is truly something more than a soap opera or a sporting match. Most of all, a trial is a contest of ideas, a process in which the law is applied to the facts. And unless that link is supplied by a comprehensive theory of the case, even the most rip-roaringly exciting story may come to nothing when the verdict is returned.

Just as a case theory rests on logic, a trial theme appeals to moral force. Rather than explain why a particular verdict is dictated by the facts and the law, a theme shows why it *should* be entered, why it is the *right* thing to do. An effective theme allows the judge or jury to believe in the underlying righteousness of the verdict.

The most compelling themes invoke shared values and civic virtues— honor, duty, friendship, commitment. In a simple contract case, for example, the lawyer might say something like, "This is a case about keeping promises." In a products liability case the plaintiff's theme might be an accusation of "profits over people." Such themes can be forceful as rhetorical devices, though neither has any independent legal weight. Of course it is important to keep promises, but that doesn't mean that this particular contract was broken. And everyone is in favor of safety.

In the Clinton impeachment the House managers constantly returned to a refrain invoking "the rule of law." This was a moral appeal rather than a legal or factual argument. The president either did or did not commit perjury, which either was or was not an impeachable offense. Strictly speaking, the rule of law was never an issue in the proceeding; there is no contrary side to that particular argument. In another sense, however, the rule of law had everything to do with it, since the senators could not ignore the greater social and historical implications of their decision. A jury trial works the same way. A trial theme underscores the theory of the case by showing why the desired verdict is both decent and good—as well as legally necessary.

Perhaps even more important than theory and theme is the "story frame."

The trial process attempts to re-create the past, but it is an imperfect process at best. Witnesses may testify about what they saw and did.

Documents and physical objects may be placed in evidence. Experts may provide relevant opinions and conclusions. In the end, however, there is an insurmountable barrier. The fact finder—judge or juror—was not at the scene of the events. Not having been there, she cannot actually know what happened. Rather, she must ultimately deduce or suppose what happened, using not only the evidence presented but also her judgment, interpretation, common sense, and other insights. This is an inevitable feature of historical fact finding—the use of one's experience and intuitions to deduce what *must have happened.*

The trial evidence allows a juror to begin creating a mental image of the events, people, locations, objects, and transactions in question. That image, however, will necessarily be incomplete, since it is beyond human capacity to describe—or absorb—all the millions of discrete details that comprise everyday life. The missing details, and inferences drawn from them, will be filled in, however, by the juror's memory and imagination. If the accident occurred on a dark road, the juror will imagine or recall a particular dark road, filling in details consistent with that image.

That act of imagination or vision constitutes a story frame, the context in which the fact finder determines what *must have happened* in the circumstances described by the evidence. In the O. J. Simpson case, for example, the prosecution labored hard to create what might be called a "domestic violence" frame. At the very outset of the trial, prosecutors introduced evidence of Simpson's ill treatment of his wife, his past threats, and her fear of him. The purpose of this evidence was to support the conclusion that given his jealousy, anger, and violent nature, he *must have been* the murderer. In contrast, the defense developed a counterstory, the "police prejudice" frame, intended to advance the theory that the officers *must have* contrived or mishandled the DNA and other evidence against Simpson.

Neither case had the benefit of direct evidence, which increased the importance of the competing frames. There were no eyewitnesses to the murder, nor was there any direct testimony that police officers had indeed monkeyed with the evidence. Instead, the jurors were asked to reach a conclusion based on an accumulation of circumstances, in light of their own judgment and past experiences. As everyone knows, the "police prejudice" frame proved convincing and Simpson was acquitted.

The story frame may well be the trial lawyer's most powerful rhetorical tool, because of its extraordinary effectiveness in the battle for the fact finder's imagination. Once a juror begins to envision events in a certain context, new information will tend to be evaluated in that same context. A thought experiment makes this point more evident.

Imagine that the defendant in a criminal case is known to be a street gang member. An image immediately springs to mind. He slouches, he is rude, he is disrespectful of the law and susceptible to peer pressure. Even if jurors do not prejudge his guilt, they will probably regard him poorly and assume that they know the answers to many questions about him. How does he dress? What sort of hours does he keep? How much does he care about school? What does he do when he hangs out with his pals? How honest is he? Does he value the rights and property of others? The answers—or at least the suppositions—are pretty obvious if the defendant is a known gang banger. The jurors will tend to look at the case in a "street gang" sort of way.

But now suppose that the defendant belongs to a youth club or a neighborhood association. Suddenly the image changes. He is more clean-cut, more responsible, more diligent in school, less aggressive toward strangers. His clothing, attitudes, and pastimes will all be imagined differently, simply because of the introductory description. The initial image dictates, or at least suggests, a variety of assumptions about the defendant's attitude, conduct, and character. Jurors will begin with a different outlook if they approach the case from a "youth club" perspective.

These assumptions are not immutable. They can be overcome or dispelled by the evidence. But a lawyer who can engage (and maintain) the jury's imagination will obviously start with a significant advantage. That is the power of story framing.

The development of a trial story is a creative process. The lawyer must imagine a series of alternate approaches, evaluating each one for coherence, simplicity, and persuasiveness. But take heart. An attorney is not free to choose a story simply because it will be effective. Trials are not merely confrontations between antagonistic fantasies. There is no room for lying. The theories, themes, and frames must be composed of truth.

Surveying all the available facts, counsel has to decide what to leave in and what to leave out. The story will be fashioned in equal parts through emphasis on the favorable details and elision of the nasty ones.

This means, of course, that trial lawyers do not tell the whole truth. Each side trumpets those facets of the truth that support its case, while doing everything legally possible to obscure or minimize that which is inconvenient or damaging. Is that process inherently cynical or corrupt, as critics contend? Or can it be redeemed, as lawyers insist?

The answer is that selectivity is inevitable. It is impossible to tell the whole truth, since life and experience are boundless and therefore indescribable. Every story will omit more than it includes. In the time-limited context of a trial, especially in the days of the famously vanishing Generation X attention span, streamlining is essential. As Marianne Wesson puts it, "Any witness who swears to tell the whole truth has just told his first lie."[1]

And there is more to it than that. The whole truth may be metaphysically honest, but nonetheless misleading and untrustworthy. For example, a criminal defendant might belong to a street gang, but still be innocent of the crime. Understanding what we do about story framing (and prejudice), are not justice and fairness actually served by excluding that feature of the whole truth? An abridgement, in fact, may be more accurate, as it removes distractions and misleading complications. The whole truth, in fact, may create a false impression.

Alas, one side's false impression is bound to be the other side's gospel, but that is inherent in the human condition—a phenomenon long predating the practice of law. In response, we have devised an adversary system designed to sort out competing claims to accuracy and justice.

For lawyers, then, virtue lies in presenting "nothing but the truth." This point can be illustrated—surprise!—through storytelling. The following chapters present a series of cases, some real and some fictional, some intricate and some straightforward. Each chapter explores the challenges, benefits, and complexities involved in expressing the truth at trial.

Although this is a book about lawyering, the emphasis in each chapter is on the story itself, rather than on the advocacy techniques. Trials occur in rich contexts, thick with facts, personalities, inferences, and implications. A thorough appreciation of the circumstances is essential to an understanding of the attorney's work. The more we know about the background of a case, the better we can understand the choices confronting the lawyers and other participants. And the more we can immerse ourselves in the details, the better we can recognize the challenges inherent in extracting a purposeful account of the truth from what is ultimately an unsettled and equivocal reality.

Perhaps the deepest lesson in this book is about witnesses rather than lawyers. Perceptions can be misleading. Memory is selective, indefinite, and undependable. Motives, though ever present, may be obscured and unrecognizable. Even the people who observe an event seldom know what really happened, much less are they able to recall and describe it with unfailing precision. A courtroom reconstruction, alas, is at best an approximation, a necessary—but still audacious—effort to extract a reliable conclusion from the ineffable secrets of past events.

Several of the chapters, therefore, may at first seem to be more about history than advocacy. But trials do not occur in a vacuum. Even simple cases, and certainly momentous ones, are strongly influenced by the times in which they take place. An obvious and well known illustration may be seen in the trial of O. J. Simpson. No aspect of that case, including the strategic and tactical decisions of the lawyers, can be truly understood without a thorough knowledge of southern California at the end of the twentieth century. Every aspect of the trial—from jury selection to cross-examination to final argument—was played out against a backdrop of race, celebrity, sex, drugs, domestic violence, police-community relations and general Los Angeles culture. To analyze F. Lee Bailey's cross-examination of Detective Mark Fuhrman, for example, one would have to appreciate the history of conflict between the Los Angeles Police Department and the African American community.

We begin with "Biff and Me," which introduces the general method of story reconstruction. Faced with the task of developing a legally effective narrative from a client's disorganized and self-interested account, a lawyer must determine which facts are relevant (and helpful) and which are distractions (or worse). Based on a real incident, the Biff story imagines a series of conversations between advocate and client, aimed at both clarifying the underlying events and interpreting them in a way that can frame a successful lawsuit.

One challenge for the lawyer is to marshal the facts within a legal context. The law has its own requirements, which may or may not be evident to a layperson. The attorney's task is to recognize and accommodate these constraints. In the Biff story, for instance, the lawyer must explain to the client that not all threats, no matter how aggressively boorish, rise to the level of a legally actionable assault. This is the mundane stuff of daily lawyering. With the applicable statute as a framework, the attorney explores the facts to see whether the client "has a case." Predictably, it turns out that what is important to the client may not be so important to the law. In other words, the lawyer must winnow "the whole truth" into a legally meaningful account that is composed of "nothing but the truth."

That same problem arises in the following chapter, the case of Edgardo Mortara, in far more tragic circumstances. In 1858 in the Italian city of Bologna, a six-year-old Jewish child was removed from his parents by the papal police. Edgardo Mortara had been secretly baptized some years earlier, and canon law therefore held that he could not be raised as a Jew. He was taken to the Vatican, where he was "adopted" by Pope Pius IX. His parents, Salomone and Marianna, engaged a lawyer to help them regain custody of their son. But, of course, their advocate had to operate within the extraordinary confines of the Roman Catholic Church's legal system. At every turn, he had to circumscribe and limit his arguments, omitting the facts most important to his clients, in a desperate effort to persuade the Pope himself to reverse his earlier decision.

To be sure, there can be no criticism of a lawyer who must operate in a system where certain truths are simply forbidden to be told. But what of the lawyer who is complicit in a client's own distortions, perhaps outright lies? That issue must be confronted in the chapter on John Brown, who gave his life in the struggle against slavery. On trial for murder and treason following the raid on Harpers Ferry, John Brown virtually reinvented himself, disavowing his violent and insurrectionary goals while claiming to have sought nothing more than the bloodless rescue of slaves. His statements at trial were palpably false, but his goal was noble—to rally the forces of abolition by becoming an admirable martyr to the cause. But may his counsel assist him in that endeavor?

The next chapter takes up the concepts of case theory and story framing while considering the forgotten trial of Wyatt Earp. Though he is remembered today as a heroic lawman, Wyatt Earp (along with his two brothers and Doc Holliday) was actually charged with murder following the legendary gunfight at the O.K. Corral. The ensuing trial lasted for nearly a month, and at times the evidence against the defendants seemed nearly overwhelming. Nonetheless, Wyatt and his colleagues were exonerated, largely because of the frontier context in which the case was decided. Defense counsel, by presenting some facts and eliding others, succeeded in framing the case as a contest between orderly society and near anarchy, while the prosecution failed to present a coherent counternarrative that might have allowed the judge to rule in its favor.

Without giving away the surprise ending to the next story, suffice it to say that the Man Who Shot Liberty Valance must confront that same antagonism between law and lawlessness. Here, the defendant has a secret that might lead to his acquittal, but perhaps at the cost of higher justice. How much should he explain to his lawyer? And how should his lawyer proceed?

Atticus Finch, on the other hand, is universally revered as a lawyer who always knew how to proceed. Atticus is the very symbol of truth and justice, standing against bigotry even at grave risk to professional success and personal safety. In 1930s Maycomb, Alabama, Atticus alone was willing to tell the truth about Tom Robinson, a black man falsely accused of raping a white woman. But what if Tom Robinson had actually been guilty of the crime? What if Atticus's compelling defense had been an artful contrivance rather than "the truth"? Would he still be a hero?

Finally, we come to the trial of Sheila McGough, which serves as the overall conclusion to this book. According to the journalist Janet Malcolm, Sheila McGough was convicted of larceny and sentenced to prison simply because she insisted on telling the whole truth. By infusing her defense with a numbing welter of shapeless details, McGough deprived her attorneys of the ability effectively to make her case. In contrast, Malcolm believes that the prosecution used bits and pieces of the truth to construct an essentially misleading narrative, leading to an unjust result. But is that really what happened? Was the case truly a clash between "the whole truth" and selective storytelling? Must naive honesty necessarily fall prey to sly advocacy? Or is there another explanation for McGough's conviction?

The answers to those questions will either validate or indict the central premise of this book, which is that purposive storytelling brings a positive ethical value to the adversary system.

NOTE

1. Marianne Wesson, *A Novelist's Perspective*, DePaul L. Rev. (forthcoming 2000).

CHAPTER ONE

BIFF AND ME

Stories That Are Truer Than True

Truth and accuracy are not the same thing. A lawyer's client may tell a story that is entirely sincere but nonetheless imprecise and unreliable. Witness accounts are often clouded by poor memory, self-interest, preconception, partiality, wishful thinking, reticence, and unwarranted conclusions about the law. In shaping a case, the lawyer has to cut through the client's misperceptions in order to arrive at a more lucid understanding of the relationship between the facts and the law.

Together, the lawyer and client may reexamine the client's own recollections and characterizations of events. Perhaps the client forgot something, or misunderstood something, or failed to comprehend the significance of one incident or another. To be sure, unscrupulous lawyers may use this process as an opportunity to put words in the client's mouth, simply in order to improve the story. But decent, ethical lawyers also review facts with their clients, helping them remember and correctly interpret the underlying occurrence.

The following account is completely true, presented here without exaggeration. Of course, I am reporting it from my perspective because that is the only one I know. There may be another side that is perfectly reasonable and plausible (although I doubt it). My biases aside, this story illustrates the ways that thoughtful counseling may actually result in a story that is "truer than true."

Arriving an hour early for my morning flight out of O'Hare, I picked up my boarding pass and looked for a place to read. There were no available seats immediately adjacent to my gate, so I headed for the circular waiting area in the middle of the concourse. I chose an empty seat at the end of an aisle. The seat next to me was also vacant, though covered with the loose sections of several newspapers. Two seats over, a man was sitting with his arms folded. I have since come to think of him as "Biff."

I sat down and dug a book out of my briefcase. My neighbor leaned over and said, "Someone was sitting there."

Not quite understanding what he meant, I looked around for the usual indicators that a seat is occupied. Seeing no bags or jackets, I turned my head to the speaker to ask what he meant.

Before I could make a reply, however, he said, "I'm telling you that my father is sitting there . . ."

Realizing what he meant, I started to pack up my briefcase so that I could move. But Biff continued talking, now in a highly agitated tone.

". . . and he's coming back." The last word was sharp.

As I pulled the zipper on my briefcase, I started to tell him that I would be gone in a moment. "Hold on a minute, mister."

Biff lost his temper before I could finish. Barely controlling himself, he angrily hissed, "Don't piss me off!"

Stunned at the threat of violence over so trivial a matter, I quickly grabbed my stuff and moved to another part of the waiting area.

I am slight, short, bespectacled, and middle-aged. Biff was far taller, much stockier, and a good fifteen years younger. Words on paper cannot begin to convey his menacing manner as he used his voice and size to intimidate me. In the otherwise orderly airport terminal, it was alarming to realize that he was actually ready to hit me if I didn't get out of that seat quickly enough to suit him. Biff left absolutely no doubt that he was threatening me with violence, at least for the purpose of frightening me into moving faster. And, of course, it worked. (Who knows whether "airport anger" may someday replace "road rage" as the latest deadly emblem of social degradation?)

The rational response to Biff's outburst was to move as far away as possible, doing my best to avoid him in the future—let's call it defensive seating. But for the purpose of story development, assume instead that my own anger, frustration, and petulance continued to mount even after I was out of harm's way. Imagine that I returned home determined to get even.

Since I lack the physique or weaponry to do the job personally, my best alternative would be to swear out a misdemeanor complaint. Being cautious, I would probably begin by consulting my own lawyer, just to make sure that I had a case. After hearing the facts, my attorney would no doubt tell me the definition of assault in Illinois: "A person commits an assault when, without lawful authority, he engages in conduct which places another in reasonable apprehension of receiving a battery."[1]

Then we would talk about how I might go about proving that I had been assaulted.[2] The first few conclusions are fairly obvious. Biff certainly acted without lawful authority and I was no doubt in apprehension of receiving a battery. (It's embarrassing to admit, but my hands were shaking. I felt scared and I probably looked scared, too.)

But now comes the hard part. Was my apprehension reasonable, or was I just overreacting? The answer to the question makes the difference between a misdemeanor and an insult, between a good case and a bad case. Let's think about how the interview might proceed:

Attorney: What has made you so angry that you want to swear out a complaint?

Client: I didn't do anything to provoke this guy, and suddenly he was threatening to hit me.

Attorney: Why do you think that he was going to hit you?

Client: Because he threatened me.

Attorney: What made it a threat?

Client: It was obviously a threat; he was trying to scare me with his words and voice.

Attorney: How can you be sure about what he was trying to do?

Client: It was obvious.

And it was obvious, dammit. It was completely clear that he was using his size and aggressiveness to frighten me into doing what he wanted. And it was unnecessary, too, since I was happy to move as soon as I understood the situation.

The law, however, does not convict people, or even take away their money, based on assertions of obviousness. The law, for very good reasons, will act only on the basis of proven facts. The problem for me, as a client, is that I don't know intuitively how to translate my impressions into proof. That is where my lawyer comes in. How can I tell my story in a way that will be meaningful and persuasive under the law? My lawyer will have to take me through the story again.

Attorney: Why do you think that he was going to hit you?
Client: Because he threatened me.
Attorney: Let's go one step at a time. Why didn't you move when he first spoke to you?
Client: He said someone "*was* sitting there," which didn't make any sense to me, so I looked around to see if anybody seemed to be coming back.
Attorney: Did you refuse to move or say anything else?
Client: No, I just tried to figure out what he meant.
Attorney: Then he told you about his father?
Client: Right, so I began gathering my stuff, but I guess I wasn't doing it fast enough.
Attorney: Why do you say that?
Client: Because that's when he raised his voice at me.
Attorney: What did he say and how did he say it?
Client: He said, "And he's coming back." But it was really the angry tone in his voice that upset me.
Attorney: What do you mean by "angry tone"?
Client: Well, I really can't describe it any better. You just know when someone is angry.
Attorney: Let's continue, then. What happened next?
Client: I said, "Hold on a minute, mister."
Attorney: Why did you say that?
Client: Because I had to gather my stuff up in order to move.
Attorney: It sounds like you were a little annoyed.
Client: I was a little annoyed. He was rushing me for no reason.
Attorney: Then what happened?
Client: That's when he threatened me.

Attorney: I think we need to do this part step by step. What did he say, exactly?

Client: He said, "Don't piss me off."

Attorney: What was his tone of voice?

Client: Angry and loud.

Attorney: Did he do anything with his hands?

Client: Yes, he made a fist.

Attorney: Did he move his fist?

Client: He clenched it and sort of shook it a little.

Attorney: Did he swing it or put it in your face?

Client: No.

Attorney: Did he move his body?

Client: He raised himself up in his seat.

Attorney: Did he stand up?

Client: No. He just lifted his backside a little bit off the chair and leaned over.

Attorney: Which way did he lean?

Client: He leaned toward me.

Attorney: Was his fist still clenched when he leaned toward you?

Client: Yes.

Attorney: Did he clench it while he was leaning?

Client: Yes.

Attorney: Did he say, "Don't piss me off" while he was leaning toward you with his fist clenched?

Client: Yes.

Attorney: Did he ever leave his seat?

Client: I don't think so.

Attorney: Did you wait around to see whether he was going to leave his seat?

Client: No, I got up and left as quickly as I could.

Attorney: How long did all of this last?

Client: Maybe a minute; not much longer.

Attorney: Are you certain he was threatening you?

Client: Absolutely. Do you think we have a case?

Attorney: I believe that you felt threatened and I think it was reasonable. We might have a case.

Client: Why wouldn't we have a case?
Attorney: It depends on the other side of the story.

You can see from my lawyer's questions that she is starting to think in terms of developing a persuasive trial story. My initial, self-generated account was adequate to explain my reason for seeking counsel, but it left too much unsaid to be useful in court. I began with an impressionistic, conclusory narrative about a perceived threat. I believe it is true. I want to tell it truthfully, but also meaningfully and persuasively. That is where my lawyer steps in.

There is more to story construction, however, than simply the addition of important details. A persuasive story will need to have

[A]ll, or most, of the following characteristics: (1) it is told about people who have reasons for the way they act; (2) it accounts for or explains all of the known or undeniable facts; (3) it is told by credible witnesses; (4) it is supported by details; (5) it accords with common sense and contains no implausible elements; and (6) it is organized in a way that makes each succeeding fact increasingly more likely.[3]

For present purposes, let us focus on the first characteristic. To succeed at trial, my case will need to include the reasons for the way the participants acted. Of course, there were only two participants, Biff and myself, and I have already explained to counsel my own reasons for sitting, pausing, and eventually moving. But that leaves a gap.

Why was Biff so aggressive? Of course, I cannot look into Biff's mind to see what actually prompted him to behave as he did. And, strictly speaking, Biff's motive would not actually be essential to my case. I only need to prove that he acted in a certain way, placing me in reasonable apprehension of receiving a battery. But my case will be stronger, more believable, if I can supply a plausible reason for Biff's aggression. After all, everyone has been in an airport at some time or another, but almost no one has ever been assaulted over an empty seat. So in many ways my story suggests a counterintuitive scenario. To justify a verdict, the fact finder will probably want to know why Biff reacted in such an unusual fashion.

Imagine a continued interview with my lawyer:

Attorney: Can you think of any reason why he might have reacted so violently?
Client: He's probably an anti-intellectual who loves to attack university professors.
Attorney: That seems unlikely. Any other possibilities?
Client: Maybe he is simply a psychopath?
Attorney: I suppose that's possible. Did you see him threaten anyone else or act in any other irrational fashion?
Client: No, I didn't. Say, doesn't crack cocaine make people violent?
Attorney: It does, but there's the same drawback as with the psychopath theory.
Client: Well, the real problem seems to be that his actions were just inexplicable. No one reacts that way!
Attorney: If "no one" reacts that way, then we'll have a tough time convincing the jury that he reacted that way. Get it? We have to tell them why someone—meaning Biff—really did react that way.

And now it is time for a little bit of lawyering. The client came to the meeting believing that his own actions were wholly reasonable and that Biff was entirely and exclusively to blame. In the case of violent threats, however, the law does not impose such a strict burden on would-be plaintiffs or complainants. In this case, I can prevail in court *even if I was inconsiderate or rude* so long as Biff's response was disproportionate or unreasonable. In other words, you are not allowed to threaten violence simply because someone has been discourteous. With that in mind, let us return to the story-framing interview.

Attorney: Do you think Biff might have felt that you were disrespecting him?
Client: I suppose it's possible. I didn't really understand what he was asking until the second or third time he said it.
Attorney: It would be rude, don't you think, to refuse to give the seat back to Biff's father?
Client: Yes, that would be really wrong. But that's not what I did.

Attorney: Well, let's try to look at it from Biff's angle, just for a moment. He did ask you three times before you moved?

Client: Not really, but I guess he could have seen it that way. Still, there was no reason for him to threaten me with his fist.

Attorney: Exactly. He might have had a reason to be annoyed, but not to become violent. That's your best case.

And now the story has taken shape. I sat down in what appeared to be an empty seat. Biff wanted me to move, but he didn't make himself very well understood. I tried to respond, but in the minute or so it took me to figure out what he meant, Biff had become livid. I probably, though unintentionally, made things worse when I said, "Hold on a minute, mister," which he might have mistaken as a refusal to move. But his reaction was out of all proportion to anything I did. He raised his voice, began to lift himself from his seat, leaned toward me, and threatened me with a clenched fist.

Of course, there will be more to the trial story than the simple outline above. My lawyer will want to fill in more details and she will definitely need to emphasize how quickly everything happened. I will also need to explain exactly why I believed that I was in "reasonable apprehension of receiving a battery." And if we file a civil case I will also have to say something about damages. Finally, my lawyer will also want to develop a theme, a shorthand introduction to the case that invokes conscience or moral force. A few possibilities spring immediately to mind. Maybe "You can't solve your problems with your fists." Counsel will no doubt come up with a better theme by the time the case gets to trial.

The most important thing about my lawyer's trial story, however, is that it is absolutely faithful to the events as I experienced them. Counsel has made my case stronger and more compelling, but not at any cost to the truth. That is, she has fulfilled the client-centered ethical obligations of the advocate as well as the system-centered duties of an officer of the court.[4]

Imagine now that my lawyer decided that the case was worth pursuing. Biff has been charged with misdemeanor assault, or perhaps served with a civil summons.[5] In either case, his first step would also be to consult a lawyer. Biff's story, we can certainly assume, will not be the same as mine. As he tells it he is no doubt entirely innocent of any wrongdoing, and I am an overwrought seat stealer.

Let us consider the initial conversation between Biff and his newly retained lawyer:

> *Lawyer:* This guy says that you threatened him at O'Hare. Did you actually do that?
> *Biff:* Not really.
> *Lawyer:* What do you mean by "not really"?
> *Biff:* Well, I wasn't going to do anything.
> *Lawyer:* But did you threaten to do anything?
> *Biff:* He wouldn't get out of my father's seat.
> *Lawyer:* Come on, Biff, did you threaten him or not?
> *Biff:* Just enough to get him to move. I wasn't really going to hit him or anything, you know.

Biff and his lawyer have a problem because they are not exactly speaking the same language. When the lawyer says "threaten" he is thinking "place him in reasonable apprehension of receiving a battery." But to Biff, "threaten" means something like "give the guy an urgent message that he ought to move his ass pronto." Compounding the problem, Biff seems to think that his actual intention—to hit or not to hit—makes a difference. The lawyer knows, however, that Biff's apparent intentions matter far more than his real ones.

From this early uncertainty the lawyer must now begin to develop his own trial story. Since Biff's "mental reservation" is not a valid defense, the lawyer will probably want to go to work on the "reasonable apprehension" angle.

> *Lawyer:* I have to tell you, Biff, that it is illegal to threaten someone with violence, even if you don't really mean to go through with it. The law is going to look at whether he thought you were threatening to hit him.

Biff: Well, I wasn't going to hit him right there in the airport.

Lawyer: Do you think he realized that?

Biff: We were in an airport, and I didn't even ask him to step outside.

Lawyer: Maybe we ought to go through it step by step. When did you first see the guy?

Biff: When he sat down in my father's seat. He didn't even ask if it was taken.

Lawyer: So what did you do?

Biff: I just told him someone was sitting there.

Lawyer: What did he do?

Biff: Nothing. He just kept sitting there, like I didn't mean anything to him.

Lawyer: What happened after that?

Biff: I said, "My father was sitting there and he's coming back," and he said, "Hold on a minute, mister," which really pissed me off.

Lawyer: Why did that piss you off?

Biff: Because he had a really snotty tone of voice and it was like he wasn't going to get up. I asked him twice and he still wasn't moving.

Lawyer: Then what did you do?

Biff: I looked him in the eye and said, "Don't piss me off."

Lawyer: Why did you say that?

Biff: Because he was pissing me off.

Lawyer: Then what happened?

Biff: He got this shocked look on his face, like I said a dirty word or something, and he grabbed his stuff and moved in a hurry.

Lawyer: Biff, did you raise your voice?

Biff: I guess I probably did. That's not illegal, is it?

Lawyer: Did you ever say you were going to hit him if he didn't move?

Biff: No.

Lawyer: Did you ever leave your seat while he was sitting there?

Biff: No.

Lawyer: Did you make any threatening gestures?

Biff: No.

Lawyer: Help me out a little, then. What would make him think you were threatening him?

Biff: He was afraid of me. I could tell by looking at him. Maybe he's the nervous type.

The story is getting better, but it still has problems. Biff makes it clear that he became upset about the seat incident. The interloper was acting like a jerk, in Biff's opinion, which was cause at least for anger. The lawyer is worried. The angrier Biff seems, the more likely it is that he made the alleged threat. For his part, Biff can't see that he did anything wrong. The seat was being saved and he did what was necessary to get me to move. This calls for a little more lawyering.

Lawyer: Let's try it this way, Biff. Did you expect the man to move after you asked him the first time?
Biff: Sure. There were plenty of seats, so why wouldn't he move?
Lawyer: Did you threaten him or raise your voice?
Biff: No, I didn't.
Lawyer: Why did you think he was going to move?
Biff: Because it was no big deal. Like I said, there were plenty of seats.
Lawyer: What were you wearing, Biff?
Biff: Jeans and a T-shirt, and my American Legion hat.
Lawyer: What was the other man wearing?
Biff: A suit and a fancy tie.
Lawyer: Were you angry when you asked him to move the second time?
Biff: Not really. I couldn't figure out why he was being such a jerk, especially after I told him it was my father's seat, but I still figured he would move.
Lawyer: Did you say anything threatening when you asked him to move the second time?
Biff: No, I just told him that my father was coming back.
Lawyer: Did you still think he was going to move?
Biff: Sure.
Lawyer: Is that when he said something?
Biff: Right, and it pissed me off. Especially the crappy way he said "mister," like he was more important than me because he was wearing a suit and tie.

Lawyer: Is there a difference between being angry and being pissed off?
Biff: Yes. And I was just pissed.

The story is now taking better shape. Two slightly unreasonable people had words with each other. Biff used one form of mildly insulting language—"pissed"—just as the seat snatcher used condescending sarcasm—"mister." The words were more heated than they really needed to be, but neither one was violent. Maybe the people were from different social classes, and that would explain why they had some trouble understanding each other. Biff's lawyer is probably already thinking of a trial theme, perhaps "Just a misunderstanding."

Astute readers will have already noticed that Biff's story left out one extremely salient detail—his clenched fist. Leaning over and shaking his fist gives some physicality to Biff's actions. Why was that fact in my account but not in his?

There are several viable explanations for the crucial disparity between the two narratives. Perhaps one of us is lying. I can guarantee you, however, that I am telling the truth. As to Biff, we'll never know. Our only post-airport information about him comes entirely from my imagination. It would seem downright unsporting for me to write Biff's story and then accuse him of lying to his own lawyer. In fairness, we ought at least to explore some other possibilities.

It could be that Biff clenched his fist without realizing it. Or he could have been tightening his hand to control himself, not recognizing it as a threatening gesture. Or he could just have forgotten about it, since it didn't mean much to him at the time. In any event, Biff doesn't think that he waved his fist at me, and his lawyer believes him.

Because of the centrality of the contradictory testimony, it is almost certain that the outcome of any trial will turn on the "fist question." If Biff did indeed lean over and shake a fist in my face, then he committed an assault and I can win. Without the fist it would seem that I am just a hypersensitive whiner, and I should lose.

Lawyers call this a credibility question. There are no other witnesses, so the verdict will go to whichever one of us turns out to be the most believable. But if that is the case, what was all the fuss about trial stories? Biff and I will each take the stand, the jury will decide whom to believe, and that will be the end of it. We should hardly need lawyers at all. Wrong. As it turns out, the trial story is an essential aspect of believability.

Juries (and judges) make their credibility determinations in a number of ways. Consciously or subconsciously, they consider demeanor, body language, speech patterns, voice inflections, and a host of other "indicators," some of which are reliable and some of which are not.[6] If Biff takes the stand and comes across as a bullying hothead, the jury will probably believe me. On the other hand, if I seem like an arrogant, pompous putz, the jury will be inclined to go with Biff. Though lawyers have been known to spend hours "sandpapering" their client's deportment, the fact is that there is usually very little a lawyer can do to change a bully into a sweetie (or a stuffed shirt into a regular guy), especially in the face of cross-examination.

But outward affect is only one component of credibility. If it cannot be disguised, it can be accommodated. And that is where the trial story becomes crucial. Let's say that Biff, all preparation to the contrary, just cannot help looking tough and overbearing. So long as he doesn't actually lose his temper on the stand, his lawyer will argue something along these lines: "Sure he's a big, strong, blunt guy—but that doesn't mean he was out to hurt anybody. Big guys are allowed to save seats for their fathers. If you look at all the facts of the case you will realize that he didn't threaten anyone with his fist."

In the same vein, imagine (completely contrary to fact, I promise you) that I testify with a supercilious smirk on my face. My lawyer will have her task cut out for her, but she will still be able to make an argument: "Okay, he's a professor and he acts like a professor. But he certainly didn't hurt anybody. If you look at all the facts of the case you will realize that Biff just lost his temper and assaulted him with his fist."

In other words, the lawyers will each bolster the credibility of their clients by invoking the facts of the case, saying, in effect, "Believe my client about the fist because he tells a logically coherent story about everything else."

On my side, a winning trial story will not only show what happened, it will also present Biff as the sort of person who would, in that situation, threaten someone with his fist. My personality quirks—a little aloof, a little hard of hearing, slow to react, annoyed at his unnecessary insistence—will be deployed to explain Biff's mounting anger and eventual near explosion. Far from portraying me as blameless, my counsel will opt to show Biff's mounting overreaction to slight or even trivial provocations. As my lawyer will explain, it will be far more credible to concede that I might actually have irritated Biff than it would be to insist that he is a completely erratic madman.

And what does this say about truth or ethics? If you review my attorney's trial story, you will see that it does not contain a single element, a single phrase, even a single thought that is not true. In fact, it is more truthful than it would have been without my attorney's intervention, since my original, emotional inclination was to portray myself as the dazed, innocent victim of an inexplicable maniac. By looking closely at both sides of the encounter, however, my good, careful counsel was able to help me say what I really meant.

Win or lose, that's got to be good lawyering.

Throughout the preceding sections of this essay I have done what I could to present the events objectively. I have tried to credit Biff's story as much as possible—going so far as to allow the possibility that I might have acted like an arrogant putz. In order to analyze the lawyering for both sides, we need to accept the variable nature of perceived reality. Here and there, of course, it was impossible to avoid vouching for myself, though I tried always to make it apparent when that was happening. If the reader detects other unacknowledged instances of reporting bias, I can only plead human frailty.

Now, however, the story is over and the point is made. I am therefore at liberty to provide more information, this time exclusively from my point of view. Because, you see, the events did not end when I hurried away from the contested seat.

As explained earlier, Biff was seated in a general waiting area in the middle of the concourse; there was no way to tell where he would be boarding. After he threatened me, I moved to another seat from which I could keep an eye on him as well as on my gate. When my flight was called, I waited to see what Biff was doing. As you have probably guessed by now, we were on the same flight.

Boarding after Biff, I made a note of his seat number so that I could alert the flight attendant to keep an eye on him. (I truly feared his erratic behavior in a way that I probably have not fully conveyed. For the subsequent purpose of my hypothetical complaint, the knowledge of his seat number would probably also allow my counsel to discovery his identity.) Fortunately, the flight was uneventful, though I did take the precaution of waiting for Biff to deplane before I left my seat.

It turned out, however, that it was not so easy to avoid Biff entirely. He and several friends stood talking in a large group right in the middle of the concourse. I stopped and tried to figure out what to do. Part of me wanted to move straight forward, asking them (politely) to get out of the way. Part of me said that I should avoid him at all cost, however such furtive circumnavigation might damage my dignity. I probably stopped and stared. (Actually, I definitely stopped and stared, in part because I was trying to read the words on Biff's cap. The idea for this essay had already occurred to me and I thought that the cap might provide an interesting detail.)

Biff saw me. He literally shouted across the concourse, "If you've got a problem with me we're going to go at it right here, you fucking worm." So it turns out that I was right in the first place—the guy was a raving psychopath.

Stunned again, I realized that a man has to do what a man has to do. I hurried out of the airport and began composing this piece in my head. All in all, I'd rather write than fight.

As for Biff, I don't expect that I will ever see him again. But judging from his temperament, I hope he knows a talented attorney.

NOTES

1. 720 ILL. COMP. STAT. 5/12-1 (1997).

2. I could also sue Biff for the tort of assault; the elements are the same and the standard of proof is lower.

3. STEVEN LUBET, MODERN TRIAL ADVOCACY 1–2 (2d ed. 1997).

4. I use this term in its generic sense, meaning a lawyer who has obligations to the administration of justice. The somewhat hoary concept of lawyer as actual court officer has been long discredited.

5. I will explain later how I would discover his full name and address.

6. See LUBET, *supra* note 3, at 42–43.

CHAPTER TWO

EDGARDO MORTARA
Forbidden Truths

We are accustomed to thinking of truth as an immediately recognizable concept. We may disagree about the content of the truth—some accept one set of facts, some believe another—but we expect consensus in the judicial system about the quality of truth itself. We want the courts to look at the occurrence (or nonoccurrence) of discrete historical events.

But what happens when an advocate must confront a system in which certain truths are simply forbidden? How can a lawyer present a case when his clients themselves are devalued and oppressed by the very forum in which he must argue? And how can the attorney explain to his clients that the truth, as they see it, has no standing in a particular court?

The story of the Mortara family, nineteenth-century Italian Jews ensnared by the power of the Papal States, illustrates this dilemma. When their son Edgardo was removed from their custody by the papal police, they were allowed to petition the Vatican for his return. With the assistance of a lawyer, they succeeded in presenting the best case available to them under the circumstances—a case that was necessarily based on the technicalities of canon law rather than the inherent rights of Jewish parents.

To the Vatican, it was an unassailable "truth" that Jewish parents had only secondary rights to raise their own children and that the protection of a boy's immortal soul was of far greater importance than the integrity of his biological family. The Mortaras adhered to an entirely different truth, one that had absolutely no standing in the papal court. It was the task of counsel to bridge that gap, to the extent possible, by conveying his clients' heartfelt position in the manner most likely to be acceptable to the reigning authorities.

∼

On the evening of June 23, 1858, an officer of the papal police knocked urgently on the door of Signor Salomone Mortara, a Jewish merchant living in the Italian city of Bologna. Marshal Pietro Lucidi, accompanied by several other of the Pope's carabinieri, demanded entry to the apartment. The Mortaras, Salomone (also called Momolo) and his wife, Marianna, were understandably apprehensive, suspecting and dreading the likely reason for police interest in their family. Their worst fears were confirmed when Marshal Lucidi began questioning them about the names and ages of their eight children. His interest quickly focused on six-year-old Edgardo.

"Your son Edgardo has been baptized," Lucidi informed the terrified parents, "and I have been ordered to take him with me."

At that moment the Mortaras' world collapsed. Through a relentless legal process, their child was removed from their custody, never to be returned. Edgardo was sent first to an institution, Rome's "House of the Catechumens," and was eventually "adopted" by Pope Pius IX himself.[1]

It seems that about five years earlier a fourteen-year-old Christian domestic servant in the Mortara home, fearing that Edgardo might die from a childhood illness, had sprinkled a bit of water on the boy's brow while he slept, whispering, "I baptize you in the name of the Father, of the Son, and of the Holy Ghost." This act, it turns out, was sufficient under canon law to constitute a baptism. Unbeknownst to him or his parents, the sleeping Edgardo was instantly transformed into a Catholic.

Edgardo soon recovered from his illness. The servant, named Anna Morisi, thought nothing more of her action, reporting it to no one at the time. In the course of the next few years, however, she mentioned the "baptism" in passing to at least one friend, who repeated the story to others. The information was eventually relayed to Bologna's inquisitor, who felt compelled under the law to take action. According to the Inquisitor, Father Pier Gaetano Feletti, his duty was clear: "[T]he boy was a Catholic and could not be raised in a Jewish household."

Clandestine baptism of their children had been a constant torment to Italy's small Jewish community, especially those in cities such as Bologna, located in the Papal States and subject to the direct civil authority of the Pope. There had been many similar occurrences over the years, continuing with some regularity right into the nineteenth century.[2] The practice was not uncontroversial, even among Catholics; so much so that the church repeatedly issued decrees forbidding, though not invalidating, secret baptisms. Nonetheless, the baptisms continued, unnerving the Jewish residents of the Papal States to the point that many families insisted that their Christian servants sign affidavits attesting that they had never baptized any of the children in their care.

While the year 1858 may seem remote, in many ways it actually lay at the beginning of the modern period in European history. Jews had already been emancipated in much of Western Europe and the Pope's temporal authority over the Papal States was widely viewed as an anachronism, if not a throwback to medieval times.[3] Consequently, the Inquisition's asportation of Edgardo Mortara became an international cause célèbre, drawing official government protests from France, England, and the United States.

Pope Pius IX, however, was unyielding. Unmoved by the anguished pleas of Edgardo's parents, he could not be swayed by the various forms of diplomatic pressure asserted by more enlightened governments, much less by the increasingly barbed attacks in the liberal press. Having assumed personal responsibility for the boy's Catholic upbringing and religious education, Pius IX came to consider Edgardo's attachment to the church as a sign of God's continued blessing of the Pope's temporal rule. "My son," he once told Edgardo, "you have cost me dearly, and I have suffered a great deal because of you." Then, speaking to others in attendance, the Pope added, "Both the powerful and powerless have tried to steal this boy from me, and accused me of being barbarous and pitiless. They cried for his parents, but they failed to recognize that I, too, am his father."

The story does not have a tidy ending. Edgardo was never returned to his parents. He continued his religious education in Rome, eventually becoming a priest of some renown, taking the name Father Pio Edgardo in honor of Pius IX. He remained completely estranged from his family and from Judaism, to the point of fleeing in disguise to avoid the possibility of being returned to his parents during Cavour's overthrow of the Papal States. In 1878 he met briefly with his then widowed mother, and thereafter remained in some contact with the other members of his family. In 1940 Father Pio Edgardo died in Belgium at age 88. David Kertzer reminds us that only one month later, "German soldiers flooded Belgium, so to begin rounding up all those tainted with Jewish blood."

In one sense, the events of the Edgardo Mortara case are almost unfathomable to modern Americans. Under no conception of the First Amendment, from extreme right to extreme left, could a child be removed from his biological parents on the basis of their religion. The very thought is offensive, evoking (with good cause) images of the Inquisition and other theocratic persecutions from which the Establishment Clause is intended to protect our citizens.

It is safe to assume, then, that the Mortara case, viewed strictly as a matter of religious coercion, is of historical interest only. Nothing like that could happen here. And if it did (as when a few overreaching judges removed children from their "hippie" parents in the 1960s), we can be confident that the courts would quickly correct the abuse.[4]

But the Mortara case was not exclusively about religion. There is also a subtext about law and good intentions, persuasion and truth. From that perspective, it turns out, the case may have contemporary lessons that are much more direct.

David Kertzer titled his book *The Kidnapping of Edgardo Mortara,* using that word repeatedly throughout his book. Other sources are in accord, the *Encyclopedia Judaica,* for example, uses the term "abduction" three times in the single paragraph it devotes to the case.[5] But there are two sides to every story, and one cannot help but observe the procedural regularity with which the matter went forward. Indeed, even today we reflexively refer to the "Mortara case," rather than, say, the Mortara affair or incident, as though to recognize the centrality of legal process.[6]

From the standpoint of the church, which is to say the papal government and its agents, the removal of Edgardo was not the story of a kidnapping at all. Rather, they regarded the events as profoundly "lawful," attended by rigorous safeguards and carried out with scrupulous concern for the rights, and even the sensitivities, of everyone involved.

The officers of the Inquisition did not react rashly or hastily to the news of Edgardo's covert baptism. The only witness to the event, Anna Morisi, was brought before the Inquisitor, Father Feletti, pursuant to a written summons. She was placed under oath prior to her interrogation, which was transcribed. Approximately six months passed before the Inquisitor ordered the gendarmes to remove Edgardo from his parents, during which time the Inquisitor consulted with his superiors in Rome in order to be certain that everything was done "punctiliously according to the sacred Canons."

No official action was taken until the authorities were satisfied that Anna Morisi's testimony had "all the earmarks of the truth without leaving the least doubt about the reality and the validity of the baptism she performed."[7] And even after the police came to remove Edgardo, the Inquisitor agreed to allow the parents a twenty-four-hour stay of his order, "if not to persuade the mother, at least to make her son's sudden departure less harsh and less painful."

Following Edgardo's remand to the custody of the papacy, the Mortaras embarked on an extended campaign of petitions and appeals. Their first plea was directed to Father Feletti, the Inquisitor of Bologna, who rejected it as beyond his jurisdiction and informed the Mortaras that their only relief lay in Rome with the Pope. The Mortaras quickly began assembling evidence in support of their cause, much of it directed at a legal technicality. It seems that, absent parental consent, Catholics were allowed to baptize Jewish children only if there was strong reason to believe that the child was about to die.

In such a case, canon law held, the importance of allowing a soul to go to heaven outweighed the customary commitment to parental (and especially paternal) authority over children.

Thus, the Mortaras and their supporters collected a series of affidavits and depositions designed to show that Edgardo had never been deathly ill, and certainly not at the time he was allegedly baptized by Morisi. By attacking the underlying legal validity of the baptism, they hoped to undo its effect and win the return of their son.

After several meetings with church officials, including Cardinal Giacomo Antonelli, the Vatican secretary of state, the Mortaras succeeded in preparing a formal legal brief for the Pope's consideration. The document was styled a "Pro-memoria and Syllabus." The Pro-memoria included the facts of the case and a seven-page section, written in Latin, citing the works of various church authorities in support of the Mortaras' plea. Another section, in Italian, listed similar instances in which baptized children had been allowed to remain with their Jewish parents.[8] The main document in the appeal was the Syllabus, a fifty-page brief, written in Latin, that rested on citation and interpretation of ecclesiastical legal sources and detailed references to prior cases of forced baptism.

The Mortaras' brief could only have been written with the assistance of a lawyer trained in canon law, but no attorney's name was signed to the document. It has been suggested that the author may have been a renegade priest. But whoever wrote the Pro-memoria and Syllabus, it is clear that his task was a difficult and perhaps even a dangerous one, well justifying counsel's evident desire for anonymity.

The appeal was addressed to the Pope himself, not only the vicar of the Roman Catholic Church, but also the absolute temporal ruler of the Papal States. Since the Inquisition had already removed Edgardo from his parents, and Pius IX had already adopted the boy, the appeal could succeed only by showing that the church had acted in error. That would be a touchy matter under any circumstances, made even more uncomfortable by the fact that the petitioners were Jews. Even an anonymous advocate could not conceivably claim that the Jewish parents were right and the Pope wrong. Such an argument, no matter how artfully phrased or well supported, would never be effective. At the time, the testimony of Jews was not even admissible against Christians in a papal court.

One can imagine the lawyer's first meeting with the grief-stricken parents. The Mortaras surely would have been frantic, desperate for help and well aware that they could not possibly present their case without the assistance of a Christian lawyer. As well, they would no doubt have been baffled by the thought that their right to the custody of their own child might be determined by something so seemingly inconsequential as the severity of a childhood illness from which he had fully recovered over five years ago.

To the Mortaras, the very seizure of their son was wrong. They had led upright, respectable lives, doing nothing to offend the authorities or challenge the dominance of the reigning church. "Signor Avvocato," they must have said, "we have been subjected to a great injustice. Please help us explain that we should not be victimized because of our religion. Even the Pope has no right to adopt our child simply because we are Jews."

"I was saddened to learn of your suffering," the lawyer would have replied. "You have harmed no one. It was unmerciful for the Inquisition to remove your child." But how much farther would he have been willing to go? Would he agree that the church was terribly destructive in its treatment of the Jewish community, or would he only acknowledge the possibility of a factual mistake regarding Edgardo? Was he morally outraged at the thought of religious oppression? Was he a liberal reformer, eager to join Garibaldi and Cavour in their march to overthrow the Papal States in favor of a secular, democratic Italian nation? Or was he merely taking the case for money, willing to sell his expertise but unwilling to embrace his clients' cause?

Whatever the lawyer's motivation, the Mortaras must have been disheartened by his ultimate strategy, which was to concede the validity of the Inquisition while arguing that its standards had been misapplied. To the Mortaras, Edgardo was not and could never be a Christian. No amount of sprinkled water, no sincerely muttered prayers, not even adoption by the Pope could convert their child against their will. Moreover, they would have denied vigorously that Christianity was spiritually preferable to Judaism, or that Edgardo, even if deathly ill, could be saved by baptism.

But those agreements could never work. Indeed, they were sacrilegious, forbidden. The Pope's authority had to be respected, the Inquisition's power could not be challenged. To be effective, to have any chance at success, the brief would have to make concession after humble concession, avoiding the "truth" of the Mortaras' oppression.

The brief was presented with a cover letter effusive in its praise of the Pope, stating the "unshakable allegiance" of the Jewish community to the Papal States. Of necessity, it was submissive and ingratiating, invoking the "charitable nature of the Catholic religion and the kindheartedness of the Pope." It must have pained the Mortaras deeply to see these sentiments expressed on their behalf. There was nothing charitable or kind about the seizure of their child. One wonders whether they pointed out to their counsel the cruel paradox inherent in appealing to the generosity of kidnappers, and whether their Christian lawyer would have been sensitive to the irony of his position.

"Advocacy is advocacy, my friends," he might have replied. "The Holy Father is judge and jury in your case, and we must praise him if we are to persuade him. And we must present the case in his terms."

The first argument was factual. According to the affidavit of Dr. Pasquale Saragoni, the family physician, Edgardo's life had never been in danger during his childhood illness. Thus, there could have been no urgent necessity for Anna Morisi's covert act. In this situation, it was argued, the involvement of a priest was required for a valid baptism. Only in exigent circumstances could a layperson administer the sacrament.

On matters of law and morality, the brief relied exclusively on Catholic authorities, quoting Thomas Aquinas for the proposition that the church had for centuries been opposed to the forced baptism of Jewish children. In the case of a child who had not reached the age of reason, consent to baptism was the exclusive right of the father. Since Momolo had never consented, Edgardo's baptism was null and void.

The argument was nimble, its form recognizable to any contemporary lawyer. Conceding the premise that the church had authority over Edgardo and his parents, notwithstanding their adherence to a different faith, the brief probed for loopholes that could cancel the effect of the baptism. Yes, a layperson can baptize a dying child, but Edgardo wasn't dying. Yes, Jewish children can be baptized, but Momolo did not consent. And besides, Edgardo had not reached the age of reason. And besides, St. Thomas opposed forced baptism in the name of the church itself.

Thus, the defense of the Mortaras had to be confined to the categories of canon law. No doubt, this must have seemed the best alternative in an excruciating situation, giving a measure of hope to Edgardo's tormented mother and father. In the past, some Jewish parents had succeeded in regaining custody of their baptized children; perhaps the Mortaras would be equally fortunate.

Reliance on church precedent, however, came at a severe analytic cost. Canon law drew a distinction between a proscribed baptism and an invalid one. Thus, Morisi's baptism might have been "illegal" or wrongful, yet still effective at rendering Edgardo a Christian. And once he was a

Christian, it followed that the child could not be raised by Jews. The invocation of Thomas Aquinas actually supported this position. St. Thomas's opposition to forced conversions was based on his fear of apostasy. Children converted over their parents' objections would necessarily be tempted to revert to Judaism, a mortal sin. Thus, it was better not to baptize them in the first place. But this did not mean that the baptism was a nullity. In fact, the logical conclusion was that such children had to be removed as much as possible from the corrupting influence of their parents.

Would the Mortaras have been better off with a more aggressive brief, taking a less conciliatory approach? Their case, as it turns out, was hopeless in any event. Pope Pius IX was determined to retain their son, raising him as a priest. There was no argument, within or outside the precedents of the church, that would have altered that result. Might it have brought them greater satisfaction to have voiced their true feelings and beliefs?

Pope Pius IX might have simply ignored the Mortaras' document, but instead he directed his legal advisors to prepare a response, also based on church law. The result was a thirty-four-page document titled *Brevi cenni*, "A brief explanation and reflections on the pro-memoria and syllabus humbly presented to His Holiness, Pope Pius IX, concerning the baptism conferred in Bologna on the child Edgardo, son of the Jews Salomone and Marianna Mortara."

Though dismissive of the Mortaras' claims, *Brevi cenni* refuted their arguments point by point in a clear effort to demonstrate the legality of the child's removal by the papal authorities. It listed five conclusions, refuting the five major points of the appeal, and distinguishing each of the prior cases relied on by the Mortaras. The Pope certainly owed no response at all to the Mortaras. Indeed, he was offended by the very idea that Jews would presume to invoke ecclesiastical precedents. Nonetheless, the length and detail of *Brevi cenni* clearly indicate the perceived importance of legality. The document was, in fact, distributed to papal representatives and ambassadors throughout Europe and Latin America as evidence that the church had acted in fairness and justice.

Emphasizing the procedural care that had been taken in reviewing the legality of Edgardo's baptism, *Brevi cenni* quickly made it clear that the strategy of obeisant advocacy was doomed from the start:

> The parents of a child who was singularly granted Divine Grace, which, having removed him from the blind Judaic obstinacy, made him by chance a son of the church, have petitioned and brought action all the way to the August throne of the Holy Father in order to get back their son, who has already been placed in the bosom of the Church.

That was that. The accidental "Divine Grace" of Morisi's baptism trumped all other considerations. Within the law of the church, "nothing more is required for the validity of the baptism than that the rite be performed according to the proper form with a suitable subject . . . and it may be performed by anybody as long as he intends to do what the Church intends."

It might be said that the agility of the Mortaras' argument may actually have backfired; it certainly did not ingratiate them, as hoped, to the papal authorities. *Brevi cenni* expressed near outrage that the Jews had dared to rely on "authorities and arguments deriving from [canon] law," which of course they misconstrued. Most important, the Jews failed to understand that they had no rights to their child superior to those of the church. "Between the two competing authorities—that of God and that of the parents—God's must prevail, for was He not the author of the natural rights that parents enjoyed?"

To the Mortaras, and no doubt to every modern observer, the terms "kidnapping" and "abduction" would be, if anything, far too mild to describe the forcible seizure of Edgardo. Nonetheless, from the Vatican's point of view the events would be more accurately characterized as a termination of parental rights, an act that occurs today with some frequency throughout the United States. And so it was that the law of child welfare, as it existed in the Papal States of 1858, did not merely allow the seizure of Edgardo, it required that he be removed from his parents for his own best interest.

From the first moment that the case came to the attention of the Inquisitor, the authorities firmly believed that they were acting in furtherance of Edgardo's obvious best interests. Since he had been made a Christian, even an unconscious one, it seemed obvious to everyone in the church—from the Pope to the police marshal—that nothing but harm could come to Edgardo if he remained in the custody of his infidel parents. The boy had to be removed for his own safety, quickly and completely.

In fact, Edgardo's new guardians feared three different sorts of misfortune that could befall the boy if they failed to do their utmost to protect him. First and foremost, they were concerned for his immortal soul. Once the children of infidels had experienced the blessings of Christianity, it was the church's duty to "protect in them the sanctity of what they have received, and to nourish them for eternal life." While the "worldly wise" might easily discount this motive, there can be no doubt that the church officials firmly and sincerely believed that they were acting with Edgardo's ultimate happiness in mind.[9] They did not seize the boy for the conscious purpose of tormenting his parents, or even to coerce the Jewish community generally. The church had no particular animus toward the Mortaras and it did not make a constant practice of depriving Jewish parents of their children. Rather, the entire impulse was protective: Edgardo's interest in salvation simply outweighed his parents' interest in custody. That is why Pope Pius IX always replied *non possimus*—impossible!—when petitioned for Edgardo's return.

The second, related fear was that a Christian child, if raised by Jews, would be exposed to the risk of apostasy. This was a deadly serious matter. It was stressful, but not illegal, to be Jewish in the Papal States. Apostasy, on the other hand, was a capital crime. Once having become a Christian, Edgardo would be liable to imprisonment or even death if he were to revert to the Judaism of his parents. Thus, it was not enough to insist that Edgardo be deemed and raised a Catholic, he had to be removed permanently from the corrupting influence of his parents.

Finally, the prejudices of the day required that Catholics be taught to fear Jews and Judaism. The oppression of the Jews was made easier and more justifiable if they could be considered menacing and dangerous. Consequently, it was thought (or at least said) that Jewish parents, consumed by their hatred of all things Christian, would "rather murder their own children than see them grow up to be Catholic." In Edgardo's case, the Inquisitor of Bologna invoked the blood libel that the boy might be "sacrificed" if returned to his parents.

Of course, every conception of Edgardo's welfare rested on utter contempt and revulsion toward Judaism. Nonetheless, given subsequent events in Europe, one must be struck by the lack of racism in the church's position. Once baptized, Edgardo was no longer considered a Jew; he was subjected to few, if any, disabilities within the Church. Indeed, he became the adopted son of the Pope and his precocity as a religious student was noted with pride. In adulthood, Father Pio Edgardo preached throughout Europe to large and admiring crowds of Christians. Moreover, Momolo and Marianna Mortara were repeatedly advised that they could regain full custody of their son if only they too would convert.

In other words, it was nothing personal; the only concern was Edgardo's best interest. Every effort was made to soften the impact of Edgardo's removal, on both the boy and his grieving parents. Delays were granted, as was visitation once Edgardo was in the firm custody of the papacy. So sympathetic were the officials to the heartache being imposed on the Mortaras that "tears flowed from the eyes of the two policemen" who took Edgardo into custody.

It may say little for the church that its position in the Mortara case appears beneficent only in comparison to the later atrocities of the Nazis. Still, it is impossible—*non possimus!*—to deny that the Pope and his agents, even the Inquisitor, were impelled in their actions by both the law and their own good intentions.

They were also concerned with Edgardo's temporal happiness, noting that he "had left his [birth] parents without protest and had gone happily with his police escort to Rome." According to one account from the Catholic press, Edgardo was given a Christian prayer book to read as he was being taken by the police from Bologna to Rome:

> He read those prayers with great pleasure, and each time the subject of the Christian religion came up in conversation, he paid great attention. Indeed, he often asked questions on particular points of our faith, showing

such great interest that it was clear how important it was to him to know the truths of our holy religion.

Whenever the carriage stopped in any town or city, the first thing that he asked was to be taken to the church, and when he entered he remained there at length, showing the greatest respect and the most moving devotion.

It was clear to the authorities that Edgardo wanted to remain within the Christian fold. They quoted him as stating, "I am baptized—my father is the Pope." In fact, it was even said that Edgardo feared returning to his birth parents, based on the specious claim that they might torture and ruin him. According to the Bologna weekly *Il vero amico*, Marianna, on seeing her son, was "filled with anger and ripped the [Christian] medallion from his chest, saying scornfully, 'I'd rather see you dead than a Christian!'"

Canon law could never respect parental rights, if that meant removing an innocent boy from the loving, spiritually supportive home of the Pope and returning him to a family of infidels. Indeed, the Jesuit newspaper *Civilita Catolica* editorialized that "[i]t would be inhuman cruelty to do so, especially when the son has the insight to see the danger himself, and himself begs for protection against it."

In a curious dialectic, it may be that the best case for the Mortaras might have been made by the argument they dared not confront. Was it in Edgardo's "best interest" to be raised a Christian? To the papal authorities, of course, the answer to the question was self-evident. Children needed to be rescued from Judaism, the sooner the better. Edgardo's baptism, even if irregular, was nonetheless a blessed deliverance. Objections to his conversion, even those based on canon law, were technicalities to be overcome.

But the Mortaras understood that their son's best interest was to remain with his mother and father. To them it was not true, as *Brevi cenni* concluded, that Edgardo could be best nourished "in the grace of Jesus Christ." It was not true that he was better off in the "bosom of the Church." It was not true in any sense that the care to be provided "by the

Church over the baptized infant is of a superior and more noble order" than that of his Jewish family.

Allowed freely to state their own case without fear of the consequences, the Mortaras surely would not have relied on the fine points of canon law. They would have presented an argument based on their own humanity. A virtuous argument, but a forbidden one.

No lawyer, of course, would have done that for them. Attorneys are trained to look for arguments that can persuade, not arguments that are faithful to the ideals of the clients. Advocacy, after all, is strictly an instrumental art, judged against a standard of actual or potential success. But instrumental advocacy will always have its limits, as in the Mortara case, where both lawyer and clients were effectively barred from speaking the truth.

To be sure, it was the quality of the law and the nature of the sovereign, not their attorney, that silenced the Mortaras. Nor is it likely that they objected to the argument that was presented on their behalf. Having lived their lives as Jews in the Papal States, they certainly understood that the Pope could not be moved by an appeal based on the equality of Judaism. If they were to succeed, it would have to be through supplication. They had no choice but to appeal to the church in its own terms.

If there had been any doubt about the necessity of that strategy, their lawyer would have explained it, perhaps as a bitter predicament: "My friends, we are confronted with bigotry, and the bigots have all the power. We can only influence their decision by the presumptions of their faith, as cruel and arrogant as they might be."

Or perhaps the lawyer was a man of his time: "As Jews, you must understand that the Church cannot allow you to raise a Christian child. It may be that your son has not been properly baptized, in which case I may be able to help you. But if Edgardo is formally a Christian, then he must stay with His Holiness. Those are my terms."

In either case, the Mortaras would have had no option but to agree. No parent would stand on principle at the risk of losing a child.[10] "Signor Avvocato, do what you think best. Our fate is in your hands. Please do whatever you can to help us regain our son."

There are cases, however, that even the best argument cannot win. There are situations where neither truth, nor justice, nor even resourceful technicality can prevail. In those circumstances, perhaps there is a place for an unconventional practice, something that we might call allegiant representation, measured solely by its ability to convey a client's deepest, most heartfelt beliefs. That sort of advocacy might not succeed in advancing discrete legal claims, but it would be truer to the claims of history.

There is a tragic denouement to this tragic story, involving another trial in another place.

In 1865 Momolo and Marianna Mortara and their family moved to Florence, a city that lay beyond the authority of the Pope. There they aspired to raise their remaining children in peace, though they never gave up hope of Edgardo's return. By the spring of 1871 they were well established in a relatively spacious apartment on the Via Pinti, Momolo working still as a merchant and Marianna caring for their two youngest children, Imelda and Aristide, who had been born after Edgardo's abduction. As was customary among middle-class Italian families, they employed a series of domestic servants. In the early spring of 1871 they hired a young woman from rural Tuscany named Rosa Tognazzi.

On April 3, 1871, barely a month after she joined the household, Rosa Tognazzi plunged to her death from a bedroom window in the Mortaras' fourth-floor apartment, landing in the courtyard below. At first her fall was thought to be suicide, brought on by her legal problems with a former employer. Soon, however, suspicion was focused on Momolo—a Jew reputed to be an angry and violent man. It was said that he had pushed his servant from the window. Although the initial police report cleared Momolo, further investigation turned up some disturbing evidence.

Still alive after the fall, Rosa was taken to a hospital where she died several hours later. A medical examination disclosed a deep, bloody laceration on her forehead. Though it was possible that such an injury could have been caused by the fall, this one was covered by a firmly knotted kerchief—suggesting that the wound had been received and stanched inside the apartment before she tumbled from the window. In other words, it seemed that she had been beaten, then murdered.

Adding further to the suspicion was the account of Signora Anna

Ragazzini, a neighbor who had run to the assistance of the semicon-
scious Rosa. "Did they throw you down?" she asked the dying girl, who
weakly answered, "Yes." "I know the Jew Momolo Mortara by sight," Signora Ragazzini told the investigating magistrate, "day and night, I always
heard loud noises, arguments, and quarreling in the Jew's house." Other
neighbors confirmed the seemingly violent nature of the Mortara
household. "You hear noises, quarreling, and swearing all the time, and
they seem to live like animals," said one. "I know the Jew Momolo Mortara," said another, he is "a violent, quick-tempered character."

On April 6, Momolo Mortara was arrested and charged with murder.

The 1860s had seen the successful struggle for Italian national unification, much of which was directed against the remaining temporal authority of the papacy. By 1870, nearly all of Italy had become a constitutional monarchy under the secular rule of King Victor Emmanuel II and
the liberal political administration of Count Camillo di Cavour. The exception, of course, was Rome itself, which was still governed by the Pope
as a much diminished Papal State. Then, on September 20, 1870, Italian
troops entered Rome, declaring it the Italian capital and confining the
Pope's authority to the few acres surrounding the Vatican.

In 1871 Florence had long been beyond the control of the church. In
fact, it had served as Victor Emmanuel's capital from 1865 until 1870.
Thus, Momolo was to be tried in a civilian court, subject to the same law
and procedures as all other Italian citizens. It could not have escaped the
court's notice that Momolo was perhaps the best-known Italian Jew in
the world and that his trial would be a test for the fairness and impar-
tiality of the new, liberal state. Though the evidence against him seemed
compelling, it was clear from the outset that Momolo, through his counsel, would be permitted to raise a vigorous and unconstrained defense.
There would be no forbidden truths in this trial.

The prosecutor's theory was straightforward. Rosa had not committed
suicide. Whatever her difficulties with her former employer, they
could not have been so serious as to cause a normal, healthy young
woman to take her own life. Instead, the prosecution argued that Momolo, in a fit of rage for which he was well known, had struck Rosa

with a cane or other object and that "following this grave wound, she was thrown from the window." At first, Momolo must have attempted to cover the gash with a kerchief, but seeing that Rosa had been mortally injured, he must have pushed her from the window in a panicked attempt to cover up his crime.[11]

Witnesses testified that Rosa was a cheerful girl, never gloomy and not the sort who would commit suicide. Ominously, however, one neighbor had testified to a shouting match between Rosa and her employer. "I knew the Jew Mortara," related Signora Enrichetta Mattei, who had seen him arguing with Rosa the day before her death. He was cursing her for having taken too long at mass. "This mass takes you an awfully long time, oh, damn you and your mass."

Among the first police officers to arrive at the scene was Pilade Masini, who stated that he had run up the stairs to the Mortaras' apartment in order to determine what had happened. Knocking loudly and repeatedly, he got no response and returned to the courtyard, assuming the apartment to be empty. Informed by neighbors that there were people in the apartment, he raced back up the stairs and kicked at the door until he was finally answered. The prosecutor used this delay to explain why neither blood nor a murder weapon had been found in the apartment. The family had used the time "to gather up all the bloodstains, which were consequently not found anywhere in the apartment by later inspections."

The medical evidence showed that Rosa had landed in a nearly upright position, causing fractures to her foot, leg, and hip. Thus, the injury to her head could not have been caused by the fall, a conclusion that was bolstered by the fact that very little blood was found near Rosa's head in the courtyard. Furthermore, the knotted kerchief was intact and not torn—more proof that it had been used to cover a preexisting wound.

In short, the foul play must have occurred in the Mortaras' apartment. The wound, the kerchief, the history of furious anger, and the delay in admitting the police—all of this added up to solid, if indirect, evidence of Momolo's guilt.

Momolo was represented by Signor Mancini, a capable attorney who provided both a theory and a "frame" for the defense. In an approach that would be immediately recognizable to every contemporary lawyer,

Mancini's theory told a story of innocence based on all the known facts, and his frame explained why Momolo was being prosecuted for a crime he did not commit.

Regarding the death of Rosa Tognazzi, Mancini first addressed the young woman's state of mind. She was being hounded and trailed by a past employer who accused her of theft, a mortifying ordeal that had driven her to despair. Of course, her friends and family would have described her as happy and cheerful—Rosa would have done everything she could to hide her predicament.

> To say that she had never before shown suicidal tendencies, as if to say that she did not have sufficient reason for such a desperate decision, is meaningless. . . . These are ideas that are spoken of when they will not be acted on, and are most likely to be carried out when they are least discussed.

The knotted kerchief, Mancini continued, was in fact a blindfold, affixed to help her steel her resolve. And why was it that the kerchief—untorn and intact—covered a bloody laceration? What explanation could there be, other than that it was applied after the infliction of the wound, especially since the physicians testified that the head injury could not have been sustained when her body struck the courtyard?

Mancini's account filled all the gaps. Rosa had jumped from the fourth-floor window with the kerchief over her eyes, obviously going forward as she pushed off from the ledge. However, it was only 2.09 meters* across the courtyard to the next building. Rosa's head obviously struck a ledge as she plunged forward and down, which explained both the nature of the wound and the absence of blood on the ground (and also, of course, in the Mortaras' apartment). And how did the kerchief come to cover the gash? It had been blown upward as she fell, in the same way that her skirts and petticoat had been blown up around her neck.

Finally, Mancini pointed out that Rosa had landed feet first, fracturing her foot and hip. That position was consistent with jumping, but not

* About 82 inches.

with being hoisted out of a window. Obviously, people desperate to shove a heavy young woman out of the window would have lifted her by the shoulders and torso, leading to a headfirst fall.

In other words, the physical evidence, far from compelling, was actually consistent with a story of suicide, and therefore innocence.

But Mancini was not done yet. Why, he asked, were these obvious conclusions overlooked by the prosecutors? Why hadn't they seen the innocent explanations for the unfortunate death of Rosa Tognazzi? To him, the answer was clear. The entire prosecution was infected with prejudice. The lawyer made his point succinctly:

> What stands out to the eyes of the dispassionate observer is the veil of prejudice under which, in this proceeding, they began to suspect that a crime had been committed by the *Jew* Mortara. It's remarkable that the witnesses do not simply refer to him by his name. Indeed, the prosecutor's office itself does not call him, in the normal manner, the *defendant Mortara*. He is, for everyone, simply *Mortara the Jew*.

Thus, the investigation became inexorable, even though no actual crime had been committed. "They assumed that it was a crime, prompted by the twisted suspicions of an old bigot . . . to the detriment of *Mortara the Jew*, and both logic and common sense were bent in search of proof."

In modern terms, we would say that Mancini played the "race card," claiming that his client was the victim of preconceptions and bias, if not an outright frame-up. He attempted to turn prejudice back against the prosecutors, demonstrating their lack of care, incomplete investigation, and rushed conclusions, all because they were biased against the defendant, *Mortara the Jew*.

And, of course, Momolo Mortara was not just any Jew. He was reviled by many conservative Catholics as a man who had attempted to rip a baptized child out of the bosom of the church. Even twelve years later, Momolo was still blamed for the scorn that had been heaped upon the Pope by liberal newspapers in Italy and across Europe. If ever a man needed the protection of the courts, it was this defendant.

From the time that the papal guards took Edgardo, his favorite child, from him, he was beset by a tremendous anguish! Everyone knows about this scandalous case, and all can imagine how it might change someone's character to see his treasured son torn from his breast and his religion, without warning, in the thick of the night, without pity, amidst the boy's, the mother's, and his brothers' and sisters' screams. From the moment of that agonizing scene . . . he became, it's true, a bit brooding and apt to grumble. But his nature was so gentle and good that, deep down, he has always stayed the same. For him, the old saying is apt: "The dog that barks doesn't bite."

The argument was persuasive, although just barely. Momolo was initially convicted by the three judges of the trial court, who held "that the wound on Tognazzi's head was inflicted by Momolo Mortara in his apartment, as a result of a sudden rage, and that Tognazzi was then thrown from the window to make it look like suicide." Their ruling was provisional, however, as a higher court—the Court of Assizes—had jurisdiction over the final decision in all murder cases.

After hearing the renewed arguments of counsel, the Court of Assizes acquitted Momolo Mortara. A broken man, already in ill health and having spent nearly seven months in jail, he died the following month.

Avvocato Mancini's trial strategy was coherent and eventually successful. It was based on true facts; indeed, it was based almost entirely on facts developed by the police and the prosecution. It was nothing but the truth. But it was not the whole truth.

For example, Mancini refused to acknowledge the substantial evidence of Momolo's nasty temper. Nor did he mention the fact that the Mortaras' other domestic servants had complained about their treatment. Erminia Poggi left the Mortaras after barely a month, complaining that Momolo was a "furious man [who] continuously mistreated" her. Poggi also described several incidents of threats and near violence in the household. Antonietta Vestri, the servant immediately before Rosa, told a similar story. She quit after less than a month because of Momolo's "furious character." Finally, a friend of Rosa's testified that the girl had been miserable in the Mortara household because "they beat her with fists and slaps and were always insulting her."

In Mancini's summation, however, Momolo was presented as a man "of the greatest tenderness." Whatever ill temper he might have shown was more than justified by the cruelty he had endured at the hands of the Inquisition. Thus, the attorney argued that the defendant himself had been victimized—an excuse-based strategy that trial lawyers would later raise to an art form in late-twentieth-century America.

And Mancini's factual theory, though derived from established facts, was fairly thin. First, it depended on a conclusion that Rosa Tognazzi would kill herself over a dispute with a former employer, rather than simply move on or run away. And even if Rosa had been suicide-prone, Mancini could only explain the injury to her forehead by positing a rather unlikely series of events. Rosa had affixed a blindfold, groped her way to the window ledge, and jumped out. Her head struck the opposite window ledge with the blindfold still in place, only to have the force of the wind subsequently blow the kerchief up over the wound, remaining there even as Rosa continued her fall and landed in the courtyard.

To sell a theory like that, Mancini would need a powerful theme that could give moral weight to the defense. Mancini could succeed only by providing the judges with a reason for *wanting* to exonerate Momolo Mortara. If they were inclined to view the defendant favorably, the "window ledge" theory would make sense; if they saw the defendant only as a raging brute, the defense would be as flimsy as a wind-blown kerchief.

Mancini took a chance on his theme, staking nearly everything on the possibility that he could evoke sympathy for "Mortara the Jew." It was a risky gamble. The judges were all Christians. And while Italian unification had cast off clerical rule, there was still an obvious residuum of sympathy and affinity for the church. The witnesses who instinctively referred to "the Jew Mortara" were, after all, ordinary Florentine citizens. And while it might have been hoped that judges would have more education and fewer biases, there was certainly no guarantee.

So Mancini played the race card. His client was not a wanton murderer, but a victim of prejudice. The police investigation had been haphazard and incomplete, jumping to an unwarranted conclusion because they wanted to pin the crime on Mortara the Jew. The adverse witnesses voiced their unreasonable suspicions, again out of aversion to the Jew Mortara. All the accusations were premised on the identity of the defendant, not the facts of Rosa Tognazzi's death.

Was it wrong for Mancini to depend so heavily on the race card? Was it merely a cynical ploy to win freedom for an abusive murderer, or was it a conscientious and admirable effort to combat bigotry in the legal system? In part, the answer would appear to depend on Mancini's knowledge and Momolo's guilt. No one would object to an exposé of intolerance when it is offered in defense of an innocent man, but it seems somehow more questionable to cry bias when the defendant is truly guilty.

Still, it is hard to conclude that the limits of advocacy are determined by the culpability of the defendant. Wouldn't a guilty Momolo nonetheless be entitled to a trial free from discrimination? Isn't it fair to caution the court against accepting the testimony of witnesses who see the defendant only as a Jew, rather than as a fellow citizen? More broadly, wouldn't the entire Jewish community of Florence be in jeopardy of unfair prosecution if the anti-Semitism directed at Momolo, whatever his involvement in Rosa's death, were allowed to go unchallenged?

The defense, however, was not unrestrained. Counsel did not claim that Momolo was the victim of a conspiracy, or even that Jews could not be tried fairly in Florence. Rather, he pointed to specific incidents in the trial where prejudice against Mortara had been exhibited. That is, he tied his use of the race card into the precise context of the case. Even his reference to the abduction of Edgardo was presented as an explanation for Momolo's temperament, which had been made an issue by prosecution witnesses.

The context of the trial—Momolo's heartbreaking fame, the witnesses' evident bias, the absence of a direct eyewitness, the ambiguity of the physical evidence, and the necessity for interpretation—placed a premium on the quality of the advocacy. There was no way fully to consider Rosa Tognazzi's death without addressing the singular identity of the defendant.

The defense attorney had no choice but to confront the story of "Mortara the Jew," lest religious prejudice play a hidden role in the conviction of his client. By bringing the question into the open, Mancini was able to do his best to counteract it. And if he managed to shame the judges into giving Momolo some extra benefit of the doubt, well, that was surely preferable to allowing pervasive biases to infect the verdict. As Mancini put it, "Indeed, we believe that because we are dealing with the *Jew Mortara*, it is all the more important that we employ some common sense." There would be no forbidden arguments so long as he was presenting the defense. Instead, there would be nothing but the truth.

NOTES

1. These sorrowful events, familiar in broad outline to most students of Jewish history, were recently explored in compelling detail in David Kertzer's brilliant book, THE KIDNAPPING OF EDGARDO MORTARA (1997). Through his own translations of documents from papal and other archives, Kertzer, a professor of anthropology at Brown University, brings to light the whole agonizing story, much of it previously unknown or only dimly understood. All quotes and other references in this chapter are taken from Kertzer's book unless otherwise indicated.

2. One well-known case occurred in Modena in 1844 and another in Reggio in 1814. *Id.* at 33–35. Such incidents continued even after the uproar surrounding Edgardo, including one in Rome in 1864.

3. It was in 1858 that Lionel Rothschild became the first Jew to serve in the British House of Commons. Kertzer, supra note 1, at 90. Rothschild had actually won several previous elections but had not been allowed to take his seat, owing entirely to his Jewish faith. Finally, in 1858, the legal restriction was removed and Rothschild was allowed to enter Parliament. Regarding Jewish emancipation, see generally JACOB KATZ, OUT OF THE GHETTO: THE SOCIAL BACKGROUND OF JEWISH EMANCIPATION, 1770–1870 (1973).

4. But see Richard Delgado, *Religious Totalism: Gentle and Ungentle Persuasion under the First Amendment,* 51 S. CAL. L. REV. 1, 3 (1977), discussing several cases in which courts countenanced parental abduction and deprogramming of their adult children who had been living in religious "cults". And compare Kit R. Roane, *Hasidic Boy Taken from Home Returns to Brooklyn,* N.Y. TIMES, Oct. 17, 1998, at A11, describing the kidnapping and return of Chaim Weill. Chaim, a six-year-old Jewish boy who suffers from cerebral palsy, was abducted by his Christian nanny, who apparently intended to take him to a "spiritual healer" in South Carolina. Despite the babysitter's professed good intentions, she was apprehended by the FBI and now faces possible life imprisonment. Chaim has been restored to his parents.

5. 12 ENCYCLOPEDIA JUDAICA 354 (1972).

6. The entry in the *Encyclopedia Judaica* is found under the heading "Mortara Case," rather than under Edgardo's (or Salomone's or Marianna's) name. *Id.*

7. Civil libertarians will want to note, however, that the proceedings lacked many of the procedural safeguards many now take for granted. There was no notice to the Mortaras of the inquisitor's interrogation of Morisi, nor would they have been allowed to attend had they learned of it. Though Morisi was questioned carefully by the inquisitor, no one represented the Mortaras' interests and, of course, there was no cross-examination.

8. It appears that the Mortaras were arguing in the alternative. First, the baptism was invalid; but even if valid, Edgardo should be restored to their custody.

9. Clay Chandler, *Scalia's Religion Remarks: Just a Matter of Free Speech?*, WASH. POST, Apr. 15, 1996, at F7 (reporting Justice Antonin Scalia's acerbic observation that the "worldly wise" consider the basic tenets of Christianity to be "absurd" and "simple-minded"). See also Steven Lubet, *Judicial Independence and Independent Judges*, 25 HOFSTRA L. REV. 745, 749 (1997), defending Justice Scalia from criticism that his remarks were improper for a judge.

10. There was one length, however, to which the Mortaras would not go. They were repeatedly told that Edgardo would be returned to them if only they and their other children would convert to Christianity. Committed to their ancestral faith, the Mortaras refused. Perhaps that was the "blind Judaic obstinacy" to which *Brevi cenni* referred.

11. A family friend, Emilio Bolaffi, was also charged with complicity in the crime, as was Ercole Mortara, Momolo and Marianna's adult son. Later, Marianna herself was indicted. The charges against all three additional defendants were dismissed for lack of evidence before the end of the trial. For the sake of brevity and simplicity, I have omitted the case against them from this account.

CHAPTER THREE

JOHN BROWN

Political Truth and Consequences

If asked to name the most important legal decisions in United States history, most Americans would quickly identify several fairly recent high-visibility Supreme Court cases such as Brown v. Board of Education, Miranda v. Arizona, *and* Roe v. Wade. *Lawyers would contribute some more, probably including* Marbury v. Madison, Dred Scott v. Sanford, *and* Gideon v. Wainwright. *Constitutional specialists would nominate a few of their own selections. Whatever the list, it is fairly certain that virtually all the cases would be chosen because of the content of the rulings.*

For that very reason, it would be harder to reach consensus regarding the most important trial in U.S. history. Most so-called trials of the century—from the Lindbergh kidnapping to O. J. Simpson—gain notoriety primarily because of media attention or inherent drama. Their actual impact rarely extends beyond the parties involved.

Sometimes, however, the very process of trying a case can focus attention on potentially transformative issues. Therefore, an argument could be made for the political significance of trials such as the Scottsboro case, the Scopes "Monkey" Trial, the Chicago Seven, or the first Rodney King case, each of which had repercussions outside the courtroom.

It may well be that the most significant, or perhaps we should say consequential, trial in U.S. history was the prosecution of John Brown following his raid on the federal arsenal at Harpers Ferry, Virginia. By one measure that choice appears unconventional, since it was a trial in name only—the outcome never having been in doubt. But the trial of John Brown, in some ways more than the Harpers Ferry raid itself, did much to hasten, and perhaps even make inevitable, the onset of the Civil War.

In the immediate aftermath of the Harpers Ferry attack, John Brown was roundly reviled across the United States. Southerners, of course, had every reason to despise the man who had threatened to incite "servile insurrection," their deepest fear. But northern reaction was not dissimilar. Brown was criticized as insane; the raid was characterized as a calamity and a wild scheme. One free state newspaper remarked that the "insane effort to accomplish what none but a madman would attempt, has resulted as any one but a madman would have foreseen, in death, to all who were engaged in it,"[1] and another put it more bluntly: "the quicker they hang him and get him out of the way the better."[2] Even the abolitionist Liberator referred to Brown's efforts as "misguided, wild, and apparently insane."[3]

Brown's trial, however, caused a dramatic shift in northern public opinion, summoning far more sympathy for his cause than he had been able to generate through force of arms. His unfair treatment by the Virginia court (or at least the perception of it), coupled with his stirring oratory in his own defense, transformed the madman into a hero.

As the trial proceeded, Brown came to be seen in the North as a noble champion of abolition, forced to take desperate action by the wicked slaveholders. And the change in northern opinion had a corresponding impact in the South. If Brown—murderer and fiend—was a hero in the North, then what chance could there be of national reconciliation? For many in the South, the conclusion followed inexorably. The only alternative to reconciliation was secession. To be sure, John Brown's trial did not create that fault line. But as we shall see, it made the fracture unmistakably clear.

The trial itself was intensely and self-consciously political. Nearly each phase and aspect—every argument and word—was measured by the participants for its political impact outside the courtroom. How interesting, then, that the case was marked by jurisdictional blunders, professional misconduct, and conflicts of interest.

Most significantly for our purposes, there was a good bit of outright lying as well, as might be expected in a proceeding conducted with the goal of establishing political, rather than legal, truth. In the battle against slavery, it would be foolish to expect a man like John Brown to be concerned about courtroom niceties. His trial counsel, of course, had different obligations. Or did they?

~

In order to understand and appreciate John Brown's trial, we will need to look fairly closely at the events leading up to the attack on Harpers Ferry.[4] Unsurprisingly, the conventional view—that John Brown was a wild-eyed fanatic pursuing a suicidal mission—is highly misleading. In fact, Brown had a long history of activism and had already become something of a national figure because of his uncompromising and increasingly violent opposition to slavery. Indeed, the relationship between Brown and the "abolition establishment" was a constant subtext at his trial.

Here is a typical description of John Brown's raid, taken from a leading high school history textbook:

> Unlike Lincoln, John Brown was prepared to act decisively against slavery. On October 16, 1859, he and a band of 22 men attacked a federal arsenal at Harpers Ferry, Virginia (now West Virginia). He hoped that the action might provoke a general uprising of slaves throughout the Upper South or at least provide the arms by which slaves could make their way to freedom. Although he seized the arsenal, federal troops soon overcame him. Nearly half his men were killed, including two sons. Brown himself was captured, tried, and hanged for treason. So ended a lifetime of failures.[5]

This account tracks the generally accepted narrative, but it is only moderately accurate and it is certainly incomplete. The actual story of John Brown's invasion of Virginia is far more complex, far more radical, and far more necessary to an understanding of his trial and the events that followed.

We can begin with the statement that Brown's life, before Harpers Ferry, had been characterized by failure. This claim is frequently used to marginalize Brown, portraying him as a ne'er-do-well or crank who was driven by frustration to an act of supreme folly. Following this characterization, the Harpers Ferry raid becomes the act of a madman, occurring outside any larger context or social movement. When we turn to the trial, however, we shall see that it was all about context. The only true dispute was over the relationship between the raid on Harpers Ferry and the forces that were tearing the nation apart. John Brown was hardly an unknown player in these events, nor had he failed in his efforts to intensify the consequences of the struggle against slavery.

While it is true that Brown's business affairs had been marked by lawsuits and bankruptcy, his career as a militant abolitionist had been considerably more successful. As a participant in the Underground Railroad, he had gained the attention, and in many cases the respect, of many of the most prominent abolitionists of the day, including Frederick Douglass, Harriet Tubman, Wendell Phillips, William Lloyd Garrison, and Gerrit Smith.

He rose to national prominence in "Bleeding Kansas," where he had been one of the most visible commanders of the Free Soil militias. Captain Brown won the Battle of Black Jack against overwhelming odds, in what has since been called the first pitched confrontation in the Civil War. Later he led the successful defense of Osawatomie against the proslavery border ruffians from Missouri. Brown also demonstrated a cruel and heartless side, which he sought to justify through claims of necessity, as when he ordered the retaliatory murder of five proslavery settlers near Pottawatomie Creek.

It was also from Kansas that John Brown embarked on his first invasion of slave territory. On December 20, 1858, Brown organized a force of about seventeen armed men for a raid into Missouri. Divided into two bands, Brown's company attacked the homes of three slave owners, killing one man who resisted, and liberating eleven slaves. The freed slaves were brought back to Kansas, where they were hidden while plans were made to carry them to freedom in Canada.

For many, especially in the South, Brown's first raid was viewed as a murderous outrage. The governor of Missouri offered a reward of $3,000 for his capture, to which President Buchanan (a proslavery Pennsylvanian) added $250. Sentiment ran against Brown even among Free State settlers in Kansas, who feared that they would all soon suffer retaliation by Missouri forces. Nor was their fear ill-founded. In the words of one ruffian, armed and outspoken, "When a snake bites me, I don't go hunting for that particular snake, I kill the first snake I meet."[6]

To be sure, none of the condemnation discouraged Brown, or even much bothered him. His goal was to incite open warfare over slavery, and armed provocation was to him an indispensable tactic. He published a detailed account of the Missouri raid in a letter to the *New York Tribune,* defending his actions to "forcibly liberate" the slaves and restore them "to their natural & inalienable rights." For John Brown, there was no room for compromise.

Notwithstanding the price on his head, Brown's next move was one of brilliantly calculated provocation. With a few companions and twelve newly liberated slaves, Brown began a very public wagon journey headed for Windsor, Ontario. Rather than move secretly at night, in the fashion of the Underground Railroad, Brown traveled boldly during the day, daring the authorities to attempt to stop him. Facing down a proslavery posse at the Battle of the Spurs, Brown's party crossed into Nebraska, eluded another posse, and eventually made its way to Iowa. Slowly, the freedom caravan proceeded north and east. Making no attempt to conceal his identity or his plans, Brown stopped frequently to preach, address crowds, and meet with newspaper reporters and editors. Switching to the railroad, they traveled on to Chicago, where they received funds that had been raised by the Cook County Bar Association. Then on to Detroit, again by rail, and finally by ferry into Canada, where the slaves became legally free on March 12, 1859.

All across Iowa, Illinois, and Michigan, Brown's procession drew cheers and support, rallying abolitionists and opponents of the Fugitive Slave Act. Not once was there an effort to interfere with his mission. The detective Allan Pinkerton even helped arrange the railroad car that took them from Chicago to Detroit.

Far from a failure, Brown's liberation train was a stunning success, galvanizing northern public opinion in opposition to slavery (or at least to the Fugitive Slave Act) and demonstrating that slaves could be freed by force. In an entirely different sense, he was a success in the south as well, where he was personally vilified as a murderous fiend. It must have heartened Brown to learn that his incursion into Missouri was perceived as a threat to the entire southern way of life, sparking frightened demands that slave state governments take immediate protective action against the possibility of invasion. That reaction—panic and outrage—was precisely the one he hoped for.

Equally inaccurate is the received description of the Harpers Ferry raid itself, which again makes it seem as though Brown's actions were an isolated outrage: "[John Brown] and a band of 22 men attacked a federal arsenal at Harpers Ferry. . . . He hoped that the action might provoke a general uprising of slaves throughout the Upper South or at least provide the arms by which slaves could make their way to freedom."

While it is true that Brown's military force consisted only of twenty-two men (including two of his sons, who were killed in the battle), he was actually supported, financed, and armed by a much larger group—or conspiracy, if you prefer—of abolitionists. Following his triumphant exodus from Missouri, Brown had launched a recruiting and fund-raising tour through the abolitionist centers in the Northeast, where he succeeded in drawing much support to his violent cause.

Though he did not reveal the specifics of his plan, Brown made it clear to his backers that he intended to liberate slaves through force of arms. Of course, that necessitated an invasion of the South. Brown's most important benefactors became known as the Secret Six—Rev. Thomas Wentworth Higginson, Dr. Samuel Gridley Howe, Rev. Theodore Parker, Franklin D. Sanborn, Gerrit Smith, and George Luther Stearns—pillars of mainstream abolitionism who provided him with encouragement and money.

Brown used the funding from the Secret Six to arm and provision his men and to rent a farmhouse in nearby Maryland, about six miles from Harpers Ferry, that he used as a staging ground. He also commissioned the production of one thousand steel-tipped pikes that he intended to distribute among freed slaves. In the process, he conducted an indiscreet and incriminating correspondence with members of the Secret Six, much of which he unforgivably brought with him (and made no effort to destroy or conceal) when he descended upon the South.

Hero or villain, John Brown was certainly tied closely to leaders of the abolitionist movement, many of whom had at least implicit knowledge of his plans. No one who encouraged or contributed money to John Brown after his bloody career in Bleeding Kansas could have expected that anything other than violence would follow. As we shall see, it was Brown's trial that made it possible for his covert supporters to begin a more public call for the forcible eradication of slavery. In turn, the evident shift of sentiment in the North went a long way toward confirming southern opinion that reconciliation within the Union would be impossible.

Nor was Brown's goal so straightforward as an attempt to "provoke a general uprising of slaves throughout the Upper South or at least provide the arms by which slaves could make their way to freedom." Rather, his "well-matured plan" was considerably more ambitious and entirely more subversive.

John Brown's design was nothing less than the establishment of a free and separate "provisional government" within the borders of Virginia, eventually to be expanded throughout the South. To that end, he had drafted a constitution, naming himself president and commander in chief.

The development of Brown's constitution had actually begun in the spring of 1858, when Brown drafted the document at the home of Frederick Douglass. Next, he convened a conference in Chatham, Ontario, where he first revealed his proposal to establish an enclave of freedom within the southern states. Described by W. E. B. Du Bois as "a frame of government . . . simplified and adapted to a moving band of guerrillas," Brown's constitution was to be the basis for a series of "permanent fortified refuges for organized bands of determined armed men."[7]

The Harpers Ferry raid was meant to be the first step toward establishing armed enclaves from which militant abolitionists and freed slaves could wage guerrilla warfare against the southern states. As Du Bois put it, they would establish their bases in the mountains "thence to descend at intervals to release slaves."[8] Then,

[H]e would continue sending armed parties to liberate more slaves, confiscate arms and provisions, take hostages, and spread terror throughout Virginia. Those slaves who did not want to fight would be funneled up the Alleghenies . . . and across the North into Canada. . . . Meanwhile, driving down Virginia into Tennessee and Alabama, Brown's guerrilla army would raid more federal arsenals and strike at plantations on the plains to

the east and west; from then on the revolution would spread sponta-
neously all through the Deep South.[9]

It was a bold and outrageous strategy, which John Brown virtually repudiated when he came to trial.

For all of Brown's preparation, the raid itself lasted little more than a day.
The small band had spent the summer at the farmhouse he rented on the
Maryland side of the Potomac River, gathering weapons and hoping for
reinforcements. Finally, on Sunday evening, October 16, 1859, Captain
Brown gave the order and the company began its march toward destiny.

Crossing the Shenandoah Bridge into Virginia, they quickly subdued
a night watchman and almost effortlessly took control of the federal arsenal and armory buildings. Taking prisoner a few unfortunate citizens
who happened to be on the street that night, they also seized the nearby
rifle works, where weapons and ammunition were manufactured for the
federal government. Brown's next step was to send a raiding party into
the countryside, with directions to take hostages and liberate slaves.
Their primary target was Colonel Lewis W. Washington, a great-grand-
nephew of the first president. Washington was reputed to own a cere-
monial sword that had been presented to his forebear by Frederick the
Great of Prussia. Along with the slaves, Brown wanted that sword as an
emblem for his own new republic.

Washington was captured without incident, as were two other slave
owners who were brought back to Brown's headquarters along with ten
temporarily emancipated slaves. Eventually Brown assembled about
thirty hostages and succeeded in cutting the telegraph lines out of
Harpers Ferry. For a while, all went according to plan.

Brown's commandos had constructed a barricade across a railroad
bridge into Harpers Ferry. Shortly after 1:00 A.M. on October 17, a Baltimore & Ohio train arrived at the blockade. In cruel irony, the railroad
employee on duty at the time was a freedman named Shephard Hayward. When he went out to investigate the situation, he was shot by one
of Brown's sentinels. He died fourteen hours later, becoming the first fa-
tality in John Brown's war against slavery.[10] The rifle shots alerted the

town that something was afoot, thus dooming the revolt within hours of its inception.

Soon the alarm was spread. A slave uprising at the arsenal! An abolitionist invasion! Church bells tolled, calling men to arms. A rider hastened to nearby Charlestown, from whence telegraph messages were quickly sent to Richmond and Baltimore. By Monday morning the raiders were surrounded by local citizens and militiamen, who poured fire down on their positions. Dangerfield Newby, a freedman who had joined the raid in hopes of liberating his wife and children, was the first of Brown's men to fall. It was clear that the insurrection had miscarried and even flight was rapidly becoming an impossibility.

Brown twice attempted to negotiate a cease-fire that would trade his hostages for the escape of his followers. But despite their display of a white flag, his emissaries were all either gunned down or taken prisoner. Nonetheless, Brown remained fairly solicitous of his own prisoners' welfare, at one point ordering breakfast for them from a local tavern. As the day wore on, more of Brown's men were shot, including his sons Watson and Oliver. Brown consolidated his forces in an engine house, the most defensible building in the armory complex, and released all but nine of his hostages. At nightfall Brown made a last-ditch attempt at negotiation, sending out a note that offered to release his prisoners if he and his men were allowed to "cross the Potomac bridge" without pursuit.[11]

Only darkness and rain prevented the assembled militias from storming the engine house and completing the rout. At about 11 P.M., Colonel Robert E. Lee arrived in Harpers Ferry, commanding a company of U.S. Marines. Plans were quickly made for an assault the next morning, when daylight would make it possible for Lee's men to distinguish between the Virginia hostages and the abolitionist invaders.

By Tuesday morning only five of Brown's raiders remained standing. Seven had fled, of whom five would escape completely, and the others were either dead or gravely wounded. No doubt expecting a frontal assault, Brown must have been heartened to see a detachment of marines approach under a flag of truce. The massive doors to the engine house had been secured with stout ropes, but Brown pushed them open slightly in order to be able to speak with the leader of the troop, J. E. B. Stuart.

Stuart presented the only terms that had been authorized by Lee. Brown was to surrender immediately and unconditionally to the federal authorities, in which case he and his men would be "kept in safety to await the orders of the President." Brown countered with a futile demand for safe passage out of Virginia, at which point Stuart jumped aside and signaled his men to storm the engine house. As the troops rushed in, Brown's party fired their rifles, but they were soon overcome. Brown himself was slashed with a saber and beaten to the ground; the extent of his injuries would become a contentious issue during his trial.

Lee's marines killed two of the raiders, capturing John Brown and four others, including Watson Brown, who had been mortally wounded the previous day. Watson was briefly interrogated by one of his captors:

"What brought you here?" he was asked.

"Duty, sir."

"Is it then your idea of duty to shoot men down upon their own hearth-stones for defending their rights?" asked the Virginian.

"I am dying," said Watson Brown. "I cannot discuss the question. I did my duty as I saw it."[12]

What would be done with the defeated John Brown? Though he had been captured on federal property and seized by federal troops, it quickly became evident that his fate would be determined by the Commonwealth of Virginia. Governor Henry Wise rushed to Harpers Ferry in order to lead the interrogation of Brown and personally take control of the prisoner.

Wise soon confronted the most critical decision of his career. How were the invaders to be punished? There were three possibilities. The governor could declare martial law and bring Brown and his men to trial before a drumhead military court, no doubt resulting in an immediate execution. Alternatively, he could turn his captives over to federal authorities—the crimes had occurred on federal property and they had been taken into custody by federal troops—insisting that the national government fulfill its responsibilities to the citizens of Virginia.

Wise, however, embraced the third option—indictment and trial in a Virginia court. This decision ultimately proved disastrous, though at the time it must have seemed like a political masterstroke.

By rejecting the path of summary execution, Wise was able to stake a claim for southern justice. Even in the face of a monstrous invasion, the governor could demonstrate that Virginia was determined to observe "judicial decencies" while protecting Brown from very real threats of lynching. At the same time, his rejection of federal jurisdiction struck a blow for state sovereignty by establishing the primacy of Virginia's courts. At a time when the authority, indeed the cohesion, of the federal government was very much in doubt, Wise was obviously determined "to enhance the prestige of Virginia at the expense of Washington."[13] Finally, a state trial gave Wise control over the framing of the indictment, which clearly reflected a political agenda:

> The Jurors of the Commonwealth of Virginia . . . do present that John Brown, Aaron C. Stevens . . . and Edwin Coppoc, white men, and Shields Green and John Copland, free negroes, together with divers other evil-minded and traitorous persons to the Jurors unknown, not having the fear of God before their eyes, but being moved and seduced by the false and malignant counsel of other evil and traitorous persons and the instigations of the devil, did, severally . . . within the jurisdiction of this court, with other confederates to the Jurors unknown, feloniously and traitorously make rebellion and levy war against the said Commonwealth of Virginia.

Brown was to be tried not only for murder, but more importantly for committing treason and waging war against Virginia on behalf of "other evil-minded and traitorous" northern abolitionists. If Brown's raid was intended as a blow against the South, the prosecution would be a counterstrike against the antislavery movement in the North. As Stephen A. Douglas would later rephrase the strategy, the attack on Harpers Ferry was the "natural, logical, inevitable result of the doctrine and teachings of the Republican Party."[14]

In brief, Governor Wise's decision to charge treason in a commonwealth court transformed John Brown's trial into something very much like a referendum on the unity of the nation. In the North, every misstep in the trial, every dereliction by the prosecution, would be seen as a reflection on the poor quality of southern justice. Prosecution in federal court would have carried with it at least a veneer of regional neutrality, but the Virginia proceeding made it clear that the case against John Brown was also intended as a defense of slavery itself. While northerners might well have supported swift trial and speedy execution of a brutal fanatic, they were not ready to condemn the abolitionist cause—especially once John Brown began to take advantage of his bloody pulpit.

The trial was convened in nearby Charlestown, the county seat, Judge Richard Parker presiding. The prosecution was led by Andrew Hunter, specially appointed by Governor Wise, assisted by Charles Harding of Jefferson County. Two local attorneys were appointed to defend John Brown, Lawson Botts and Thomas C. Green, the mayor of Charlestown. Consistent with the governor's instructions, the prosecutors were determined to follow the proper forms of adjudication, albeit as rapidly as possible. Brown was ready both to exploit and disdain them:

> Virginians, I did not ask for any quarter at the time I was taken. I did not ask to have my life spared. The Governor of the State of Virginia tendered me his assurance that I should have a fair trial; but, under no circumstances whatever will I be able to have a fair trial. If you seek my blood, you can have it at any moment, without this mockery of a trial.... There are mitigating circumstances that I would urge in our favor, if a fair trial is to be allowed us: but if we are to be forced with a mere form—a trial for execution—you might spare yourselves that trouble.

Of course, John Brown had no interest in hastening his own execution. Indeed, his primary trial strategy was to delay it at every turn. It was not that he feared death. He wrote to his supporters that "I cannot now better serve the cause I love so much than to die for it; and in my death I may do more than in my life." Rather, he intended to fight for every possible moment in which he could proclaim his cause to the watching public.

Moreover, Brown's persistent efforts to stall the case played neatly against the prosecution's insistence on proceeding at "double quick time." The trial commenced less than a week following the raid, beginning on the very day that the indictment was returned, and the prosecution was adamant that it reach its conclusion without interruption. Relying on Virginia's speedy trial statute, Judge Parker denied every request for a continuance, no matter what the stated reason.

Brown's first claim was that he was too badly injured to face immediate trial. He had been stabbed and beaten when Stuart's brigade stormed the engine house. Declaring that he was too weak from his wounds, Brown initially refused to leave his jail bed. Judge Parker ordered that the prisoner be carried into court on a cot, from which Brown made his first request for a continuance:

> I do not intend to detain the court, but barely wish to say, as I have been promised a fair trial, that I am not now in circumstances that enable me to attend a trial, owing to the state of my health. I have a severe wound in the back, or rather in one kidney, which enfeebles me very much. But I am doing well, and I only ask for a very short delay of my trial, and I think I may be able to listen to it; and I merely ask this that, as the saying is "the devil may have his dues," and no more. I wish to say further that my hearing is impaired and rendered indistinct in consequence of wounds I have about my head. . . . I could not hear what the Court has said this morning. . . . I do not presume to ask more than a very short delay, so that I may in some degree recover, and be able at least to listen to my trial, and hear what questions are asked of the citizens, and what their answers are. If that could be allowed me, I should be very much obliged.

A court-appointed doctor, however, advised the judge that Brown's injuries were not so serious as to impair his memory or his hearing, and the continuance was denied.

Other continuances were sought throughout the trial, some based on Brown's repeated claims of ill health, others on the ground that new counsel was about to arrive from the North. The judge would have none of it. "[T]he expectation of further counsel," he ruled, "does not constitute a sufficient cause for delay since there is not certainty about their coming." And when two new attorneys actually did arrive, one from Washington and the other from Cleveland, the judge would not even allow them a few hours in which to study the indictment and prepare the defense, insisting bluntly that "the trial must go on."

The court succeeded in bringing the trial to a speedy conclusion, but only at the cost of engendering tremendous sympathy for John Brown. In the words of the *Lawrence (Kansas) Republican,*

> We defy an instance to be shown in a civilized community where a pris-
> oner has been forced to trial for his life, when so disabled by sickness or
> ghastly wounds as to be unable even to sit up during the proceedings, and
> compelled to be carried to the judgment hall upon a litter.... Such a pro-
> ceeding shames the name of justice, and only finds a congenial place amid
> the records of the bloody Inquisition.[15]

The *Boston Transcript* made the same observation: "Whatever may be his guilt or folly, a man convicted under such circumstances, and, especially, a man *executed* after such a trial, will be the most terrible fruit that slavery has ever borne, and will excite the execration of the whole civilized world" (emphasis in the original).[16]

Since the outcome of the case was never in doubt—Virginia had the power and resolve to see Brown hang—sympathy is all that was truly at stake. Thus, every denied continuance brought John Brown closer to his ultimate goal, a consequence that he seems to have well understood, as the requests for delay persisted throughout the trial.

Brown's appointed attorneys, Botts and Green, were capable members of the Charlestown bar. While they no doubt were appalled and angered by Brown's acts, their defense of him was not perfunctory—an impressive accomplishment in an extraordinarily difficult situation.

For example, Botts and Green exercised all their peremptory challenges, excusing eight of the twenty-four proffered veniremen, although the effort at finding dispassionate jurors in Jefferson County was surely an exercise in futility. Each of the twelve who were eventually seated swore that he could "try this case impartially from the evidence alone without reference to anything [he had] heard or seen of this transaction." Of course, the promises of objectivity must have been transparent to everyone in the courtroom. Still, Botts and Green evidently did the best they could under the circumstances.

More debatable was counsel's decision not to seek a change of venue. The trial began scarcely a week after the outrage at Harpers Ferry, with both panic and fury still thick in the air. A biased jury was the least of Brown's fears, a lynch mob being an ever present possibility. Judge Parker made it clear that he intended to protect the prisoner, announcing in open court that a lynching would be "nothing else than murder, for which its perpetrators might themselves incur the extreme penalty of the law." Of course, moving Brown to another county in Virginia would have had at best a minimal effect on the predisposition of the jury pool, while perhaps exposing him en route to an even greater risk of lynching. The Jefferson County jail, situated directly across the street from the courthouse, was probably the safest place for Brown in the entire commonwealth.

Botts and Green rightly concluded that an insanity plea was the only conceivable hope of saving Brown's life. Apparently without consulting their client, they obtained a telegram from A. H. Lewis of Akron, Ohio, attesting to a history of insanity in Brown's family. Immediately after the jury was impaneled, Botts read the telegram aloud in open court. According to Lewis, "Insanity is hereditary in [Brown's] family."

> His mother's sister died with it, and a daughter of that sister has been two years in a lunatic asylum. A son and daughter of his mother's brother have also been confined in the lunatic asylum, and another son of that brother is now insane and under close restraint. Those facts can be conclusively proven by witnesses residing here, who will doubtless attend the trial if desired.

There would be no opportunity to assess the effectiveness of the strategy. Brown was far more interested in making his point than in avoiding the noose, and he quickly recognized that a claim of insanity would undermine everything he stood for. He repudiated the defense at once, rising from his cot for the first time during the trial:

I look upon [the insanity defense] as a miserable artifice and pretext of those who ought to take a different course in regard to me, if they took any at all, and I view it with contempt more than otherwise. . . . Insane persons, so far as my experience goes, have but little ability to judge their own sanity; and, if I am insane, of course, I should think I know more than all the rest of the world. But I do not think so. I am perfectly unconscious of insanity, and I reject, so far as I am capable, any attempt to interfere in my behalf on that score.

Botts and Green acted well beyond their authority in raising the question of Brown's sanity, but there can be little doubt that their intentions were honorable (or at least sincere). It would have been far easier for them to have mounted a superficial defense, or none at all, while watching or even hastening the inevitable conviction. Instead, they employed what must have seemed to them the only viable strategy on Brown's behalf. True, they were more or less heedless of Brown's larger, political design for the trial, but it surely would have been well nigh impossible for two Virginia lawyers—both men would later serve in the Confederate army, Botts dying in the Second Battle of Bull Run—to have assisted him enthusiastically. Even so, Botts, in his opening statement, while careful to avoid vouching for his client, was able to bring himself to argue that "it was due to the prisoner to state that he believed himself to be actuated by the highest and noblest feelings that ever coursed through a human breast."

The conflict of interest was palpable, as the advocate was plainly torn between duty to his client and loyalty to his community. Perhaps the best evaluation of the professionalism of Botts and Green came from one of the northern lawyers who eventually replaced them: "I must say that their management of the case was as good for Brown as the circumstances of their position permitted."

Notwithstanding the evident integrity of Botts and Green, John Brown repeatedly requested access to attorneys of his own choosing. When the question of a lawyer first arose, Brown attempted to reject the appointment of local counsel.

I have sent for counsel. I did apply, through the advice of some persons here, to some persons whose names I do not now recollect, to act as counsel for me, and I have sent for other counsel, who have had no possible opportunity to see me. I wish for counsel if I am to have a trial; but if I am to have nothing but the mockery of a trial, as I have said, I do not care anything about counsel.

Brown clearly understood that sympathetic lawyers would make it easier for him to manage his own defense, both as it was proffered in the courtroom and as it was presented to the public. In 1859 every common law jurisdiction prohibited criminal defendants from testifying under oath in their own defense. Strange as it might seem to modern sensibilities, it was thought at the time that sworn testimony would constitute either an invitation to perjury or a violation of the privilege against self-incrimination. Consequently, defendants such as Brown were wholly dependent on their attorneys if they wanted to be heard.

Seeking legal assistance from Judge Daniel Tilden of Cleveland and Judge Thomas Russell of Boston, both of whom also practiced law in accordance with the standards of the time, Brown made his needs clear. Without a lawyer committed to the cause, "neither the facts in our case can come before the world; nor can we have the benefit of such facts (as might be considered mitigating in the view of others) upon our trial." Exquisitely sensitive to the importance of his public image, Brown added, "Do not send an ultra Abolitionist."

In fact, he devised his own outline for the trial:

We gave to numerous prisoners their liberty.
Get all their names.
We allowed numerous other prisoners to visit their families, to quiet their fears.
Get all their names.
We allowed the conductor to pass his train over the bridge with all his passengers, I myself crossing the bridge with him, and assuring all the passengers of their perfect safety.
Get that conductor's name, and the names of the passengers, so far as may be.

We treated all our prisoners with the utmost kindness and humanity.
Get all their names, so far as may be.
Our orders, from the first and throughout, were, that no unarmed person should be injured, under any circumstances whatever.
Prove that by ALL the prisoners.
We committed no destruction or waste of property.
Prove that.

Brown's aim was not only to defeat the charge of murder, which he hoped to do by demonstrating that he had shown compassion rather than malice toward his captives, and by extension that he had no intention to murder anyone. But that goal was subordinate to his larger purpose, which was to enhance the image of his entire endeavor by emphasizing its humanitarian, rather than military, objectives. It would have been nearly impossible to engender sympathy in the North for a bloody invasion of peaceful Harpers Ferry (hence the need for a lawyer who was not an ultra-abolitionist). A much stronger case, however, could be made for a tempered mission to rescue slaves in which no property was to be damaged and "no unarmed person should be injured under any circumstances whatsoever." And there began the reinvention of John Brown.

Of course, the claim was false. Brown had no particular respect for southern property or for the lives of slave owners. He had proven as much by the killings in Kansas and Missouri. In fact, he believed that he was completely justified in taking lives, as he had explained early in the raid to his second hostage, the watchman Daniel Whelan: "I came here from Kansas, and this is a slave state; I want to free all the negroes in this State; I have possession now of the United States armory, and if the citizens interfere with me I must only burn the town and have blood."

Truthfully or otherwise, Brown's case could best be presented to the world with the assistance of cooperative counsel. While the trial began with Botts and Green at the defense table, they were eventually dismissed.

One northern lawyer did arrive near the beginning of Brown's trial. In strictly professional terms, his conduct was far more questionable than anything done by Botts and Green.

George H. Hoyt was a neophyte lawyer from Athol, Massachusetts. Only twenty-one years old, he appeared even younger. Within days of the Harpers Ferry raid, Hoyt was retained by John Le Barnes, a Boston abolitionist, and sent directly to Charlestown, ostensibly to assist in Brown's defense.

In reality, however, Hoyt was sent not as a lawyer but as an advance scout with directions to begin planning an escape attempt. Hoyt was instructed to send Le Barnes

> an accurate and detailed account of the military situation at Charlestown, the number and distribution of troops, the location and defences of the jail, and nature of the approaches to the town and jail, the opportunities for a sudden attack and the means of retreat, with the location and situation of the room in which Brown is confined, and all other particulars that might enable friends to consult as to some plan of attempt at rescue.

Both Judge Parker and prosecutor Hunter were skeptical of Hoyt. It seemed unlikely that an inexperienced youngster was the only lawyer in Massachusetts available to assist so famous an abolitionist as John Brown. Hunter communicated his misgivings to Governor Wise, reporting, "A beardless boy came in last night as Brown's counsel. I think he is a spy." The prosecutor promised that the young man, as well as all other strangers, would be "watched closely."

(Hunter was right to be wary. Le Barnes was not the only abolitionist who was working on rescue efforts for John Brown. Though none of the plans matured into action, Virginia had already experienced one invasion and the authorities could hardly discount the possibility of another.)

The prosecutor's suspicions notwithstanding, Judge Parker accepted Hoyt's credentials and allowed him to appear as additional counsel for Brown. He was thereafter given free access to the prisoner, sharing with him the true purpose of his presence in Charlestown. This raises the distinct likelihood that the constant attempts to prolong Brown's trial were, at least at some point, intended to facilitate escape. Certainly Hoyt continued in a dual role as both counsel and conspirator; even after the trial he was involved in evaluating a plan to launch a rescue mission from

Ohio. There is no evidence that Brown's other northern attorneys were actively complicit in such efforts, but it is altogether possible that they were aware of what might follow from an extended trial. That conclusion is supported by an enigmatic note, received by Brown near the trial's conclusion: "My brave but unfortunate friend, Protract to the utmost your trial. Your delivery is at hand. [signed] W.L.G."[17]

Brown himself rejected the possibility of escape, reasoning with great clarity that he could better serve the cause as a martyr. "Let them hang me," he said. "I am worth inconceivably more to hang than for any other purpose." Many of his supporters among the abolitionist elite eventually agreed. Rev. Theodore Parker predicted that "Brown will die . . . like a martyr and also like a saint."[18] Rev. Thomas Higginson put it more bluntly: "I don't feel sure that his acquittal or rescue would do half as much good as being executed, so strong is the personal sympathy with him."[19]

Brown's dismissal of escape, however, does not exonerate George Hoyt, who was manifestly willing to use his law license to facilitate an armed raid on the courthouse itself, if that had been possible. To be sure, history has absolved his ardent abolitionism, and there was genuine courage, indeed heroism, in his willingness to challenge hostile Virginia—either as counsel or spy—on behalf of the cause. As a lawyer, however, he knowingly violated both criminal statutes and professional conventions, and he no doubt would have done more had circumstances allowed. Hoyt's actions can best be understood as civil disobedience— illegal conduct in service of a higher law and pursuit of a greater ideal. If discovered, he would have borne the consequences.

John Brown was not the only one who wanted to use the courtroom to make a larger point, as became apparent from the very beginning of the trial. Governor Wise was determined to address the issue of the supposed northern threat to southern autonomy, believing that Brown's invasion could only have been the result of a "powerful and well-organized conspiracy." And while it is true that Brown was a confederate of the leading abolitionists, he was a very independent and unconstrained member of the movement. If not quite an abolitionist renegade, he was surely the quintessential loose cannon. In the days following the raid, it might well have been possible to separate Brown from the "passive abolitionists" of the North who, in Robert Penn Warren's words, listened to sermons, went home, and "were content to mind their own business."[20]

In the autumn of 1859 the threat of further abolitionist violence was very much a phantom menace, but Wise and his colleagues still chose to prosecute Brown as though he were the vanguard of an invasion. Informed that Judge Daniel Tilden was en route from Ohio to assist Brown's defense, Hunter "asked tartly if Tilden was a lawyer or a leader of a band of desperadoes."

The prosecutor's opening statement gave primacy to the indictment's treason count, with its pointed allusion to "other evil-minded and traitorous persons to the Jurors unknown." He asserted that Brown's goal had been "to rob Virginia's citizens of their slaves and carry them off by violence," continuing proudly that the attempted manumissions had been "against the wills of the slaves, all of them having escaped and rushed back to their masters at the first opportunity."[21]

No argument could have been more forceful in the South or more inflammatory in the North. By tying his case to the virtues of slavery, the prosecutor implicitly asserted that the execution of Brown would be a blow for the protection of slavery—a claim that even moderates in the North could not abide. Many who would never otherwise have condoned the tactics of Harpers Ferry found it necessary to defend Brown, since the alternative was defending slavery.

A more restrained prosecution theory could have been equally successful without sharpening regional tensions. Rather than focus on the political crime of treason, the prosecutor could have sought Brown's execution based on the simple crime of murder. Imagine the impact, in both North and South, if he had presented an argument such as this:

This is not a case about slavery; it is a case about violence. No matter what anyone thinks about the question of slavery, you will have to agree that John Brown committed murder in the course of his invasion of Harpers Ferry. Shephard Hayward was a freed slave, not a slave owner, yet he became Brown's first victim. More men died because of John Brown's belief that he is above the law, that he is empowered to destroy those with whom he disagrees. Perhaps slavery will endure and perhaps it will be abolished, but the decision is not to be made by John Brown's weapons. Justice demands that he be convicted of the murders that he caused.

That theme would have found support in the North as well as the South, by invoking what was still perceived as a common interest in preserving the Union through peaceful means. It is too much to claim, of course, that even the most conciliatory prosecution theory would have had a healing effect on the growing divisions between North and South, but it could have avoided framing the trial as a simple battle between slavery and abolition. And it was precisely that characterization—you are either for slavery or for Brown—that allowed John Brown to take the national stage as a spokesman for the cause of freedom.

Perhaps the prosecutor was playing to his audience, mindful of the need to reassure Virginians that they were secure in their lives and property, including their human property. Perhaps he was zealously determined to make the maximum case against John Brown. Perhaps he was taking directions from Governor Wise, whose broader political ambitions were no secret. Whatever the reason, he played directly into John Brown's hands. By maintaining an extreme theory of the case, he enabled Brown, against all previous odds, to reinvent himself as a heroic icon (at least according to northern lights).

The prosecution case began with Andrew Phelps, conductor of the railroad train that had been stopped by Brown's blockade, who described the shooting of Shephard Hayward. Phelps had also been present at the initial interrogation of Brown following his capture, during which Brown had been asked about his plans. Phelps testified about Brown's proposed constitution for a "provisional government" with himself as commander in chief. In addition, Phelps continued, there was to be a secretary of state, a secretary of war, and a general government that would include "an intelligent colored man."

On cross-examination, Phelps conceded that Brown had stated "it was not his intention to harm anybody or anything. He was sorry men had been killed. It was not by his orders or with his approbation."

The prosecution's most notable witness was Colonel Lewis Washington, who was said to bear a striking resemblance to the first president.

Washington described his kidnapping by Brown's men and his subsequent imprisonment at the armory. Brown, Washington testified, realized that his position was surrounded, and therefore took Washington and nine other men "whom he supposed to be the most prominent" of his hostages, and isolated them in the engine house. Brown had advised Washington that "I shall be very attentive to you, Sir," explaining that "I may get the worst of it in my first encounter, and if so, your life is worth as much as mine." The colonel did not say whether he interpreted that particular statement as a reassurance or a threat. Washington added, however, that "No negro from this neighborhood appeared to take arms voluntarily."

Following Washington's testimony, the prosecution required Brown to identify a series of documents, recovered from the farmhouse in Maryland, linking him to his abolitionist backers in the North.

Other prosecution witnesses included the hostages Armsted Ball, a machinist from the armory, and John Allstadt, a plantation owner who had been abducted by the same expedition that seized Washington. Ball testified that the raiders had fired from their redoubt, killing Harpers Ferry Mayor Fontaine Beckham. Allstadt observed that Brown had kept his rifle "cocked all the time." He also noted that the released slaves "did nothing" and that "some of them were asleep nearly all the time." The latter pronouncement drew laughter in the courtroom, though some of the observers must have recognized it as preposterous even at the time.[22] Still, the idea that slaves might sleep through their own liberation had powerful mythic force, undermining the claims of abolitionism and reinforcing the image of slavery as a benign (and even necessary) institution.

The first defense witness was another hostage, Joseph Brewer, who was asked to affirm Brown's directions that his men avoid unnecessary bloodshed. This was to be the defense theme throughout. Brown had been moved by moral necessity to attempt the emancipation of slaves, but he had made every effort to refrain from violence, even in the face of extraordinary provocation. The prosecution objected, claiming that Brown's asserted restraint was no more relevant than the "dead languages," but Judge Parker allowed the testimony.

To press the point, the defense called Harry Hunter, son of the special prosecutor, who had been present for one of the most demoralizing events of the entire raid. In the early afternoon on Monday, October 17, Brown had attempted to negotiate a cease-fire by sending William Thompson out of the armory under a white flag of truce. Thompson, whose brother was married to Brown's daughter, was immediately seized by the local militia, white flag notwithstanding. Despite the failure of this tactic, Brown tried it again a few hours later, with even more disastrous results. This time the messengers—Aaron Stevens and Brown's son Watson—were both shot. Watson was mortally wounded, although he did manage to make it back to the temporary refuge of the armory; Stevens was captured and held for trial.

Thompson was not so lucky. Following his capture he had been taken to the Wager House hotel, where a mob, led by Harry Hunter and George Chambers, tracked him down and killed him. Hunter described the events in his testimony:

> We . . . caught hold of him, and dragged him out by the throat, he saying: "Though you may take my life, [80,000] will arise up to avenge me, and carry out my purpose of giving liberty to the slaves." We carried him out to the bridge, and two of us, leveling our guns in this moment of wild exasperation, fired, and before he fell, a dozen or more balls were buried in him; we then threw his body off the trestlework. . . . I had just seen my loved uncle and best friend I ever had, shot down by those villainous Abolitionists, and felt justified in shooting any that I could find; I felt it my duty, and I have no regrets.[23]

Hunter's testimony caused Brown to show emotion for the only time during the entire trial. The prisoner groaned and "cried out" for details.[24] Brown's distress in hearing the story of Thompson's murder was no doubt genuine, but he must also have realized the value of the testimony in advancing his overall strategy. The evidence now showed that Brown had harmed no prisoners and had not even sought to use them as shields when Stuart's detachment stormed the engine house. In contrast, the Virginians had repeatedly ignored his flags of truce, shooting down Aaron Stevens and Watson Brown and then cold-bloodedly murdering the captured William Thompson. Harry Hunter might have felt justified in killing as many "villainous Abolitionists" as he could find, but the expression of that sentiment was one more step in turning the commonwealth's murder case against John Brown into a national contest between slavery and freedom.

Harry Hunter's testimony was received with complete and excruciating silence in the courtroom. The special prosecutor must surely have been shaken by his son's story of deliberate execution of a man who was "unarmed and pleading for his life."[25] Nor could Botts and Green have been unmoved, though it is impossible to know whether they sympathized more with their client or with the elder Hunter, a fellow Virginian and colleague at the bar.

The stage was set for drama, and Brown provided it soon after Hunter left the stand. Defense attorneys Botts and Green called out the names of several additional witnesses, but none came forward. Clearly unnerved by Hunter's testimony, Brown rose from his cot and protested loudly:

> I discover that notwithstanding all the assurances I have received of a fair trial, nothing like a fair trial is to be given me, as it would seem. I gave the names, as soon as I could get them, of the persons I wished to have called as witnesses, and was assured that they would be subpoenaed . . . but it appears that they have not been subpoenaed as far as I can learn; and now I ask, if I am to have anything at all deserving the name and shadow of a fair trial, that this proceeding be deferred until tomorrow morning; for I have no counsel, as I before stated, in whom I feel that I can rely, but I am in hopes counsel may arrive who will attend to seeing that I get the witnesses who are necessary for my defence.

Whether offended or relieved, the appointed attorneys immediately petitioned the court for leave to withdraw as counsel. As Green put it,

> Mr. Botts and myself will now withdraw from the case, as we can no longer act in behalf of the prisoner, he having declared here that he has no confidence in the counsel who have been assigned him. Feeling confident that I have done my whole duty, so far as I have been able, after this statement of his, I should feel myself an intruder upon this case were I to act for him from this time forward.

He continued candidly, "I had not a disposition to undertake the defense, but accepted the duty imposed on me, and I do not think, under these circumstances, when I feel compelled to withdraw from the case, that the court could insist that I should remain in such an unwelcome position."

Green was of the same mind: "I have endeavored to do my duty in this matter, but I cannot see how, consistently with my own feelings, I can remain any longer in this case when the accused whom I have been laboring to defend declares in open court that he has no confidence in his counsel."

Judge Parker quickly agreed, releasing both men from their obligations as counsel. This left the novice George Hoyt as the only available attorney for Brown. Hoyt petitioned for a delay based on his own inadequacy as trial counsel (he did not mention his dual role as spy): "[I] cannot assume the responsibility of defending him myself for many reasons. First it would be ridiculous in me to do it, because I have not read the indictment through . . . and have no knowledge of the criminal code of Virginia, and no time to read it."

Informing the court that experienced attorneys were expected to arrive shortly, Hoyt pleaded for a continuance until at least the next morning. The judge was impassive. Disinclined throughout to wait for northern lawyers, he also disapproved of Hoyt's proposal because "the idea of waiting for counsel to study our code through could not be admitted." Botts, however, did one last service for his erstwhile client, imploring Judge Parker to allow Hoyt at least a night of preparation and volunteering to "sit up with him all night to put him in possession of the law and facts in relation to this case." The court relented, allowing Hoyt one night to become schooled in both criminal defense and Virginia law.

Although we can only speculate as to his reasons, it is certainly understandable that Brown seized the opportunity to discharge Botts and Green. Notwithstanding their technically competent representation, Brown needed ideological allies, more than merely capable advocates, if he was to carry out his plan. Perhaps he was truly aggrieved at Botts and Green's failure to obtain the desired witnesses (though it would hardly have seemed likely that northern lawyers could have been more effective in that endeavor); perhaps he simply saw an opportunity to assail the quality of Virginia justice; and perhaps the story of Thompson's murder impelled him to take some action, any action—the discharge of his Virginia lawyers being the only power that he had. Most likely, however, it seems that Brown would rather have faced trial unrepresented than place his fate—and, more importantly, his ability to communicate—in the hands of southerners.

Whatever his motive, the disavowal of Botts and Green brought him no sympathy in Charlestown. According to the *New York Herald,* "the indignation of the citizens scarcely knew bounds." Brown was denounced as "an ungrateful villain, and some declared he deserved hanging for that act alone."[26]

Hoyt's hastily acquired skills as an advocate, however, were not to be tested. Experienced reinforcements had arrived by morning—Samuel Chilton of Washington and Hiram Griswold of Cleveland. The new attorneys requested several hours in which to read the indictment and study the record, but Judge Parker was willing to allow them only a few minutes to interview their client. Brown had chosen to dismiss his very capable local attorneys; he would have to bear the consequences. "The trial must go on."

And go on it did. The defense continued to call hostages who testified that their lives had never been threatened, even after Watson and Oliver Brown had been fatally shot. Most of the direct examinations were conducted by young Hoyt, but in a bizarre turn Brown himself took part in some of the questioning without rising from his cot. Hunter protested the repetitive testimony, calling it a waste of time. Hoyt replied that it was relevant to "prove the absence of malicious intention," which seemed to satisfy the court. Hunter waived cross-examination of these witnesses, surely hoping both to expedite the trial and to belittle the validity of that particular line of defense.

Once the last witness had testified, Chilton argued for the first time that there was a defect in the indictment. It was unfair, he maintained, to require Brown to defend himself in one proceeding against three such disparate charges as murder, treason, and inciting servile insurrection. Thus, he requested that the prosecution be required to elect a single count and dismiss the other two.[27] The reasoning behind this strategy is not entirely clear, unless it was simply another effort at delay. All three charges were capital crimes and all three were supported by roughly the same evidence. And even if forced to choose, the prosecution would obviously select its strongest, best-supported count, which would be sufficient to send Brown to the gallows.

The prosecutors objected mightily, though their motivation is easier to understand. Having chosen to indict Brown as a threat to the southern way of life—meaning, of course, the preservation of slavery—they were not about to temper their case at its very conclusion. All three counts were necessary to tell their story. In their eyes, John Brown was not merely a murderer, he was an abolitionist murderer. Indeed, he was a murderer because he was an abolitionist. If Brown's abolitionism itself was tantamount to a crime, then the charges of treason and servile insurrection were necessary to establish the connection.

Judge Parker promptly ruled for the prosecution, holding that "distinct offenses may be charged in the same indictment," and directed the attorneys to proceed immediately to their final arguments. Again the defense protested at being pressed to go forward, but the prosecution claimed there was urgent need to bring the trial to a conclusion. Resuming his theme of the abolitionist threat, Hunter successfully argued that the very length of the trial endangered the welfare of society: "[T]here could not be a female in this county who, whether with good cause or not, was not trembling with anxiety and apprehension."

By that point it was already late Saturday afternoon and Brown was again maintaining that he was too ill to proceed. Though clearly mistrusting Brown's claims, Judge Parker struck a compromise intended "to avoid all further cavil at our proceedings." The prosecution would begin its argument that evening, but the defense argument and the prosecution rebuttal would be held over until the following Monday. Having insisted that the jurors were being unfairly separated from their families, the prosecution was now constrained to argue only briefly before adjourning for the balance of the weekend. That task fell to Charles Harding, the second-string prosecutor known for his ineptitude, who limited his remarks to about forty minutes. Harding addressed none of the legal issues, but instead condemned Brown as the leader of a band of "murderers and thieves," declaring that he had "forfeited all rights to protection of any kind whatsoever."

Brown spent much of the next day meeting with his attorneys in order to outline his defense, no doubt conferring over precise tactics. Represented at last by trusted and supportive counsel, Brown declared that he was "perfectly satisfied" with their plans.[28] The prisoner clearly understood that his life was forfeit, and realized that the audience for his defense lay well beyond the courtroom. "He seems," observed George Hoyt, "to be inspired with a truly noble Resignation."[29]

The defense argument on Monday morning rested in equal parts on technicalities and misrepresentations. Doing his best under difficult circumstances, Hiram Griswold began by asserting that Brown could not be guilty of treason as charged because he was neither a citizen nor a resident of Virginia. Moreover, Virginia had no jurisdiction over the murder charges since Brown had remained almost exclusively on federal property.

But the heart of the argument, evidently presented with his client's input and approval, consisted of an artful denial of Brown's very principles. Far from a danger to slavery and the South, Brown was depicted as an idealistic dreamer, noble in his intentions but incapable of incitement. There could be no conviction for conspiracy to incite insurrection because the slaves simply failed to join. The provisional constitution, Chilton claimed, was never a serious plan, but instead was an "imaginary government for a debating society . . . a wild and chimerical production." As to Brown's influence on the abolitionist movement,

Can it be supposed, gentlemen, even for a moment, that there is fear to be apprehended from such a man, who, in the zenith of his power, when he had a name in history, and when something might be hoped for the cause in which he was engaged, could only, throughout the whole country, raise twenty-one men?

Is it to be supposed for a moment, I ask, now, when he is struck down to the earth, his few followers scattered or destroyed—now, when the fact is known that the south is alarmed and armed in every direction ready to repel any enterprise of this kind, that anything is to be feared? No, gentlemen, there is not the remotest danger of your ever again witnessing in your State anything akin to that which lately occurred.

Of course, even to his death, Brown intended just the opposite. He had failed to incite rebellion directly; it was his hope and aspiration to achieve it posthumously through martyrdom.

It cannot be known whether Griswold was fully aware of his own tacit deceptions. He had not met Brown before arriving in Virginia, though he must certainly have known of him, including Brown's pitched battles in Kansas and probably the Pottawatomie murders as well. Attorney and client counseled together at some length as Griswold prepared his speech, but we do not know whether the prisoner was candid or cagey during their meeting. There is reason to suspect, however, that Griswold was knowingly complicit in the effort to reinvent John Brown as a mainstream abolitionist, as will become apparent when we consider Brown's own address to the court. But whatever the lawyer's actual knowledge, it is certain that Brown himself initiated the strategy.

Griswold's argument was not actually intended to assuage the fears of the Virginia jurors or save Brown's life, but rather to magnify the enormity of the certain verdict. If Brown could be characterized as less than a menacing firebrand, then his execution could be characterized as an attack against the entire abolitionist movement—an attack that would in turn motivate a response. Ironically but effectively, it appeared that the denial of violence could be used to inspire violence.

Special prosecutor Hunter delivered the rebuttal. He addressed the alleged technical deficiencies in the indictment, dismissing them as legally without merit, but he saved his real fire for Brown's "nefarious and hellish purpose of rallying forces into this Commonwealth . . . as the starting point for a new government."

To Hunter, Brown was the vanguard of an abolitionist invasion. Brown's conduct showed "that it was not alone for the purpose of carrying off slaves" that he came to Virginia. Rather, his intention was to overthrow the commonwealth, establishing an abolitionist regime—or worse—in its place. "His 'Provisional Government' was a real thing and not a debating society . . . and in holding office under it and exercising its functions, he was clearly guilty of treason." Hunter warned that Brown "wanted the citizens of Virginia calmly to fold their arms and let him usurp the government, manumit our slaves, confiscate the property of slaveholders, and without drawing a trigger or shedding blood, permit him to take possession of the Commonwealth and make it another Haiti."[30]

There was no space for reconciliation in the prosecutor's scorching argument, which has been referred to as a "whiplashing" of Brown, but was at least as much a scourging of the entire abolitionist cause.[31] To Hunter, freeing the slaves was the equivalent of assassinating their masters, and he drove that point home in his allusion to Haiti. But if that logic served to rally the frightened people of the South, it would have an entirely different impact in the North, where most abolitionists had previously supported emancipation without violence. But Hunter, in essence, denied the possibility of peaceful emancipation—manumission leads to Haiti—thereby pushing the abolitionist movement in exactly the direction that John Brown intended.

It took the jury only forty-five minutes to reach its determined verdict of guilty on all charges. John Brown, however, was yet to have the last word.

Allowed to address the court before sentencing, Brown delivered extemporaneous remarks that were directed "not [to] the men who surrounded him, but the whole body of his countrymen, North, South, East and West."[32] Speaking six years later at Abraham Lincoln's funeral service, Ralph Waldo Emerson would refer to Brown's speech as one of the two greatest of the century (the other being the Gettysburg Address).[33]

Certainly, Brown's speech galvanized the North, drawing praise from those who had previously denounced him. It was fashioned for that very purpose, and was therefore devised with no deep regard for the truth. As Robert Penn Warren would say, "It was so thin that it should not have deceived a child, but it deceived a generation."[34]

Brown did not hesitate to conceal the extent of his true plans:

In the first place, I deny everything but what I have all along admitted: of a design on my part to free slaves. I intended certainly to have made a clean thing of that matter, as I did last winter, when I went into Missouri and there took slaves without the snapping of a gun on either side, moving them through the country, and finally leaving them in Canada. I designed to have done the same thing again on a larger scale. That was all I intended. I never did intend murder, or treason, or the destruction of property, or to excite or incite slaves to rebellion, or to make insurrection.[35]

Brown's Missouri rescue had been popular in the North, so it is understandable that he would attempt to wrap himself in the mantle of that success. But even so he tampered with the truth. In fact, there had been gunfire in Missouri and a slave owner had been killed. Moreover, the Missouri liberation had been an almost incidental event during the Kansas battles, during which Brown had ordered the execution of five unarmed men for the crime of sympathy with slavery.

It was flatly untrue that Brown intended no more at Harpers Ferry than to deliver slaves to Canada. His "well matured plan" actually called for the establishment of a permanent military enclave to be used as a base for continuing raids on slaveholders. If successful, Brown would have spread his encampments further into the South to encourage and facilitate insurrection, though he continued to deny as much: "I never had any design against the liberty of any person, nor any disposition to commit treason or incite slaves to rebel or make any general insurrection. I never encouraged any man to do so, but always discouraged any idea of that kind."

Lies again. Brown had specially ordered one thousand steel pikes for the express purpose of arming freed slaves for a general insurrection. He brought cases of handguns and rifles with him to Virginia, far more than could possibly have been needed to equip his force of twenty-two men. "General insurrection" was so much his intention that he had printed forms for the "commissions" of the officers in his provisional army, which was to be organized into battalions, companies, bands, and sections. And far from discouraging men from joining him, Brown had actively recruited others, castigating those who lost their resolve and failed to join the mission.

But Brown was not lying to save his life. Having scorned an insanity defense, he knew full well that he would be sentenced to die and he was determined to make the most of his martyrdom. His protestations of nonviolence were intended to aid his greater cause by making him the victim, rather than the killer, of Harpers Ferry. And so, when he turned to the cause itself he was able to speak with sincere nobility:

> I believe that to have interfered as I have done, as I have always freely admitted I have done, in behalf of His despised poor, I did no wrong, but right. Now, if it is deemed necessary that I should forfeit my life for the furtherance of the ends of justice, and mingle my blood further with the blood of my children and with the blood of millions in this slave country whose rights are disregarded by wicked, cruel, and unjust enactments, I say, let it be done.

Thus, John Brown was able to turn attention from his own excesses and recklessness to the evils of slavery. The strategy could not have been more effective. All across the North, people rallied to Brown's cause, lionizing him as the hero of Harpers Ferry and denouncing the malevolence of southern justice that would enslave millions and then dare to execute their liberator. As though governed by physical laws, the reaction in the South was equal and opposite, condemning both Brown (literally) and his northern supporters (figuratively) as a mortal threat to their lives and homes.

At a distance now of over 140 years, it is impossible to chastise John Brown for lying about his tactics in order to advance the cause of abolition. The struggle for human freedom was the greatest movement of the nineteenth century and John Brown, for all his extremism, understood more clearly than most that it would take a civil war to emancipate the slaves. Measured against that goal, a few flashes of oratorical deception seem well justified, perhaps imperative. And in any event, Brown certainly felt no moral obligations to the slaveholders' court. In a sense, he was speaking the whole truth when he told his captors that his acts were "worthy of reward rather than punishment." Bound by

God to "remember them that are in bonds," he had done nothing more than to "act up to that instruction."

It is fair to ask, however, whether his lawyers were aware of the deceit. Under no conception of legal ethics have attorneys ever been entitled to "counsel or assist a witness to testify falsely."[36] It may be that professional misconduct is morally vindicated under extreme circumstances, but that question cannot be answered unless we know whether the standard was violated in the first place.

As it turns out, there is good reason to believe that Chilton and Griswold were willing participants in John Brown's plan to suppress the truth about his intentions at Harpers Ferry. First, we know that Brown was adamant about his need for northern lawyers who were not known as ultra-abolitionists. Notwithstanding the determined efforts of Botts and Green, and the possibility that highly regarded local lawyers might actually have been more effective before the Charlestown jury, Brown dismissed them at the first opportunity, even if that meant placing his trial in the hands of the novice (though politically dependable) George Hoyt. Hoyt, of course, was completely trustworthy and deserving of Brown's confidence, having traveled to Virginia for the purpose of facilitating an escape.

Chilton and Griswold, the senior lawyers who eventually took over the defense, were not part of any rescue scheme. They did, however, spend hours closeted with Brown in preparation for the trial's final arguments, following which Hoyt himself pronounced the client "well pleased with what has transpired."

A further implication arises from the manner in which the defense was conducted. John Brown was not called to make a statement on his own behalf until after the verdict had been returned, and then the invitation came from the court. Although Virginia law at the time prohibited a criminal defendant from testifying under oath, common law precedent did allow defendants to address the jury directly, either in narrative or through direct examination.[37] Judge Parker had earlier shown an inclination to indulge Brown's unconventional participation in the trial, allowing him to address the court on a number of occasions and also to question several of the witnesses. There is much reason to believe, therefore, that he would have permitted Brown to make a statement to the jury prior to the verdict. Moreover, the denial of such a request would have provided even more ammunition for northern newspapers, ever eager to condemn Virginia justice.

Since the goal of the defense was to give Brown an opportunity to speak to the nation, why did they forgo an opening to put him on the witness stand, even if unsworn? Why wait until after the conviction to ask him to speak? And indeed, why not at least attempt to provide two such occasions rather than one?[38]

For a trial strategist, one answer seems evident. A mid-trial statement by Brown, unlike his speech at sentencing, could have been followed immediately by rebuttal evidence. For some reason, Brown's lawyers apparently did not want to expose him to contradiction by the prosecution, or perhaps even cross-examination if the court had allowed it. It is unlikely that they seriously feared the possibility of implicating his backers in Massachusetts or elsewhere. Brown could readily have dealt with that problem simply by refusing to answer questions about his supporters, as he had done when interrogated by Governor Wise shortly following his capture. Facing a certain conviction and death sentence, he hardly needed to be concerned about a contempt citation; nor would his reputation have suffered as a result of shielding his associates from indictment.

We are left, then, with the distinct possibility that Brown's statement was withheld from the trial itself for fear of the uncomfortable questions that would have followed about the true nature of his intentions. Confronted with his papers, maps, commissions, and letters, would he have been credibly able to deny the plan for a general insurrection? Would he have been able to maintain his crucial calm composure for the balance of the proceeding, as well as his artfully devised story? Knowing that he would later have the option of an unchallenged speech at sentencing, a capable lawyer would have chosen to avoid that risk—especially if he was aware of Brown's intention to lie.

That is as far as we can go based upon the available evidence. We know that Brown dissembled, the better to make his point. We know that his attorneys facilitated that stratagem, knowingly or otherwise, thus enabling Brown to play his crucial role in "heightening the contradictions" between North and South.

~

Here is an example of the northern reaction to John Brown's exploits immediately after the raid on Harpers Ferry: "We are damnably exercised here about the effect of Brown's wretched fiasco in Virginia [and] about the moral health of the Republican Party. The old idiot—the quicker they hang him and get him out of the way the better."[39]

Salmon Chase, a Republican candidate for president and eventually Lincoln's secretary of the treasury, put it this way: "How sadly misled by his own imaginations! How rash—how mad—how criminal then to stir up insurrection which if successful would deluge the land with blood and make void the fairest hopes of mankind!"[40]

Virtually all the northern newspapers had the same initial response to the raid, calling Brown a "lawless brigand," a "madman," and worse. The *New York Times,* then a moderate Republican paper, was typical in saying, "The great mass of our people look on this with horror and execration."[41]

With the progress of the trial, however, northern reaction changed dramatically in a direction that could only be viewed with alarm, if not outright panic, in the South. Many editors took the position that the raid was an inevitable response to the evils of slavery, in essence saying that the slave owners got what they deserved: "If a man builds his house on a volcano, it is not those who warn him of the danger who are to blame for its eruptions."[42]

The *New York Independent* was among the most outspoken, expressing the conviction that Brown's raid demonstrated that "God has in view the overthrow of slavery." Decrying the "indecent haste of the court to obtain a verdict of Guilty, the rude treatment of counsel from abroad, the disregard for the forms and proprieties of law," the editorial went on to make an ominous prediction:

> Not John Brown but slavery will be gibbeted when he hangs upon the gallows. Slavery itself will receive the scorn and execration it has invoked for him. . . . When John Brown is executed, it will be seen he has done his work more effectively than if he had succeeded in running off a few hundred slaves. The terror by night that rules in every household on her soil, drawing sleep from mothers and children, the anxieties and

fears that for months to come will burden her population, the spirit of revenge—all these will make the cost of slavery to Virginia greater than she can bear.[43]

Leading northern abolitionists drove home the same point. Ralph Waldo Emerson called Brown a "new saint awaiting his martyrdom" who "will make the gallows glorious like the cross."[44] Henry Wadsworth Longfellow said that Brown's raid would mark the "date of a new Revolution—quite as needed as the old one."[45] Wendell Phillips proclaimed that Brown "has twice as much right to hang Governor Wise, as Governor Wise has to hang him."[46] For Virginia, the execution of Brown was "sowing the wind to reap the whirlwind, which will come soon."

The reaction in the South was fiery from the first news of the raid, and it continued in that vein without surcease. The *Richmond Whig* presciently declared, "Immediate shooting or hanging without trial is the punishment they merit. In regard to the offenders, the just and safe principle is hang them first and try them afterward."[47] The *Fredericksburg Herald* was, if anything, even more enraged: "Hang these villainous wretches, offenders against the public peace, without the benefit of clergy. . . . The wheel and the rack are not a whit too hard for them. Shooting is a mercy they should be denied."[48]

As it became clear that northern opinion had become sympathetic to Brown, indeed openly supportive of him, the anger in the southern press turned in a new direction. If Brown was a hero in the North, then what chance could there be for security within the Union? "The day of compromise is passed," declared one editor, "there is no peace for the South in the Union. The South must control her own destinies or perish."[49] The *Charleston Mercury* made the point explicitly:

> The great source of the evil is that we are under one government with these people, that by the Constitution they deem themselves responsible for the institution of slavery and therefore they seek to overthrow it. . . . If we had a separate government of our own, the post office, all the avenues of intercourse, the police and military of the country, would be under our

exclusive control. Abolitionism would die out in the North or its adherents would have to operate in the South as foreign emissaries.[50]

It was too late to turn back. John Brown's trial had rubbed raw the wound of slavery, exposing the impossibility of reconciliation. Perhaps the South could have endured the raid, but there was no tolerating the transformation of John Brown into a northern hero: "Though it convert the whole Northern people without an exception into furious, armed abolition invaders, *yet Old Brown will be hung!* That is the stern and irreversible decree, not only of the authorities of Virginia but of the people of Virginia without a dissenting voice."

Counterfactual history is always questionable, and surely it is too much to claim that the Civil War could have been forestalled if only the trial of John Brown had been handled differently. On the other hand, the argument is compelling that the Harpers Ferry prosecution inflamed regional antagonisms, thus hastening the war and perhaps even making it unavoidable. Which straw broke the camel's back? Was it Bleeding Kansas that made the war inevitable? Was it only the election of Lincoln that assured secession? Whatever the answer, it seems certain that the trial of John Brown, and the subsequent public reactions, placed a heavy burden on the fragile, splintering Union.

In that sense, Brown was successful beyond any expectation. Reconciliation between North and South would assuredly have meant compromise on the question of slavery, preserving the institution at least where it already existed and thus condemning to continued bondage another generation or more of black Americans. By using his trial to push the abolitionist movement toward open approval of violence, thus enraging even "moderates" in the South, Brown achieved one of his dearest goals. It is therefore possible to say that the defense strategies, candid and otherwise, prevailed. In contrast, the prosecution ultimately resulted in disaster for the men who directed it, assuming that they wanted to protect their lives and property.

As he left jail for the gallows on his execution day, John Brown handed a note to one of his guards, speaking prophetically to his allies in the North:

I John Brown am now quite *certain* that the crimes of this *guilty land*: *will never be purged away*; but with Blood. I had *as I now think*: *vainly* flattered myself that without *very much* bloodshed; it might be done.

As though to underscore Brown's role in inspiring the looming war between the states, the officer in charge of his execution spoke these last words on the scaffold as the trapdoor was released: "So perish all such enemies of Virginia! All such enemies of the Union!"

NOTES

1. OSWALD GARRISON VILLARD, JOHN BROWN 473 (1911), quoting the *Atchison City (Kansas) Freedom's Champion*.

2. Quoted in STEPHEN B. OATES, TO PURGE THIS LAND WITH BLOOD: A BIOGRAPHY OF JOHN BROWN 310 (1970).

3. Quoted in VILLARD, *supra* note 1, at 473.

4. Unless noted otherwise, the facts of the raid and subsequent trial have been taken from the following sources: VILLARD, *supra* note 1; W. E. B. DU BOIS, JOHN BROWN (1973); JULES ABELS, MAN ON FIRE: JOHN BROWN AND THE CAUSE OF LIBERTY (1971); OATES, *supra* note 2; THOMAS FLEMING, THE TRIAL OF JOHN BROWN (1967); RICHARD B. MORRIS, FAIR TRIAL (1953); ROBERT PENN WARREN, JOHN BROWN: THE MAKING OF A MARTYR (1929); OTTO J. SCOTT, THE SECRET SIX: JOHN BROWN AND THE ABOLITIONIST MOVEMENT (1979).

5. GARY NASH & JULIE ROY JEFFREY, THE AMERICAN PEOPLE: CREATING A NATION AND A SOCIETY 496 (1998). They go on to say, "In death, however, Brown was not a failure. His daring if foolhardy raid, and his impressively dignified behavior during his trial and speedy execution, unleashed powerful passions, further widening the gap between North and South." *Id.*

6. Quoted in ABELS, *supra* note 4, at 220.

7. Du Bois, *supra* note 4, at 259.

8. *Id.* at 276.

9. OATES, *supra* note 2, at 278.

10. ABELS, *supra* note 4, at 279–80. In yet a further irony, the Sons and Daughters of the Confederacy later erected a plaque to Hayward, claiming that he "exemplif[ied] the character and faithfulness of thousands of Negroes, who under many temptations throughout subsequent years of war so conducted themselves that no stain was left upon a record which is the peculiar heritage of the American people." *Id.*

11. Brown's precise terms were strikingly unrealistic, given his desperate position: In consideration of all my men, whether living or dead, or wounded, being

soon safely in and delivered up to me at this point with all their arms and am-munition, we will then take our prisoners and cross the Potomac bridge a lit-tle beyond which we will set them at liberty; after which we can negotiate about the Government property as may be best. Also we require the delivery of our horse and harness at the hotel.

Quoted in *id.* at 292.

12. OATES, *supra* note 2, at 302.

13. *Id.* at 308. As Oswald Garrison Villard put it, "Wise had no desire to have it said that the State of Virginia was forced to hide behind the skirts of the Federal Government, and to obtain its help to punish those who violated her soil and killed her citizens." VILLARD, *supra* note 1, at 477.

14. Quoted in OATES, *supra* note 2, at 310.

15. Quoted in VILLARD, *supra* note 1, at 480.

16. Quoted in *id.* at 481.

17. Quoted in MORRIS, *supra* note 4, at 282. The initials would appear to be those of William Lloyd Garrison.

18. Quoted in ABELS, *supra* note 4, at 341.

19. Quoted in *id.*

20. WARREN, *supra* note 4, at 391.

21. The myth of contented slaves was essential to southern peace of mind. Of course, once Brown had been overwhelmed and captured, the "liberated" slaves did everything they could to distance themselves from any cooperation with his plan. It was worth their lives even to suggest otherwise. W. E. B. Du Bois, however, believed that an unknown number of slaves had cooperated with Brown. DU BOIS, *supra* note 4, at 346. At least one slave, known only as Phil, was arrested and jailed for as-sisting Brown in defending the engine house. He is reported to have died in prison, from either fear or mistreatment.

22. In fact, it was Allstadt's own slave, recorded only as Phil, who was arrested for cooperating with Brown. Phil died in the Jefferson County jail before he could be tried.

23. Hunter's uncle Fontaine Beckham, mayor of Harpers Ferry, had been shot and killed by one of Brown's raiders.

24. VILLARD, *supra* note 1, at 491.

25. *Id.*

26. Quoted in *id.* at 492.

27. *Id.* at 494.

28. *Id.* at 495.

29. Quoted in *id.* (capitalization in the original).

30. Quoted in MORRIS, *supra* note 4, at 289.

31. *Id.*; OATES, *supra* note 2, at 326.

32. VILLARD, *supra* note 1, at 498.

33. ABELS, *supra* note 4, at 331.

34. Quoted in *id.* at 332.

35. Quoted in Villard, *supra* note 1, at 498.

36. The contemporary iteration is found in the American Bar Association's Model Rules of Professional Conduct Rule 3.4(b) (1999), but the concept itself is as old as the legal profession.

37. Every United States jurisdiction followed some version of "interested party" incompetence well into the nineteenth century. Virginia did not abolish the rule until 1886. Under common law precedent, however, judges had discretion to allow criminal defendants—especially in capital cases—to make unsworn statements on their own behalf, either in narrative form or with the assistance of counsel's direct examination.

38. Following the jury's verdict on November 2, Judge Parker set Brown's execution for December 16. In the intervening six weeks, Brown was allowed to write hundreds of letters expressing his views and goals. When Griswold and Chilton opted to forgo a statement by Brown, however, it could not have been known that there would be such a lengthy delay between conviction and execution, or that Brown would be allowed such free access to public opinion.

39. Quoted in Oates, *supra* note 2, at 310.

40. Quoted in *id.* at 313.

41. Quoted in Abels, *supra* note 4, at 317.

42. Quoted in *id.*

43. Quoted in *id.* at 313–14.

44. Quoted in Oates, *supra* note 2, at 318.

45. Quoted in *id.* at 319.

46. Quoted in *id.* at 318.

47. Quoted in Abels, *supra* note 4, at 319.

48. Quoted in *id.*

49. Quoted in Oates, *supra* note 2, at 320.

50. Quoted in Abels, *supra* note 4, at 316.

CHAPTER FOUR

WYATT EARP

Truth and Context

The evidence presented in court is only part of the "truth" that judges and juries consider in reaching their verdicts. Trial lawyers understand that every fact finder is accompanied by his or her own set of life experiences, past observations, social preferences, and general inclinations. These factors and others like them constitute the context of the trial, the backdrop against which all decisions will be made.

This observation serves to emphasize the crucial importance of case theory and story framing, as is demonstrated by the story of a forgotten trial.

Wyatt Earp is well known as the quintessential frontier hero. He cleaned up Dodge City, Kansas, and Tombstone, Arizona, with the help of his fearless brothers and the maverick Doc Holliday. In a moment that virtually defined the mythic western gunfight, he faced down the Clanton and McLaury brothers in the legendary gunfight at the O.K. Corral.

It is far less known, however, that Wyatt and his colleagues were immediately arrested and charged with murder in the aftermath of the shoot-out. And it seemed at the time that the prosecution had a compelling case. Of course, the defendants were ultimately exonerated—witness the enduring fame and heroization of Wyatt and company—but historians have wondered ever since whether justice was truly done.

Looking back at the trial itself, we will see that the prosecutors presented a powerful and well-supported account that was as gripping as it could possibly be, filled with suspense, intrigue, heroism, and betrayal. Nonetheless, the events occurred in a broader context that made conviction of the lawmen difficult and unlikely. To succeed, the prosecutors faced an acute need to reframe the story, but their theory of the case fell short and the defendants walked free.

It is early afternoon on a fateful day—October 26, 1881–in the frontier town of Tombstone, Arizona. Four heavily armed men have decided to take the law into their own hands. Gamblers and possibly thieves, a notorious gunslinger among them, they are determined to take vengeance for a series of trivial insults and imagined threats. Ignoring the orders of the county sheriff, they march grimly to an alley between a rooming house and a photographer's studio where they catch sight of their intended victims—four terrified men, two of whom they had already pistol-whipped that day, who are trying desperately to saddle their horses and ride out of town ahead of the trouble. It was not to be. With cool precision, the killers stride down the alley, guns ready, while horrified townsfolk watch from the nearby buildings. Barely pausing to shout an angry taunt—"The fight has now commenced! Go to fighting or get away!"—they begin firing at their cornered prey. In less than half a minute it is over. Three men lie dead or dying from multiple gunshot wounds; only one has managed to escape. Arrogantly and unemotionally, the leader of the gang again brushes off the bewildered sheriff: "I won't be arrested, but I am here to answer what I have done. I am not going to leave town."

For most readers, the preceding narrative will seem both familiar and dissonant—almost, but not quite, a story that has been heard many times before. And well it should, because it is an account of the legendary "Gunfight at the O.K. Corral," though not told from the customary perspective of the celebrated Earp brothers. Rather, it is the losers' story, as it would have been related by partisans of the Clanton and McLaury brothers, three of whom were "hurled into eternity" by the bullets of the Earps and Doc Holliday. Of course, the losers' story is barely acknowledged today. Wyatt Earp is a hero, Doc Holliday an intriguing rogue, and the Clantons and McLaurys are identified, if at all, simply as generic bad guys. In gunfights as in war, the winners write the history.

And Wyatt Earp, it turns out, won the historic gunfight in two different venues. As we all know, his first victory came in the dusty streets of Tombstone, Arizona. But he also won for a second and equally important time—at least as far as his legend is concerned—in a territorial courtroom. Wyatt Earp and his companions were prosecuted for murder in the weeks following the gunfight. The charges were ultimately dismissed by Judge Wells Spicer, but not before many days of testimony from eyewitnesses who swore that the Earps had gunned down unarmed men begging for their lives.[1] So seriously were the charges taken that at one point Judge Spicer revoked bail for Wyatt and Doc, ordering them to jail on the prosecution's motion that "the proof so far was conclusive of murder."

Wyatt Earp would be remembered far differently today if he had been hanged as a murderer, rather than glorified as the definitive frontier marshal. So it is not hard to see that his myth depends as much on the outcome of the trial as it does on his survival of the shoot-out.[2]

Trials, like gunfights, tend to have two sides. And as we shall see, the context—which is to say, the story frame—can be as important as the events themselves.[3]

The Earp brothers—Wyatt, Virgil, Morgan, and James—arrived in Tombstone in the fall of 1879. Although Wyatt and Virgil had already achieved considerable reputations as lawmen in Kansas, they came to Arizona not as peace officers but as fortune seekers. Their various investment plans enjoyed varying degrees of success, and they eventually found themselves once again employed in law enforcement.

Tombstone itself was every bit the frontier boom town portrayed in the western movies. Sitting on a high plateau and surrounded by rugged mountains, the town was a scant thirty miles from the Mexican border, a fact that would assume some importance in the clashes that led to the famous gunfight. The economy of Tombstone was based primarily on the rich silver mines in the nearby hills. By the time the Earps arrived, capital was flowing into Tombstone from Boston, Philadelphia, Chicago, and New York. Along with the money came the businessmen's predictable desire for stability and order, another factor in the coming battle and its denouement.

The wealth of the silver mines also brought "development." Though the Earps spent only two years in Tombstone, they saw its population grow from 1,200 to at least 6,000, with some estimates placing the peak population at 10,000 and more. There were saloons, hotels, theaters, French restaurants, oyster bars, an opera house, a photographer's studio, even ice cream parlors.

But the easterners were not the only relative newcomers to the Arizona Territory. There were also the "Cowboys," a loose gang of "rootless ex-cowhands and saddle tramps [who] gravitated toward the small towns of southeastern Arizona, attracted to the climate and the relative lack of law enforcement on either side of the [Mexican] border."[4] Most of the Cowboys, including the Clantons and McLaurys, came from Texas; some were Confederate veterans. The Cowboys, it seems, had a penchant for conducting cattle-stealing raids into Mexico. Eventually their rustling led to a virtual border war, much to the dismay of the mine owners and townsfolk, not to mention the federal authorities.

With so much money to be made and such a volatile and transient population, the civic life of Tombstone was unruly and divided. Although the factions tended to shift somewhat, it is fair to say that they broke down roughly along regional, economic, and political lines. On one side there were the town-dwelling, Republican, eastern-oriented business interests. On the other side there were the Cowboys and their sympathizers. Mostly southerners and Democrats, they lived on ranches and in the small satellite towns in the countryside surrounding Tombstone. To rural Arizonians, cattle theft from Mexico was barely a crime, and more than a few of the local ranchers were eager to acquire the stolen livestock at bargain prices.

In the fractious and disorganized politics that characterized the Arizona Territory, each side had its own claim to law enforcement. The Tombstone town marshal was generally elected by Republicans, while the Cochise County sheriff was an office for the Democrats. In the struggle for legitimacy, however, the easterners held the trump, since the territorial marshal was a federal official appointed by Republican governor John Fremont. (This, of course, riled the Cowboys, former Confederates who detested the encroachments of federal power.) There were even dueling newspapers in Tombstone. The *Epitaph* was Republican and pro-business, and consequently pro-Earp, while the *Nugget* tended to support the Democrats and the Cowboys.

The Earps might not have had advance knowledge of Tombstone's various conflicts, but it was always clear which side they would be on. They were staunch Republicans. Virgil and James fought in the Union army, and Wyatt tried to (he was too young). Coming originally from Iowa, and most recently from Kansas, they were considered easterners by Arizona standards (then as now). Most important, they stood for law and order. Virgil and Wyatt had served as peace officers in the railheads of Dodge City and Abilene, where their primary task was keeping a tight rein on rowdy Texas trail hands, an experience that could not have endeared them to the ex-Texan Cowboys. The wild card of the Tombstone deck, in more ways than one, was John Henry "Doc" Holliday, who had been a practicing dentist before heading west. A well-known gambler and gunslinger, notorious for carrying a nickel-plated revolver, Doc Holliday was a native of Georgia and the son of a Confederate officer. Nonetheless, Doc allied himself with the Earp faction, by virtue of his long and close friendship with Wyatt.

By 1881, three of the Earp brothers had set aside most of their assorted business speculations in favor of full-time work as peace officers, which was the job they did best. (The exception was James, who tended bar in a saloon and was not involved in the defining gunfight.) Virgil, the oldest of the brothers, had secured a federal appointment as deputy territorial marshal for southeastern Arizona, and was also acting town marshal (sometimes called chief of police) for Tombstone. Wyatt and Morgan served as Virgil's special deputies. All three brothers occasionally rode shotgun for the stage lines in and out of Tombstone, and there is good reason to believe that Wyatt additionally worked as an undercover "detective" for the Wells Fargo Company.

The Earps' rival in law enforcement, and Wyatt's rival in other ways as well (more on that later), was Sheriff John Behan of Cochise County—a southerner, a Democrat, and a Cowboy sympathizer. Behan played a crucial role in both the gunfight and the trial. If things had turned out differently in either arena, we might hail him today as "brave, courageous, and bold." As it is, he is barely remembered.

This being a western epic, the story would not be complete without a stagecoach robbery. Stage holdups were a constant problem for Tombstone, and each side often blamed the other for the crimes, though the accusations often seemed grounded as much in politics as in reality. It was just such a robbery that set in motion the chain of events that would lead to the gunfight at the O.K. Corral.

On March 15, 1881, the Tombstone–Benson stage was attacked by four outlaws. Though the robbery was unsuccessful, leaving behind a Wells Fargo shipment of at least $26,000, the bandits killed the driver, Bud Philpot, as well as one of the passengers. Two posses were formed as soon as the news of the murders reached Tombstone. One posse, under the leadership of Virgil Earp, included Wyatt and Morgan, Bat Masterson, Doc Holliday, and a Wells Fargo agent named Marshall Williams. The other was headed by none other than John Behan.

The Earp posse managed to track down and apprehend a man named Luther King, who confessed his involvement (though claiming he had only held the horses) and implicated three others still at large, all with known Cowboy associations: Harry Head, Billy Leonard, and Jim Crane. Behan soon arrived on the scene and argued in favor of releasing King, but the Earps insisted that he be arrested. Turning the prisoner over to Behan and a deputy, the Earp posse continued to hunt for Head, Leonard, and Crane.

Returning to Tombstone after several days of hard riding, the Earps learned that King had escaped from Behan's loosely guarded jail. More dismaying, they discovered rumors flying around town that they themselves might have been responsible for the robbery. At one point Behan actually arrested Doc Holliday for the crime, based on an affidavit extracted from Doc's girlfriend, Kate Elder, who seems to have been drunk at the time. The charge had to be dropped, however, when Kate sobered up and recanted.

Even with Doc's release, rumors continued to spread about the murder of Bud Philpot, making the capture of Leonard, Head, and Crane a matter of both pride and honor (and maybe more) for the Earps and Holliday.

By the end of the summer, however, all three robbers were dead. In June, Leonard and Head were gunned down in an internecine Cowboy feud. In August, Crane was killed in the Guadalupe Canyon Massacre by Mexican soldiers who crossed the border to apprehend cattle rustlers; among the four other victims was Old Man Clanton, father of Billy and

Ike.[5] There followed a series of retaliatory raids that inflamed the border. This cycle of cross-border violence and reprisal led to repeated calls for intervention by the United States army and for more vigorous law enforcement by the local federal marshals, meaning Virgil Earp and his deputized brothers. This, of course, would only heighten tension between the Cowboys and the Earps.

In the midst of all this, and before the massacre at Guadalupe Canyon, Wyatt Earp made a deal with Ike Clanton. Figuring that Ike might have information about Crane's whereabouts, Wyatt proposed to give Ike the hefty reward offered by Wells Fargo, if Ike would snitch on his sometimes pal. The deal had to be kept secret, since Ike could hardly let it be known that he had agreed to inform on a fellow Cowboy. As for Wyatt, he was apparently willing to forgo the reward money in exchange for an opportunity to arrest Crane. As Wyatt later explained, "I had an ambition to be sheriff of this county at the next election, and I thought it would be a great help to me with the people and businessmen if I could capture the men who killed Philpot." Of course, the bargain between the Cowboy and the lawman fell through when the Mexican army dispatched Crane at Guadalupe Canyon, but it nonetheless turned into a source of continuing friction between Wyatt and Ike, resulting in a deadly confrontation later that year.

In the following months, more stages were robbed,[6] more outlaws escaped, and more tension built between the Earps and the Cowboys as the Earps attempted to enforce federal law and the Cowboys, with the apparent toleration if not outright support of Sheriff Behan, were having none of it. In one well-reported incident, Frank McLaury and several other Cowboys confronted Morgan Earp on Tombstone's main street. "I'm telling you Earps something," McLaury boasted, "you may have arrested Pete Spence and Frank Stilwell, but don't get it into your heads that you can arrest me. If you ever lay hands on a McLaury, I'll kill you."[7] Similar threats were made to Virgil, who was acting town marshal at the time. It was clear that a showdown was coming, and in the small hours of October 26, 1881, it began.

Tombstone lived on a twenty-four–hour schedule. The bars, theaters, gambling halls, and opium parlors all operated around the clock, as trail hands and miners were ever anxious to sample the pleasures of the town. So it was not surprising when, nearing midnight on October 25, Ike Clanton and Tom McLaury rode into town with a wagon load of beef (remember, they were rustlers) and immediately headed for their favorite gambling halls. At about 1:00 A.M. on October 26, Ike showed up at the Alhambra Saloon for "lunch," where he ran into Doc Holliday. The two began a shouting match, instigated by a drunken Ike, who apparently suspected that Wyatt and Doc were going to expose his deal to betray Crane. As Ike continued to mouth threats, Doc taunted him to make good: "You son of a bitch of a Cowboy, go heel [arm] yourself."[8] Morgan Earp, also present in the Alhambra, told Ike to leave.

Not long after, Ike confronted Wyatt in the street, telling him that they would soon have to go "man for man." According to Wyatt, he replied, "Go home Ike, you talk too much for a fighting man."

Then, in either a temporary gesture of conciliation or a bizarre continuation of the feud by other means, nearly all the principals repaired to the Occidental Saloon to play poker. John Behan, Ike Clanton, Tom McLaury, Doc Holliday, and Morgan, Virgil, and Wyatt Earp sat at the same table for nearly five hours; history did not record the name of the big winner.[9] Though the game was peaceful enough, Ike followed Virgil into the street once it was over, this time threatening Doc Holliday, "The damned son of a bitch has got to fight."

Virgil Earp went home to sleep, but Ike Clanton did not. Instead, he roamed the streets of Tombstone, openly carrying a gun and continuing to threaten the Earps and Holliday. At noon he was standing in front of a saloon waving a Winchester rifle. Reports of Ike's aggressive behavior came to the Earps, who could not ignore such a flagrant breach of the peace and violation of the gun ordinance. They began to search for Ike, finding him on Allen Street. Virgil quickly grabbed the rifle from Ike's hand and just as quickly used his own revolver to club him to the ground.

Bleeding from a scalp wound, Ike continued the verbal assault: "If I had seen you a second sooner, I'd have killed you."

"You cattle thieving son-of-a-bitch," shouted Wyatt, "you've threatened my life enough, and you've got to fight."

"Fight is my racket," replied the still angry Cowboy, "and all I want is four feet of ground."

Wyatt openly challenged Ike Clanton, "You damned dirty cow thief, you have been threatening our lives, and I know it. I think I would be justified in shooting you down any place I should meet you. But if you are anxious to make a fight, I will go anywhere on earth to make a fight with you."

In an odd scene that could not be repeated today, the Earps brought the disarmed Cowboy before a magistrate, who fined Clanton on the spot (twenty-five dollars plus costs) and set him free. Virgil Earp even asked Clanton where he would like to pick up his confiscated guns.

On leaving the courthouse, Wyatt was confronted by Tom McLaury, who continued Ike's threats. McLaury was not visibly armed, but Wyatt took no chances, pulling his pistol and striking the Cowboy across the head.

By this time, everyone in Tombstone knew that a fight was brewing. There were dozens of eyewitnesses to the following events, many of whom later gave accounts to the press and the court. People virtually lined the streets to see what was going on. And what they saw could not have been encouraging, since Ike and Tom, now joined by their brothers, Billy Clanton and Frank McLaury, proceeded to Spangenburg's gun shop. Virgil and Wyatt stood outside, watching the Cowboys load their weapons.[10] Virgil wasted no time walking to the nearby Wells Fargo office to get a short-barreled shotgun.

The Cowboys headed to the O.K. Corral, located at the end of Fremont Street. They were overheard threatening to shoot the Earps on sight, a fact that was reported to Virgil by a bystander named H. F. Sills. Eventually, the Cowboys moved to a vacant lot behind the corral, adjacent to Camillus Fly's photography studio.

Spotting John Behan, Virgil asked the county sheriff to help disarm the Cowboys. Behan refused to help the Earps, but did go to the corral to talk to the Clantons and McLaurys. Frank McLaury, however, refused Behan's request to give up his weapons, saying he would not be disarmed unless the Earps were as well.

Meanwhile, Virgil and Wyatt, standing near Hafford's Saloon at the corner of Fourth and Allen Streets, were joined by brother Morgan and

Doc Holliday. Virgil handed the shotgun to Doc, and the four men began their famous shoulder-to-shoulder walk toward the corral. Behan tried to intervene, but the Earps strode past him. According to both Virgil and Wyatt, Behan falsely claimed to have disarmed the Cowboys— perhaps setting up the Earps for an ambush—though this is one of the many disputed facts that have never been fully resolved.

Arriving at the lot, Virgil announced, "I have come to disarm you. Throw up your hands." Someone fired a shot and, in Ike Clanton's phrase, "the ball opened." Within thirty seconds, the most famous gunfight in American history was over. But who started it, and why? And could it have been avoided even as the Earps faced down the Cowboys at that last critical moment? It would take a trial to answer those questions, even though many events of the gunfight itself were more or less uncontroverted.

Two pistol shots were fired almost simultaneously, followed by perhaps thirty more from both sides, as well as two blasts from the Wells Fargo shotgun. Frank McLaury was killed on the spot, Tom McLaury and Billy Clanton were mortally wounded—all three men "Hurled into Eternity," as the *Tombstone Epitaph* reported in a headline the following morning. Virgil, Morgan, and Doc were also wounded, though not extremely seriously. Ike Clanton, the man who started it all, ran for cover and escaped unharmed.[11]

Wyatt, the only participant who was not hit, was soon confronted by Behan. "Wyatt, I am arresting you," he said. "For murder."

Wyatt Earp would have none of it. "I won't be arrested. You deceived me Johnny, you told me they were not armed. I won't be arrested, but I am here to answer what I have done. I am not going to leave town." Behan backed off, though not for long.

While most of Tombstone's citizenry supported the Earps, the Cowboy faction had its defenders as well. The bodies of Tom, Frank, and Billy were displayed outside the local undertaker's establishment, propped up beneath a sign reading "Murdered in the Streets of Tombstone." Their funeral was attended by thousands of mourners, as the town band led the cortege to the graveyard on Boot Hill.

Within a few days of the gunfight it became clear that the Earps' chief accuser would be Sheriff John Behan. According to Behan, Billy

Clanton had called out to the Earps, "Don't shoot me, I don't want to fight," and Tom McLaury had cried, "I have got nothing," while opening his shirt to show that he was unarmed." With some elaboration, this would become the anti-Earp story, as developed by the prosecution at the hearing before Judge Spicer (the pro-Earp story was told by the defendants themselves).

Who fired the first round? Did Frank McLaury shoot first, or at least draw his gun, prompting Wyatt to return fire in self-defense? Or was it an unprovoked Doc Holliday, wielding his notorious nickel-plated revolver against men who had no desire to fight? That was the crucial issue confronting Tombstone as the inquiry into the gunfight proceeded. The rest of the details receded in significance compared to that one question—who drew first? As is so often the case, the presence of numerous eyewitnesses only added to the confusion, since their accounts were sharply at odds. The task of judgment would fall to Justice of the Peace Wells Spicer. In order to determine what happened, he had to decide whom to believe.

On October 31, 1881, Ike Clanton filed murder charges against all three Earp brothers and Doc Holliday, a coroner's inquest having heard from nine witnesses who swore that the Earps had provoked the fight. The city council had already suspended Virgil as town marshal, pending the outcome of an investigation. Wyatt and Doc were arraigned and bail was set at $10,000 for each of the defendants, including Virgil and Morgan, whose wounds prevented them from appearing in court. As was required by territorial law, the initial step in the proceeding was a preliminary hearing, which began immediately. The sole legal question was whether the defendants would be held for trial in the district court.

The district attorney at the time was Lyttleton Price. A Republican who might otherwise have been thought to support the Earp faction, he was obligated to lead the prosecution. Friends and supporters of the dead Cowboys raised $10,000 so that several private lawyers could assist the prosecution, including Ben Goodrich, a native Texan and former Confederate officer. On the third day of the hearing, another lawyer arrived from Texas—William McLaury, brother of Frank and Tom. Will

McLaury was immediately made an associate prosecutor, a task he accepted with all the passion one would expect under the circumstances: "This thing has a tendency to arouse all the devil there is in me—it will not bring my brothers back to prosecute these men but I regard it as my duty to myself and family to see that these brutes do not go unwhipped of justice. . . . I think I can hang them."[12]

The Earps were represented by Tom Fitch, a native New Yorker whose personal history was as colorful as might be expected of a criminal defense lawyer on the Arizona frontier. He had previously worked as a newspaper reporter and had served in the California legislature. He had also been elected to Congress from Nevada (where he had reportedly made friends with Mark Twain). After a stint in Utah as counsel for the Mormon Church, he moved to Tombstone in 1877, where he served in the territorial legislature. Doc Holliday was separately represented by another local attorney, T. J. Drum.

The first prosecution witness was William Allen, a friend of the McLaurys, who testified that he had followed the Earps down Fremont Street and heard one of them call out, "You sons of bitches, you have been looking for a fight." At the same time, "Tom McLaury threw his coat open and said, 'I ain't got no arms.' . . . William Clanton said, 'I do not want to fight' and held his hands out in front of him."

The prosecution theory became rapidly clear. As much as the Cowboys might have misbehaved and postured earlier that day, they brandished no guns and posed no actual threat. Instead, it was the Earps who stalked the Cowboys, determined to have it out with them, firing before the Clantons and McLaurys even had a chance to surrender. As to the critical question of the first shot, Allen believed that it came from Doc Holliday ("the smoke came from him"), and that the second shot also came from the Earp party.

That latter point was pivotal to the prosecution. Virgil Earp was well respected in Tombstone, even by most of his political adversaries. Since he held the position of both town and federal marshal, it would be hard to tar him—or by extension, his brothers—as a wanton killer. In contrast, Doc Holliday was widely regarded as a renegade, "the fastest, deadliest man with a gun" in Tombstone, so it would be far easier to target him as the instigator of the crime.[13]

Moreover, it does not appear that Doc was actually deputized when he joined Virgil Earp's posse.[14] At the very least, it might be seen as criminally negligent for Virgil to bring the notoriously erratic Doc into what was already a tense situation. And of course, if Doc Holliday could be shown to have opened fire, that would explain the shots from the Cowboys that wounded Virgil and Morgan. So Doc Holliday and his nickel-plated gun became the cornerstone of the prosecution case.

Other damning witnesses followed, including Martha King, a Tombstone housewife who observed the Earp party on their way to the showdown. Before the fight ever started, she heard one of the Earps say, "Let them have it," to which Doc Holliday replied, "All right."

Sheriff John Behan testified over a period of several days, explaining that he had tried to stop the Earps, who shoved him aside. Proceeding to the scene of the fight, he heard Wyatt yell, "You sons of bitches have been looking for a fight," and another of the Earps ordered the Cowboys to "Throw up your hands." Then the firing began.

I saw a nickel-plated pistol in particular [which] was pointed at one of the party. I think at Billy Clanton. My impression at the time was that Holliday had the nickel-plated pistol. I will not say for certain that Holliday had it. These pistols I speak of were in the hands of the Earp party. When the order was [given] to "Throw up your hands," I heard Billy Clanton say, "Don't shoot me, I don't want to fight." Tom McLaury at the same time threw open his coat and said, "I have nothing" or "I am not armed," or something like that. . . . My attention was directed to the nickel-plated pistol for a couple of seconds. The nickel-plated pistol was the first to fire, and instantaneously a second shot—two shots right together simultaneously—these two shots couldn't have been from the same pistol—they were too near together. The nickel plated pistol was fired by the second man from the right, the third man from the right fired the second shot, if it can be called a second shot. Then the fight became general. . . . The first two shots were fired by the Earp party.

The sheriff added that at least two of the Cowboys, Ike Clanton (who survived) and Tom McLaury (who did not), had been unarmed, and that "there was as many as eight or ten shots before I saw arms in the hands of any of the McLaury or Clanton party."

Behan's testimony allows for two possibilities, one bad for the Earps and the other worse. The worst interpretation, of course, is that the town marshal called for the Cowboys to surrender, and then shot them down when they raised their hands as told. But if that was too harsh, the prosecution could fall back on the theory that Virgil, at least initially, might really have meant to disarm the Cowboys, but recklessly fell to shooting when he heard the report of the "drunken, dangerous dentist's" infamous weapon.[15] Behan's repetition of "nickel-plated pistol" was obviously meant to drive home Doc Holliday's role, since everyone in Tombstone knew that only he used such a gun.

When Behan was tendered for cross-examination, the defense faced a difficult decision. His well-known antagonism toward the Earps would lend support to a claim of bias, but as sheriff of Cochise County he nonetheless brought a good deal of credibility to the stand. Could the defense afford to attack him head on, claiming that he had adjusted his story to convict the defendants? There was plenty of ammunition to that effect. For example, Behan had apparently given an interview to the *Tombstone Nugget* immediately after the gunfight, in which he informed the paper that "Frank McLowry [*sic*] made a motion to draw his revolver" just before the shooting began, an observation conspicuously at odds with his "nickel-plated" testimony at trial.[16] There was also the matter of Behan's Cowboy associations and sympathies, including the fact that his deputy, Frank Stilwell, had twice been arrested by Virgil Earp for robbing the Bisbee stage. At one point Behan had operated a faro table at a local saloon, law enforcement and gambling not being regarded as mutually exclusive professions on the frontier. But Wyatt broke the bank at Behan's table, putting him out of business and no doubt occasioning some resentment as well.[17]

And there was one more plausible line of cross-examination, this one potentially explosive. Since the fall of 1880, Behan had been living with a woman named Josephine "Sadie" Marcus, a dancer and actress from San Francisco who had come to Tombstone with a traveling production of Gilbert and Sullivan's *H.M.S. Pinafore*. The daughter of a middle-class German-Jewish family, Josephine was obviously adventurous and said to be stunningly beautiful. Bat Masterson described her as "the belle of the honky-tonks."[18] By the time of the trial, however, it appears that Josephine's affections had strayed in the direction of Wyatt Earp.

Wyatt himself was still living with a woman named Mattie Blaylock, often referred to as his second wife (and therefore called Mattie Earp) though there is no record of a marriage. But it seems clear that Wyatt was seeing Josephine at the time.[19] According to the memoirs of Virgil's wife, Allie,

> We all knew about it, and we knew Mattie did too. That's why we never said anything to her. We didn't have to. We could see her with her eyes all red from cryin', thinkin' of Wyatt's carryin'-on. I didn't have to peek out at night to see if the light was still burnin' at daylight when I got up.
>
> Everything Wyatt did stuck the knife deeper into Mattie's heart. Polishin' his boots so he could prance into a fancy restaurant with Sadie. Cleanin' his guns to show off to Sadie. You never saw his hair combed so proper or his long, slim hands so beautiful clean and soft.[20]

In the end, Wyatt succeeded in "stealing" Josephine from John Behan.[21] As much animosity as Behan might have felt toward the Earps because of their law enforcement and gambling conflicts, it would have paled compared to his romantic rivalry with Wyatt for the woman Bat Masterson called "the prettiest dame" in Tombstone.[22]

Tom Fitch must have been tempted indeed to attack Behan on cross-examination. Could he make the sheriff contradict himself? Would Behan even be able to maintain composure if confronted with the story of Wyatt and Josephine? But that tactic also had its risks. Taking aim so directly at a prosecution witness might suggest weakness in the defense case. And bringing Josephine into the trial would surely breach Victorian decorum, not to mention the possibility that it might backfire by making Wyatt himself look like a two-timer.

At least in part, Fitch opted for a safer course that challenged Behan concerning the "nickel-plated" gun. Holliday was known to have carried a shotgun into the fight, so where did the revolver come from? Why would a man with a shotgun in his hands stop to pull out a pistol? And since the shotgun was unquestionably fired twice in the course of a thirty-second battle, how could Doc Holliday have started the fight with a nickel-plated pistol? Behan had no good answer, a deficit that has undermined the prosecution theory from that day to this.

But Fitch could not restrain himself entirely, and the cross-examination he conducted on bias was not nearly so effective. Did Behan meet with William Allen before trial to coordinate their testimony? "No," said the sheriff. Had the witness contributed to the fund collected to pay the private prosecutors? "I have not contributed a cent, nor have I promised to."

Venturing into the rivalry between Behan and the Earps, the defense made only slightly more headway: "Were not you and Wyatt Earp applicants to General Fremont for the appointment of sheriff of Cochise County, and did not Wyatt Earp withdraw his application upon your promise to divide the profits of the office and did not you subsequently refuse to comply with your part of the contract?" Behan admitted the existence of the bargain, but claimed it fell apart because of Wyatt, at one point adding cryptically, "something afterwards transpired that I did not take him into the office." Whatever the reason for the failed arrangement—jealousy, perfidy, fortuity—it did not terribly undermine Behan's testimony about the gunfight.

In addition to Behan and Allen, two more witnesses testified that the Earp party, and Holliday in particular, fired the first shots and that the Clantons and McLaurys had raised their hands at Virgil's command before they were gunned down. The evidence was sufficiently compelling that Judge Spicer revoked bail for Doc and Wyatt and remanded them to jail (because of their wounds, Morgan and Virgil were still confined to bed at the time). In a bitter irony, they were taken into custody by John Behan and remained in his charge for the next sixteen days. Recognizing the perils inherent in the situation, over a dozen Earp supporters stood guard in front of the jail, lest any Cowboy enthusiasts be tempted to take the law into their own hands.[23]

The capstone of the prosecution case should have been the testimony of Ike Clanton, the only Cowboy who survived the gunfight. After giving his occupation as "stock raising and cattle dealer," he provided an account consistent with those of the other prosecution witnesses, a story filled with high drama and professions of personal courage. The Earps had bullied and intimidated the Clantons and McLaurys for nearly twenty-four hours before the battle, though Ike himself had "never threatened any of the Earps nor Holliday." The fight itself was started by Doc and Morgan, quickly followed by a barrage from Virgil and Wyatt, despite the unarmed Cowboys' efforts to surrender. According to Ike, he heroically tried to take Wyatt out of the fight:

> He shoved his pistol up against my belly, and told me to throw up my hands. He said, "You son-of-a-bitch, you can have a fight!" I turned on my heel, taking Wyatt Earp's hand and pistol with my left hand and grabbed him around the shoulder with my right hand and held him for a few seconds. While I was holding him he shot. . . . I then went on across Allen Street. . . . As I jumped into the door of the photograph gallery, I heard some bullets pass my head.

At this point the prosecution case was strong on details and weak on motive. Five witnesses had testified that the Earps started the fight and that the Cowboys were either unarmed, had tried to surrender, or both. But something was lacking. It was unlikely that Judge Spicer would conclude that Virgil Earp was a cold-blooded killer who murdered the Cowboys for sport. After all, Virgil was a well-respected lawman, holding the positions of both town and federal marshal, with no record of extravagant force. It would be unconvincing to make him out simply as triggerhappy, especially since the most damning eyewitnesses were all known adversaries of the Earps. The case against the defendants would be truly coherent only if the prosecution could explain why the Earps would suddenly turn from peace officers into assassins.

The defense set out to underscore that deficit in the cross-examination of Ike Clanton. First, however, there would be a bit of impeachment, as Clanton was compelled to admit that, contrary to his direct examination, he had indeed threatened the Earps during the night before the gunfight.[24]

Tom Fitch next went to work, asking Ike Clanton about the agreement to rat on Leonard, Head, and Crane, the Cowboy robbers of the Benson stage. The defense theory was that Ike's overnight rampage against the Earps was motivated by the fear that he might be discovered as an informer. It was no surprise, therefore, that Clanton, while admitting an approach by Wyatt, denied making any such deal.

And then Ike Clanton continued, claiming that Wyatt and Morgan had secretly confided in him that the Earps themselves, along with Leonard, Head, and Crane, had been responsible for the stage holdup and the murder of Bud Philpot. He added that the Earps had "piped off" the money to Doc Holliday (whom Clanton later accused of being the man who actually shot Philpot). Wyatt, fearful that Leonard, Head, or Crane might squeal, had offered Clanton six thousand dollars to help liquidate them. Ike, however, told Wyatt, "I would have nothing to do with helping to kill Crane, Leonard, and Head."

There was the missing motive. The Earps, having divulged their secret criminality to Ike Clanton, now had to eliminate him in order to avoid detection.

I found out by Wyatt Earp's conversation that he was offering money to kill men that were in the attempted stage robbery, his confederates, for fear that Leonard, Crane and Head would be captured and tell on him, and I knew that after Leonard and Head was killed that some of them would murder me for what they had told me.

That would explain why the Earps, and especially Holliday, fired so quickly, refusing the offer of surrender by the Clantons and McLaurys. It would also explain Ike's earlier claim that Wyatt seemingly risked his life by firing at the unarmed, fleeing Ike Clanton rather than at the other Cowboys who had drawn their guns and were returning fire.

This testimony posed a perplexing challenge for defense counsel, confronted with the demanding task of showing that the alleged confessions of Wyatt, Morgan, and Doc had never occurred. It is always tough to prove a negative, and tougher still on cross-examination. Tom Fitch chose sarcasm as his weapon, hoping to make clear that Ike's story was not worthy of belief. "Did not Marshall Williams, the agent of the [Wells Fargo] Express company at Tombstone, state to you ... that he was personally [involved] in the attempted stage robbery and the murder of Philpot?" "Did not James Earp, a brother of Virgil, Morgan, and Wyatt, also confess to you that he was [a] murderer and stage robber?"

It wasn't great cross-examination, or even admissible, but it made the point.[25] The validity of the prosecution now hung on the extraordinary story of Ike Clanton.

Throughout the prosecution case, defense counsel made a series of tactical decisions. Behan was handled fairly gingerly on cross-examination, the subject of his pro-Cowboy partisanship barely being raised. In contrast, Ike Clanton was allowed to ramble on in an anti-Earp tirade, a move that was no doubt intended to give him enough rope to hang himself figuratively, rather than hang the Earps in reality. But perhaps the boldest strategy came into play when Wyatt himself took the stand as the first witness for the defense.

Rather than proceed in standard question-and-answer format, Wyatt took advantage of a territorial law that allowed a defendant in a preliminary hearing to give narrative testimony without facing cross-examination.[26] In fact, Wyatt began reading from a lengthy prepared statement, which both surprised and outraged the prosecution. Perhaps the defendant can avoid cross-examination, they claimed, but he should not be allowed to write out his testimony in advance. Judge Spicer, however, ruled that "the statute was very broad [and that] the accused could make any statement he pleased whether previously prepared or not."[27]

Early in his narrative, Wyatt set the scene, describing the Clantons and McLaurys as dangerous criminals who contributed to the atmosphere of lawlessness surrounding Tombstone:

It was generally understood among officers and those who have information about criminals, that Ike Clanton was sort of chief among the cowboys; that the Clantons and McLaurys were cattle thieves and generally in the secret of the stage robbery, and that the Clanton and McLaury ranches were meeting places and places of shelter for the gang.

Then he brought up the matter of the Benson stage robbery and the murder of Bud Philpot, explaining the soured deal with Ike Clanton and reinforcing the Cowboy's reasons for threatening the Earps just prior to the gunfight.

I had an ambition to be sheriff of this county at the next election, and I thought it would be a great help to me with the people and businessmen if I could capture the men who killed Philpot. There were rewards offered of about $1200 each for the capture of the robbers.... I thought this sum might tempt Ike Clanton and Frank McLaury to give away Leonard, Head, and Crane, so I went to Ike Clanton, Frank McLaury ... when they came to town. I had an interview with them in the back yard of the Oriental Saloon. I told them what I wanted. I told them I wanted the glory of capturing Leonard, Head, and Crane and if I could do it, it would help me make the race for sheriff at the next election. I told them if they would put me on the track of Leonard, Head, and Crane, and tell me where those men were hid, I would give them all the reward and would never let anyone know where I got the information.

Wyatt proceeded to outline a long history of threats against the Earps by the Clantons and McLaurys, including many that had occurred in front of witnesses. He detailed the crimes of other Cowboys as well, as though to emphasize guilt by association: "I knew all those men were desperate and dangerous men, that they were connected with outlaws, cattle thieves, robbers and murderers.... I heard of John Ringo shooting a man down in cold blood near Camp Thomas. I was satisfied that Frank and Tom McLaury killed and robbed Mexicans in Skeleton Canyon." A prudent lawman could draw only one conclusion. "I naturally kept my eyes open and did not intend that any of the gang should get the drop on me if I could help it."

Wyatt was adamant that the Cowboys had initiated the confrontation, threatening Morgan, Doc, and Wyatt at various times, including an incident in the Oriental Saloon when Ike, wearing his six-shooter, warned, "You must not think I won't be after you all in the morning." Ike had been even more explicit to Ned Boyle, a bartender, who had reported to Wyatt that Ike had said, "[a]s soon as those damned Earps make their appearance on the street today the ball will open, we are here to make a fight. We are looking for the sons-of-bitches!"

Next came the subject of Behan's betrayal of his fellow lawmen. Wyatt recounted that as the Earps marched down Fremont Street headed for the O.K. Corral, Behan called out, "I have disarmed them." Wyatt continued, "When he said this, I took my pistol which I had in my hand under my coat, and put it in my overcoat pocket," thus making himself an easier target for the Cowboys, who had not been disarmed at all.

When they arrived at the lot behind the corral, "Frank McLaury's and Billy Clanton's six shooters were in plain sight." Virgil called to the Cowboys, "Throw up your hands, I have come to disarm you," but instead, Billy Clanton and both McLaury brothers went for their guns:

> I had my pistol in my overcoat pocket, where I put it when Behan told us he had disarmed the other parties. When I saw Billy Clanton and Frank McLaury draw their pistols, I drew my pistol. Billy Clanton leveled his pistol at me, but I did not aim at him. I knew that Frank McLaury had the reputation of being a good shot and a dangerous man, and I aimed at Frank McLaury. The first two shots which were fired were fired by Billy Clanton and myself, he shooting at me, and I shooting at Frank McLaury. I don't know which was fired first. We fired almost together. The fight then became general.

As to Ike Clanton's testimony, Wyatt's attitude was at first dismissive:

> After about four shots were fired, Ike Clanton ran up and grabbed my left arm. I could see no weapon in his hand, and thought at the time he had none, and so I said to him, "the fight has now commenced. Go to fighting or get away." At the same time I pushed him off with my left hand. . . . I never fired at Ike Clanton even after the shooting commenced because I thought he was unarmed.

Later, he became contemptuous: "The testimony of Isaac Clanton that I ever said to him that I had anything to do with any stage robbery . . . or any improper communication whatever in any criminal enterprise is a tissue of lies from beginning to end."

Wyatt added two statements that may provide a certain insight into the conduct of the trial. First, he addressed the legal justification for his actions:

I believed then, and believe now, from the acts I have stated and the threats I have related and other threats communicated to me by other persons, as having been made by Tom McLaury, Frank McLaury and Ike Clanton, that these men last named had formed a conspiracy to murder my brothers, Morgan and Virgil, Doc Holliday and myself. I believe I would have been legally and morally justifiable in shooting any of them on sight, but I did not do so, nor attempt to do so. I sought no advantage when I went, as deputy marshal, to help to disarm them and arrest them. I went as a part of my duty and under the directions of my brother, the marshal. I did not intend to fight unless it became necessary in self-defense or in the rightful performance of official duty. When Billy Clanton and Frank McLaury drew their pistols, I knew it was a fight for life, and I drew and fired in defense of my own life and the lives of my brothers and Doc Holliday.

Finally, Wyatt commented on the broken deal with Sheriff Behan, saying cryptically that Behan's sworn claims about the reasons "for not complying with his contract [were] false in every particular."

The story was powerfully told, but not without undertaking a certain risk. True, the narrative testimony insulated Wyatt from what might have been a withering cross-examination at the hands of Will McLaury, but only at the cost of suggesting that he might have something to hide. Furthermore, the decision to have Wyatt read his statement had its own drawbacks. Would Judge Spicer believe that the words were actually Wyatt's? Surely, one can see counsel's guiding hand in some of the language. It seems almost impossible that the relatively unschooled Wyatt Earp would have been able to summarize so neatly the law of justifiable homicide: "I sought no advantage when I went, as deputy marshal, to help to disarm them and arrest them. I went as a part of my duty and under the directions of my brother, the marshal. I did not intend to fight unless it became necessary in self-defense or in the rightful performance of official duty." Might the judge also infer that the very details of the narrative had been composed (and therefore improved) by the attorneys?

We can only speculate about counsel's reason for adopting this maneuver, but it is made all the more enigmatic by the wide-open approach taken by the defense to the balance of the proceeding. Rather than limit their evidence at the preliminary hearing, keeping their cards close to the vest and saving their key witnesses for a possible trial, Fitch and Drum opted to present a full-fledged case. They called another eleven witnesses in addition to Wyatt, all of whom were readily tendered for further questioning by the prosecution.[28] Even Virgil Earp, so badly wounded that court had to convene at his bedside, was subjected to the rigors of cross-examination. Why was the defense so much more protective of Wyatt than of Virgil? Were they worried that Wyatt would lose his temper under questioning from Will McLaury? Or were they afraid that he would be forced to make damaging admissions? Perhaps he knew something that his brother did not?

It was Wyatt who had the most pointed rivalry with John Behan, including their failed agreement to split the proceeds of the job of Cochise County sheriff. What might the prosecution have discovered by inquiring into Wyatt's mysterious assertion that Behan's reasons "for not complying with his contract are false"? Recall that Behan's own testimony on this point was equally obscure: "something afterwards transpired that I did not take him into the office." Could this all have been an effort to shield the reputation of Josephine Marcus? Though the romantic triangle might well have been the best means to expose Behan's duplicity, defense counsel did not question Behan on the subject, nor did they put Wyatt in a position to be questioned about it himself. Was the lawman willing to hazard his own freedom—as well as that of his brothers and friend—in the name of gallantry?

There is at least one more possibility. It was Wyatt who had firsthand knowledge of the aborted arrangement with Ike Clanton for the betrayal of the Benson stage robbers. Perhaps there was more to that story than Wyatt was willing to tell. While it is hardly imaginable that Wyatt was actually involved in the murder of Bud Philpot, his connections to Leonard, Head, and Crane might have been closer than he cared to admit—at least while he was on trial for his life. Perhaps Wyatt's version of the ill-fated deal might have unraveled if probed too searchingly on the stand.

Wyatt Earp's prepared statement provided a coherent narrative of the defendants' theory, though his refusal to be cross-examined could not help but make it somewhat suspect. Given the explicit testimony of Behan and company, would Judge Spicer be willing to dismiss the charges based on an account that could not be tested in court? Surely the easier course of action would be to bind the defendants for trial, subjecting Wyatt, Virgil, Morgan, and Doc to the uncertain mercies of an Arizona jury. To avoid that danger—and it was a danger, given the jury pool in Cochise County—defense counsel would have to provide witnesses who could demonstrate the indicators of credibility that Wyatt's testimony had eschewed.

After producing several witnesses to bolster the details of Wyatt's story, the defense heightened the trial's drama by calling Virgil Earp to the stand. Well, not exactly to the stand. The town and federal marshal was too severely injured to come to the courthouse, so Judge Spicer reconvened the hearing in Virgil's room at the Cosmopolitan Hotel.

Virgil affirmed Wyatt's testimony about Behan's treacherous claim to have disarmed the Cowboys, and explained his own unsuspecting response: "I had a walking stick in my left hand and my right hand was on my six-shooter in my waist pants, and when he said he had disarmed them, I shoved it clean around to my left hip and changed my walking stick to my right hand."

When he came in sight of the Cowboys, however, it was obvious to Virgil that they were well armed. Billy Clanton and Frank McLaury had their hands on their six-shooters and Tom McLaury was reaching for a Winchester rifle on a horse. Virgil called out, "Boys, throw up your hands. I want your guns." At that point, "Frank McLaury and Billy Clanton drew their six-shooters and commenced to cock them, and [I] heard them go 'click, click.'"

Virgil still attempted to avoid a fight. "At that I said, throwing up both hands, with the cane in my right hand . . . 'Hold on, I don't want that.'" But to no avail. Billy Clanton fired his pistol and Tom McLaury drew the rifle from its scabbard, using the horse as a shield. On cross-examination, Virgil agreed that Wyatt had also fired an initial shot, simultaneously with Billy Clanton.

Several more defense witnesses followed, upright citizens of Tombstone including two bartenders (an honorable and important profession in territorial Arizona), the town clerk, an army surgeon, and a hotel keeper. Several testified that the Clantons and McLaurys had threatened violence against the Earps; others had seen the Cowboys, including the supposedly unarmed Tom McLaury, carrying guns just before the shoot-out.

For example, the hotel keeper Albert Bilicke testified that he had seen Tom McLaury at Everhardy's butcher shop shortly before the fight. "When he went into the butcher shop his right-hand pants pocket was flat and appeared as if nothing was in it. When he came out his pants pocket protruded as if there was a revolver therein." This evidence was not devastating, but the prosecutor (who should have known better) could not bring himself to leave it alone: "How did it happen that you watched him so closely the different places that he went and the exact position of his right-hand pantaloons pocket when he went into the butcher shop and the exact form of a revolver in the same right-hand pocket when he came out?" Asked to explain his answer, Bilicke took full advantage of the prosecutor's classic mistake: "Every good citizen in this city was watching all those cowboys very closely on the day the affray occurred, and as [Tom] was walking down the street my attention was called to this McLaury by a friend, and so it happened that I watched him very closely." At a stroke, the defense theory crystallized. The Cowboys were a menace to the "good citizens" of Tombstone. They had to be watched and kept under control, meaning that Virgil Earp had only been doing his job. As will become evident, Judge Spicer was keenly attuned to such testimony.

Next to the Earps themselves, the most important defense witness was H. F. Sills, a railroad engineer from New Mexico who just happened to be visiting Tombstone on October 26. A complete stranger in town, he had no prior contact with either the Earps or the Cowboys. Sills testified that shortly after arriving in Tombstone he passed by the O.K. Corral and overheard one of the Cowboys talk about killing "the whole party of the Earps" on sight. Later, when the fight began, he saw Virgil raise his cane and he believed that Wyatt and Billy Clanton had fired the first shots.

Sills's testimony was significant for two reasons. First, he was one of the few truly neutral witnesses at the hearing. Nearly everyone else was closely identified with one side or the other. And since he was neutral, it was particularly significant that Sills undercut the "nickel-plated pistol" theory by testifying that Wyatt and Billy Clanton fired first. By taking Doc Holliday out of the picture, he deprived the prosecution of its possible fallback position that the unstable gunslinger had impulsively fired as the Cowboys tried to surrender—which would make Virgil, at a minimum, criminally negligent for enlisting the erratic Holliday's assistance in the first place. But if it was Wyatt who shot first, Judge Spicer could only find for the prosecution if he concluded that the deputy sheriff was a deliberate murderer—a strikingly harder story to sell.[29] (Of course, the prosecution would have no case at all if Billy Clanton or Frank McLaury could be conclusively shown to have fired the first shot, but even the staunchest Earp partisans were unwilling to go completely out on that limb; the best they could hope to establish was that Wyatt and one of the Cowboys fired almost simultaneously.)

The prosecution cross-examined Sills relentlessly, hoping either to shake his story or to expose some hidden bias. Neither tactic worked.

The defense also called Addie Bourland, a dressmaker who lived across from Fly's photography studio, the scene of the gunfight. Though Bourland was not able to say who started the gunfight, she stated that she did not see the Cowboys with their hands in the air. This testimony was obviously important to Judge Spicer, who took the extraordinary step of visiting her at her home during a break in the trial. Following that *ex parte* interrogation, Spicer recalled Bourland to the stand, over the strenuous objections of the prosecution, and proceeded to question her himself. Could she be more explicit about the beginning of the fight? "I didn't see anyone hold up their hands," she said. "They all seemed to be firing in general on both sides. They were firing on both sides at each other. I mean by this, at the time the firing commenced."

Then the prosecution, having been granted further cross-examination, blundered in a manner still all too familiar to contemporary trial lawyers, by asking one question too many. What had Miss Bourland told Judge Spicer during their private interview? Her answer: "He asked me one or two questions in regard to seeing the difficulty, and if I saw any men throw up their hands, whether I would have seen it, and I told him I thought I would have seen it."

Until that moment, it was possible that Bourland had simply missed the Cowboys' gesture of surrender, in what was, after all, merely a thirty-second confrontation. It was the improvident cross-examination that allowed her to shore up her testimony by adding that "I would have seen it" if it had happened.

The defense rested, turning the case over to the prosecutors for rebuttal. Will McLaury and Lyttleton Price now faced a decision of their own. An adverse decision at this point would terminate the proceeding, never allowing them to present further evidence to a jury. What could they do to reinvigorate their case, which had been badly damaged by the defense presentation? Should they recall John Behan, allowing him to refute the charges in Wyatt's statement (and perhaps to expose Wyatt as an adulterer)? Could they locate additional witnesses who might impeach the reputations of Sills and Bourland? Was there more to be offered regarding the deal between Wyatt and Ike? And was there anything at all more to be said about Ike's claim that the Earps' attack was an effort to silence him concerning their participation in the Benson stage robbery?

Any testimony along those lines would have enhanced the prosecution theory, but it seems that there was no such information at hand. Instead, they called a single rebuttal witness, a butcher named Ernest Storm who had purchased the McLaurys' beef shortly before the gunfight. Storm offered the nearly irrelevant testimony that Tom McLaury did not appear to be armed when in "my shop about two or three o'clock in the afternoon." Storm somewhat refuted Albert Bilicke's testimony that McLaury had emerged from the butcher shop with a pistol visible in his front pocket, but not with any great force. The balance of the defense case was untouched.

Many lawyers believe that it is essential to call at least one rebuttal witness, if only to make sure of having the crucial last word. Nonetheless, the prosecution here may actually have damaged itself by closing its case with a witness who had so relatively little to say.

As we look back on the Tombstone murder trial, it is interesting to note the evidence that appears to have been omitted in the month-long hearing. From the defense side, relatively little was made of Sheriff Behan's connection to the Cowboys, including the arrest of his own deputy for robbing the Bisbee stage. In fact, the very idea of an organized outlaw faction was barely developed, save for an inaccurate reference to Ike Clanton as "sort of a chief among the Cowboys." True, many defense witnesses testified that the Clantons and McLaurys were dangerous habitual criminals, but the larger story of nearly open communal warfare stayed out of the record.

The prosecutors were hardly eager to underscore the connection between the victims (not to mention their own key witnesses) and the epidemic of cattle theft, border raids, stagecoach robberies, and occasional murders that had plagued the growing community. On the other hand, they might have used the deep divisions in Tombstone society to strengthen their case as well. What else could explain the Earps' posited determination to gun down the surrendering Cowboys? Without more context, the prosecution was left arguing either the implausible theory that the entire gunfight was a plot to shut up Ike Clanton, or the less culpable theory that a jumpy Doc Holliday had started the battle, drawing the Earps in almost by misadventure.

Judge Spicer delivered his decision on November 30, 1881, and it happened that the story frame made all the difference in the case. He was troubled by the inclusion of Wyatt and Doc in Virgil's posse, given the evidence of their history of bad blood with the Cowboys:

> In view of these controversies between Wyatt Earp and Isaac Clanton and Thomas McLaury, and in further view of this quarrel the night before between Isaac Clanton and J. H. Holliday, I am of the opinion that the defendant, Virgil Earp, as chief of police, subsequently calling upon Wyatt Earp and J. H. Holliday to assist him in arresting and disarming the Clantons and McLaurys—committed an injudicious and censurable act.

But it turned out that he was troubled more by the deeper background of the fight, and he did not confine himself to circumstances that had been introduced at trial:

> [Y]et when we consider the conditions of affairs incident to a frontier country; the lawlessness and disregard for human life; the existence of a

law-defying element in [our] midst; the fear and feeling of insecurity that has existed; the supposed prevalence of bad, desperate, and reckless men who have been a terror to the country and kept away capital and enterprise; and consider the many threats that have been made against the Earps, I can attach no criminality to [Virgil's] unwise act. In fact, as the result plainly proves, he needed the assistance and support of staunch and true friends, upon whose courage, coolness and fidelity he could depend, in case of an emergency.

Remarking that there were "witnesses of credibility" on both sides, Spicer nonetheless rejected the argument that the Cowboys had been shot while trying to surrender: "Considering all the testimony together, I am of the opinion that the weight of the evidence sustains and corroborates the testimony of Wyatt Earp, that their demand for a surrender was met by William Clanton and Frank McLaury drawing, or making motions to draw their pistols."

But this conclusion alone should not have been sufficient to free the defendants. The proceeding was simply a preliminary hearing, held only for the purpose of determining whether there was sufficient evidence to warrant a full trial. Ordinarily, the existence of "witnesses of credibility" would be enough to allow the prosecution to go forward, with the "weight of the evidence" being left for decision by a jury. In this case, however, there was an added element. The Earps claimed lawful justification for the shootings. That, as Judge Spicer determined, was a legal defense well within his jurisdiction to decide:

Was it for Virgil Earp as chief of police to abandon his clear duty as an officer because its performance was likely to be fraught with danger? Or was it not his duty that as such officer he owed to the peaceable and law-abiding citizens of the city, who looked to him to preserve peace and order, and their protection and security, to at once call to his aid sufficient assistance and persons to arrest and disarm these men? There can be but one answer to these questions, and that answer is such as will divest the subsequent approach of the defendants toward the deceased of all presumption of malice or of illegality. When, therefore, the defendants, regularly or specially appointed officers, marched down Fremont Street to the scene of the subsequent homicide, they were going where it was their right and duty to go; and they were doing what it was their right and duty to do; and they were armed, as it was their right and duty to be armed when approaching men whom they believed to be armed and contemplating resistance. . . . To constitute a crime of murder there must be proven, not only the killing, but the felonious intent. . . . [I]n looking over this mass of testimony for evidence upon this point I find that it is anything but clear.

Considering "the conditions of affairs incident to a frontier country," Judge Spicer would require specific evidence of intent before he would order the lawmen to stand trial. But here the prosecution failed badly, offering only the allegations of Ike Clanton, which the judge rejected in their entirety:

> The testimony of Isaac Clanton that this tragedy was the result of a scheme on the part of the Earps to assassinate him, and thereby bury in oblivion the confessions the Earps had made to him about "piping" away the shipment of coin by Wells, Fargo & Co. falls short of being sound theory, [on] account of the great fact most prominent in this matter, to-wit: that Isaac Clanton was not injured at all, and could have been killed first and easiest, if it was the object of the attack to kill him. He would have been first to fall, but as it was, he was known, or believed to be unarmed and was suffered, as Wyatt Earp testified, told to go away, and was not harmed.

Which led inexorably to a single result:

> In view of all the facts and circumstances of the case, considering the threats made, the character and positions of the parties, and the tragical results accomplished in manner and form as they were with all surrounding influences bearing upon the *res gestae* of the affair, I cannot resist the conclusion that the defendants were fully justified in committing these homicides—that it [was] a necessary act done in the discharge of an official duty.

All charges against the Earps and Holliday were dismissed.

With "witnesses of credibility" on both sides, the preliminary case against the Earps should have belonged to the prosecution. Their burden was relatively modest, requiring only the production of sufficient evidence to merit a complete trial. In fact, at one point Judge Spicer virtually ruled that the prosecution had met its burden, when he revoked bail for Wyatt and Doc and remanded them to custody.

So what went wrong?

For one thing, the defense strategies all paid off. By producing a maximum series of favorable witnesses at the preliminary hearing, rather than reserve them for trial, the defense succeeded in creating a favorable frame for Judge Spicer's evaluation of the facts of the case. The same approach underscored the "civic" nature of the Earps' actions, since many of their witnesses were solid, town-dwelling citizens: an army surgeon, various hotel- and saloonkeepers, a dressmaker, even an assistant district attorney, a probate judge, and the clerk of the board of supervisors. Though some of the witnesses were clearly central to the defense, others were cumulative or even superfluous. It seems highly likely that the parade of notables was intended to influence the court in ways that were not strictly evidentiary.

When it came to evidence, the defense also succeeded when it chose a "minimalist" approach. The narrative statement of Wyatt Earp apparently did not backfire. More important, the risky decision to take it fairly easy on John Behan seems to have worked out as intended. In determining the significance of the evidence, Spicer stated that he gave greater "weight to the testimony of persons unacquainted with the deceased or the defendants, [than] to the testimony of persons who were companions or acquaintances, if not partisans of the deceased." By this he could only mean that he accepted the testimony of Sills and Bourland, rather than John Behan's. The further implication is that the judge was convinced that Sheriff Behan was a companion, perhaps even a partisan, of the slain Cowboys. The defense could have pounded away further at the connection, but in this case understatement appears to have worked well.

Though Judge Spicer was said to lean "toward the Republican law-and-order crowd," he was still willing enough to ship Wyatt Earp and Doc Holliday off to the cold and perilous comforts of John Behan's jail.[30]

In fact, the trial began with a defense challenge to Spicer's jurisdiction, claiming that as a justice of the peace he lacked authority to preside over the hearing. Whatever his biases, they were not so pronounced that the Earps considered their exoneration a mere formality.

But as much as he might have aspired to objectivity, Spicer had to be aware of Behan's sympathies even in the absence of explicit courtroom proof. Living in Tombstone, he must have known about the lawlessness in the surrounding countryside, including the various stage robberies, raids into Mexico, and outright murders that had been attributed to the gang of Cowboys.[31] Indeed, as the murder hearing was about to begin, Tombstone's mayor, John Clum, was requesting federal troops to help safeguard the town against the outlaw threat. It should have come as no surprise, therefore, when Spicer characterized the Clantons and McLaurys (and their friends) as "reckless men who have been a terror to the country and kept away capital and enterprise." The defense did not have to prove that the Cowboys meant trouble for Tombstone, it was in the juridic air.[32]

It was the task of the prosecution to neutralize this judicial bias—possibly by distancing the victims from the Cowboy circle, conceivably by showing that the gang was more myth than reality. Perhaps that goal could not have been accomplished at all, but it certainly could not have been achieved through timid measures. The prosecution did attempt to establish that the Clantons and McLaurys had only been in a few "rows," but they never presented a sustained counternarrative to the Earps' story (and Spicer's evident assumption) of Tombstone-in-peril.

To persuade Judge Spicer to rule against the "regularly or specially appointed" peace officers, the factual assertions of partisan witnesses were bound to be insufficient. To win, the prosecution needed a compelling theory that explained not simply how but also *why* the Earps would murder the Cowboys.

One such theory has since been offered by the Earp researcher Paula Mitchell Marks, who suggests that the fight may have grown out of the Earps' efforts to ingratiate themselves with Tombstone's financial interests, either to enhance Wyatt's chance of being elected county sheriff or simply to remain in the good graces of the local mine owners and businessmen. In either case, they could score points by coming down hard on the Cowboys and impressing the locals with their "tough brand of police work."[33]

So when Ike Clanton showed up in Tombstone on October 26, mouthing threats and displaying his weapons, the Earps responded with force, "buffaloing" first Ike and then Tom McLaury. The Clantons and McLaurys, however, did not have the good sense to get immediately out of town. Instead, they gathered at the O.K. Corral, at least two (and possibly three) of them armed, in seeming defiance of Virgil Earp's lawful, though excessive, authority. The Earps and Holliday then marched over to the lot on Fremont Street, perhaps intending only to intimidate the Cowboys, perhaps intending to administer new beatings, but not with the settled purpose of committing murder. Unfortunately, things got out of hand; either the Cowboys did not respond quickly enough or the Earps and Holliday were too jumpy. Guns were drawn and shots were fired, the first shot coming from the volatile Doc Holliday. After that, the fight "became general" and the Cowboys' fate was sealed.

We can never know whether Marks's suppositions are historically true; they have been rejected by other researchers. As advocacy, however, her proffered theory has the advantage of plausibility. To sustain a finding of probable cause, Judge Spicer would only have to believe that the Earps were overaggressive and reckless, not that they were assassins. Consequently, Ike Clanton's wild charges would have been irrelevant to the case, making it far less likely that the prosecution would fall along with Ike's flimsy credibility. Of course, the great drawback to the theory is that it would only support a charge of manslaughter, not murder (at least against the Earps; a murder charge against Holliday might still have been a possibility). But a tempered case was exactly what the prosecution needed in the first place. The cold-blooded murder theory was almost certain to fail, given the Earps' badges and Judge Spicer's predisposition.[34]

Why did the prosecution choose to "roll the dice," gambling that they would succeed in proving murder at the cost of abandoning the more promising manslaughter charge? Though documentary evidence is lacking, it seems a good bet that Will McLaury, aggrieved and vindictive over the killing of his two brothers, played a key role in pushing the prosecution to pursue its immoderate, and ultimately unsuccessful, approach. McLaury had a great emotional stake in proving that his brothers were innocent victims and the Earps vicious killers, leading him to accept uncritically Ike Clanton's fanciful claims.[35] The virtues of familial loyalty aside, the prosecution team clearly could have benefited from more detached associate counsel.[36]

For most of the last century frontier historians have debated the fine points of the gunfight at the O.K. Corral. Hollywood, of course, has been firmly in the pro-Earp camp, at least since the 1950s when Burt Lancaster won *The Gunfight at the O.K. Corral,* and Hugh O'Brien brought the role to television in *The Life and Legend of Wyatt Earp.* Most recently, Kevin Costner and Kurt Russell have starred as Wyatt—a hero, of course—in separate feature films. Allen Barra and Casey Tefertiller more or less concur with the general tenor, if not necessarily the documentary accuracy, of the Hollywood portrayal, concluding that the Cowboys started the fight and the Earps had to end it in order to carry out their duties as lawmen.[37] Other researchers, such as Paula Mitchell Marks, are decidedly more skeptical, suggesting that the Cowboys were mostly a nuisance and that the Earps gunned them down in an unnecessary show of force (and lied about it afterward).[38]

While the weight of opinion seems to favor the Earps, a review of the lawyering at the preliminary hearing certainly allows the possibility that the revisionists may have a point. To be sure, the accounts of John Behan and Ike Clanton, if believed, could support a murder conviction, but their stories are made suspect by obvious (and not so obvious) bias and self-interest. In any event, the testimony of the unquestionably impartial H. F. Sills would seem at least to create reasonable doubt no matter what Behan and Clanton had to say.[39] The murder story was just too intricate, requiring that every dispute be determined in favor of the prosecution in order to justify a decision adverse to the Earps. Thus, the most cogent account of the Earps' guilt would have to focus on a lesser crime such as manslaughter—not so dramatic as outright murder, but still a serious felony.

In advocacy terms, the best cases are both "simple" and "easy to believe." A simple story makes maximum use of undisputed facts, while relying as little as possible on evidence that is either hotly controverted or inherently unbelievable. In the same sense, a story cannot be easy to believe if it depends on implausible arguments or if it requires proof that the opposing witnesses have lied or falsified evidence. Trials can sometimes be won by stories that fail the tests of simplicity and ease, but it will be an uphill struggle. The best and most effective trial theories are able to encompass the entirety of the other side's case and still result in victory by sheer logical force.

A simple story actually seeks to narrow the scope of disagreement between the parties by incorporating (and accommodating) as many of the other side's facts as possible. No matter how vigorously presented, the murder case against the Earps and Holliday could never be simple. It required the resolution of too many contradictory facts: Who made the first move? How serious were the Cowboys' threats? Did Sheriff Behan mislead the Earps? If the judge believed Virgil and Wyatt regarding any one of these questions, the prosecution would fail. At trial, that is the cost of complexity.

A manslaughter prosecution, however, would have had the simple virtue of making most of those questions irrelevant. Indeed, it could have accommodated nearly all of Wyatt's and Virgil's testimony concerning Ike's threats, the march down Fremont Street, and even the eventual moment of truth. Imagine how the prosecutor could have presented the final argument if manslaughter had been the charge:

> Wyatt and Virgil Earp claim that the Clantons and McLaurys reached for their guns, but sometimes you see what you want to see. After spending the previous night and morning contending with Ike Clanton and Tom McLaury, the Earps were ready for a showdown. They wanted to have it out with the Cowboys once and for all. So when Tom McLaury threw back his jacket to show that he was unarmed, the Earps and Holliday just couldn't wait to start shooting. Even a moment of calm hesitation would have shown that Tom had no weapon, but the defendants were all fired up. They didn't wait, they didn't think, they just started shooting. And that is manslaughter in this territory.

In a murder prosecution, any number of smaller questions might also have turned the case in favor of the defense, but they simply vanish under a manslaughter theory. For example, one of the greatest weaknesses in the murder case was John Behan's inability to explain how Doc Holliday could have fired—in the space of twenty-five seconds—both a shotgun and a nickel-plated pistol. But that anomaly has no bearing on the lesser charge, since the alternative—that Wyatt fired the first shot—can be made equally probative of manslaughter.

If the murder case was not simple, even less was it easy to believe, resting as it did on both implausible elements and the necessity of harsh judgments. Ike Clanton's outlandish story may have been the death knell of the prosecution case.[40] Of course, even fantastic tales may sometimes be true, but it was just too much to ask of Judge Spicer that he believe that Deputy Marshal Wyatt Earp would have helped rob the Benson stage *and* have confided the deed to the disreputable Ike.

In this case, it appears that the prosecution put the conclusory horse ahead of the theoretical cart (or perhaps stagecoach). If indeed the Earps were murderers (and Will McLaury certainly was not about to see it any other way), then there had to be a reason. And if there had to be a reason, then Ike's story was probably the best they could muster. A more fruitful approach, however, would have been to consider the plausibility of the alleged motives before deciding the nature of the offense to be charged. Such an analysis would have revealed that there was scant motive for murder, but that the underlying reasons for manslaughter might well be established.

The prosecution case was not easy to believe for yet another reason. It required the judge to conclude that Wyatt and Virgil lied on the stand. In contrast, a manslaughter theory could have accommodated virtually all of the Earps' testimony, perhaps even turning it against them. For example, Wyatt testified that Frank McLaury and Billy Clanton had their six-shooters in "plain sight" as the Earps approached the Cowboys. When Virgil called for them to hold up their hands, "Billy Clanton and Frank McLaury commenced to draw their pistols." Wyatt continued, "I had my pistol in my overcoat pocket, where I put it when Behan told us he had disarmed the other parties. When I saw Billy Clanton and Frank McLaury draw their pistols, I drew my pistol."

But Wyatt also testified that he succeeded in getting off the first shot, an impressive achievement given that he had to pull his weapon out of his overcoat pocket, while Frank and Billy already had theirs out and in plain sight. Could it be that Wyatt was a bit readier to begin firing that he admitted or recalled? Or perhaps the Cowboys were not really reaching for their pistols after all, as evidenced by the fact that Wyatt apparently had plenty of time to pull his six-shooter out of his pocket after he saw them move their hands. In either case, there is a feasible implication that Wyatt acted recklessly, shooting without thinking. Importantly, Judge Spicer could have come to that conclusion without assuming that Wyatt lied on the witness stand.

Trial lawyers understand how difficult it is to re-create the past even a few months or years following the events themselves. After nearly 120 years, it seems impossible to determine with certainty exactly what happened in Tombstone that October afternoon. It is clear, however, that many contemporary observers—not limited to the Cowboy crowd—then believed that the Earps acted with unnecessary brutality. One newspaper, for example, reported in mid-hearing that "public sentiment, which was at first in [the Earps'] favor, has turned now since the evidence shows that it was the gratification of revenge on their part, rather than desire to vindicate law which led to the shooting."[41] Nonetheless, the prosecution badly overplayed its case, leading to Judge Spicer's exoneration of the defendants. Today, the Earp brothers and Doc Holliday are lionized as the heroes of the O.K. Corral, the few dissenting revisionist voices being drowned out by the accolades of history. And all because the prosecution gambled in its theory choice—and lost.

NOTES

1. The longhand transcript of the hearing before Judge Spicer, as well as the transcript of the inquest that preceded it by several days, survived until the 1930s, when both documents came into the possession of a Works Projects Administration writer named Hal L. Hayhurst. Hayhurst produced an edited, typewritten version of the transcripts, including much of the verbatim record along with his own summaries and editorial comments. The Hayhurst document was published in 1981 by Alford Turner under the title THE O.K. CORRAL INQUEST. Turner himself critiques the Hayhurst document as incomplete and anti-Earp. Nonetheless, Turner's edition is acknowledged today as the best, most accessible, and most complete version of

the trial record. Unfortunately, the original transcripts were destroyed along with Hayhurst's personal effects when the writer died.

Unless otherwise noted, all quotations from the trial record are taken from Turner's INQUEST.

2. Even survival plus acquittal might not have been enough to secure his legend. The Earp persona was further magnified by his longevity. Not only did he live until 1929, but he also made his home in Los Angeles, where he was able to spin his stories of the frontier days for writers and movie stars, Tom Mix among them. His story, which took him from Dodge City to Tombstone and eventually to Alaska, was made even more engaging by the presence of real-life characters with names like Doc Holliday, Big-Nose Kate, Curly Bill Brocius, Johnny Behind-the-Deuce, Old Man Clanton, Bat Masterson, Buckskin Frank, and Johnny Ringo. No doubt, the existence of an extensive written record—newspaper reports of the gunfight and the transcript of Judge Spicer's hearing—also contributed to the long-term popular fascination with Earpiana.

3. General information regarding the Earps and the situation in Tombstone is taken from the following three sources: ALLEN BARRA, INVENTING WYATT EARP: HIS LIFE AND MANY LEGENDS (1998); CASEY TEFERTILLER, WYATT EARP: THE LIFE BEHIND THE LEGEND (1997); PAULA MITCHELL MARKS, AND DIE IN THE WEST: THE STORY OF THE O.K. CORRAL GUNFIGHT (1989). Unless noted, facts included in this chapter represent a consensus among the three sources.

4. At the time, the word "cowboy" had not yet come into general use to refer to the men who drove cattle for a living—they were usually called cowhands, drovers, or stockmen. "Cowboy," when the term was first introduced, was slightly derisive and eventually became nearly synonymous with cattle rustler. The Tombstone Cowboys themselves embraced the description, rather in defiance of conventional society. Adopting the approach of Allen Barra, I capitalize "Cowboy" to distinguish the disreputable louts from honest, hardworking ranch hands—the cowboys we have all come to know and admire.

5. The Mexican army was acting in reprisal for an earlier incident, usually called the Skeleton Canyon Massacre, in which as many as nineteen Mexican nationals had been murdered by a band of Cowboys, said to have included the McLaury brothers.

6. Including the robbery, on September 8, 1881, of the Sandy Bob stage from Tombstone to Bisbee, in which the prime suspect was Frank Stilwell, one of John Behan's deputy sheriffs.

7. Quoted in BARRA, *supra* note 3, at 161. Stilwell was Behan's deputy, arrested by Morgan Earp for robbing the Bisbee stage.

8. It was illegal to carry a gun in Tombstone, and it is most likely that both men were unarmed.

9. BARRA, *supra* note 3, at 167.

10. Mr. Spangenburg, however, refused to sell a weapon to Ike Clanton, though that was probably unknown to the Earps at the time.

11. The following morning, the *Tombstone Nugget* ran this account of the gunfight:

[W]hen within a few feet of them the marshal said to the Clantons and McLowrys: "Throw up your hands boys, I intend to disarm you."

As he spoke Frank McLowry made a motion to draw his revolver, when Wyatt Earp pulled his and shot him, the ball striking on the right side of his abdomen. About the same time Doc Holliday shot Tom McLowry in the right side, using a short shotgun, such as is carried by Wells-Fargo & co.'s messengers. In the meantime Billy Clanton had shot at Morgan Earp, the ball passing through the left shoulderblade across his back, just grazing the backbone and coming out at the shoulder, the ball remaining inside of his shirt. He fell to the ground but in an instant gathered himself, and raising in a sitting position fired at Frank McLowry as he crossed Fremont Street, and at the same instant Doc Holliday shot at him, both balls taking effect, either of which would have proved fatal, as one struck him in the right temple and the other in the left breast. As he started across the street, however, he pulled his gun down on Holliday saying, "I've got you now." "Blaze away! You're a daisy if you do," replied Doc. This shot of McLowry's passed through Holliday's pocket, just grazing the skin.

While this was going on Billy Clanton had shot Virgil Earp in the right leg, the ball passing through the calf, inflicting a severe flesh wound. In turn he had been shot by Morgan Earp in the right side of the abdomen, and twice by Virgil Earp in the right wrist and once in the left breast. Soon after the shooting commenced Ike Clanton ran through the O.K. Corral, across Allen Street in Kellogg's saloon, and thence into Toughnut Street, where he was arrested and taken to the county jail. The firing altogether didn't occupy more than twenty-five seconds, during which time thirty shots were fired.

Quoted in Barra at 184–85 (orthography original).

12. Quoted in TEFERTILLER, *supra* note 3, at 135.

13. BARRA, *supra* note 3, at 197.

14. Most scholars believe that Doc, a trusted friend, was brought along to guard the rear, which perhaps explains why he had been given Virgil's shotgun. At trial, Virgil explained that he had deputized his brothers, but of Holliday he would say only that "I called on him on that day for assistance to help disarm the Clantons and McLaurys."

15. TEFERTILLER, *supra* note 3, at 132.

16. BARRA, *supra* note 3, at 184.

17. *Id.* at 129.

18. *Id* at 113.

29. Josephine remained living in a house once shared with Behan, but the sheriff moved out and Wyatt spent much of his time there. According to one researcher, "Wyatt was away one night when Behan appeared to demand that [Josephine] get

out or move the house, as the lot was in his name. Morgan Earp had thoughtfully shown up to protect her in Wyatt's absence . . . and flattened the demanding Behan." MARKS, *supra* note 3, at 160.

20. Quoted in BARRA, *supra* note 3, at 234–35. Allen Barra doubts the full veracity of Allie Earp's memoirs, but does conclude that Josephine and Wyatt were involved with each other by the time of the trial. At a minimum, "they must have talked and made some kind of pact to meet outside Arizona later." *Id.* at 233–36.

21. In fact, the two would live together for almost fifty years, until Wyatt's death in 1929, sharing adventures at "every mining camp and racetrack from Texas to Mexico to Alaska." *Id.* at 101.

22. *Id.* at 113.

23. Their fears were far from illusory. Prosecutor Will McLaury bragged at the time that he had "a large number of my Texaᴗ friends here who are ready and willing to stand by me and with Winchesters if necessary." Quoted in MARKS, *supra* note 3, at 283–84. As history records, the Cowboys did indeed take matters into their own hands following the trial, maiming Virgil and murdering Morgan in separate ambushes. Wyatt took his own revenge in what has since come to be known as the "Vendetta Ride."

25. Clanton admitted having said something to the effect of "the Earp crowd had insulted [me] the night before when [I was] unarmed—I have fixed or 'heeled' myself now, and they have got a fight on sight." "Heeling" oneself was Arizona slang for arming oneself.

25. Judge Spicer sustained objections to both questions.

26. The statute is described in the court record as Section 133, page 22 of the laws of Arizona, approved February 12, 1881.

27. TEFERTILLER, *supra* note 3, at 142, quoting the *Tombstone Nugget*.

28. They may also have been exposed to threats of murder, as Tombstone's tense atmosphere made it a very real possibility that Cowboy partisans might attempt to eliminate adverse witnesses.

29. Sills's testimony was significant for a third reason as well. Shortly after he left the stand, defense counsel argued that the prosecution evidence had become so weak that Wyatt and Doc should be restored to bail. Judge Spicer agreed, setting bond at $20,000 each. The money was easily raised, and Doc and Wyatt remained free for the balance of the hearing.

30. TEFERTILLER, *supra* note 3, at 156.

31. For example, on the very day of the gunfight, General William Tecumseh Sherman had written to the U. S. secretary of war requesting permission for the army to pursue American raiders into Mexico. Wrote Sherman, "[I]t is notorious that the civil authorities of Arizona on that extensive frontier are utterly powerless to prevent marauders from crossing over into Sonora and to punish them when they return for asylum with stolen booty." Quoted in MARKS, *supra* note 3, at 298.

32. Mayor John Clum, for example, saw the gunfight, and therefore the trial,

strictly in terms of the good Earps against the dangerous Cowboys: "Was the police force of Tombstone to be bullied and cowed?" he asked rhetorically. Quoted in *id.* at 298.

33. *Id.* at 298–99.

34. Spicer said as much himself, noting that the prosecution claimed that the Earps "precipitated the triple homicide by a felonious intent then and there to kill and murder the deceased, and that they made use of their official characters as a pretext. I cannot believe this theory, and cannot resist the firm conviction that the Earps acted wisely, discreetly and prudentially, to secure their own self-preservation."

35. Will McLaury went even further than Ike Clanton, apparently believing that his brothers were murdered because they "had got up facts intending to prosecute ... Holliday and the Earps, and Holliday had information of it." Quoted in MARKS, *supra* note 3, at 263.

36. Will McLaury suggested more than once that he would have been happy to gun down the Earps himself. Writing to his law partner about the revocation of bail for Wyatt and Doc, he said, "I did not think they ... would make a move and did not fear them. The fact is I only hoped they would as I would be on my feet and have the first go. And thought I could kill them both before they could get a start." Quoted in MARKS, *supra* note 3, at 268. A recent widower, McLaury left behind his two young children when he came to Tombstone, a fact that caused his sister to reprimand him for neglect. McLaury replied, "My children will be provided for and I don't think a father would be any great advantage to them who would leave it to god to punish men who had murdered their uncles." *Id.* at 283.

37. BARRA, *supra* note 3; TEFERTILLER, *supra* note.

38. MARKS, *supra* note 3.

39. Given that the hearing convened less than a week following the gunfight, one wonders whether the prosecutors were even aware of Sills as they shaped their theory and presented their case.

40. There has been much suggestion that Ike's farfetched story may have been drug-induced. He requested and obtained a few days off in the middle of his testimony in order to obtain medical attention for persistent headaches (due to the pistol-whipping by Virgil Earp). At the time, administration of cocaine was the accepted remedy for headaches.

41. Quoted in MARKS, *supra* note 3, at 277.

CHAPTER FIVE

LIBERTY VALANCE
Truth or Justice

Out of the east a stranger came, a law book in his hand.
A man, the kind of a man the west would need to tame a troubled land.
But the point of a gun was the only law that Liberty understood.
When the final showdown came to pass, a law book was no good.

Gene Pitney's hit song is better known than John Ford's classic motion pic-ture,[1] which in turn is much better known than the Dorothy Johnson short story on which it was loosely based.[2] But whatever the source, the image is nearly universal. A quiet, educated man brings order to a western town, making it safe for women and children by showing the courage to stand up to a villainous outlaw.

Of course, it could never be quite that easy. Somewhere along the line the hero will be forced to abandon his law books in favor of a firearm. Before justice can prevail, there will have to be a gunfight. And so it was in The Man Who Shot Liberty Valance, *when Ransome Stoddard, played nobly by James Stewart, challenged the cruel and arrogant Liberty Valance, leer-ingly portrayed by Lee Marvin.*

Everyone heard two shots ring out. One shot made Liberty fall.
The man who shot Liberty Valance, he was the bravest of them all.

It was a fight that Liberty would not win. By the time the smoke cleared, he was lying dead on the ground, the improbable victim of the mild-man-nered lawyer who had somehow managed to get off a lucky—or perhaps it was destined—shot.

Ransome Stoddard was immediately celebrated for his courage. He gets the girl, of course, and goes on to an honorable career as a statesman and diplomat, though the plotline has a twist or two and a bit of a surprise ending. The last thing anyone seriously suggests is that Ransome Stoddard be prosecuted. The man who shot Liberty Valance is a hero, a champion writ large, not a criminal. Who would ever dream of prosecuting the man who saved the town from that swaggering, gunslinging bully?

> *When Liberty Valance rode to town, the women folks would hide. They'd hide.*
> *When Liberty Valance walked around the men would step aside.*
> *Cause the point of a gun was the only law that Liberty understood.*
> *When it came to shootin' straight and fast, he was mighty good.*

All of which fits the formula for a western legend so long as Liberty had been killed in self-defense. And while only a few ruffians mourned his death, one must wonder what might have happened if there had been just one more lawyer in town—say, a prosecutor who was tempted to look a bit more deeply into the gunfight. Perhaps he would have sought to enhance his reputation as the Man Who Indicted the Man Who Shot Liberty Valance.

It all began on a westbound stagecoach.[3] Ransome Stoddard, for reasons never disclosed, was headed for the tiny town of Shinbone, located somewhere "south of the Picketwire" on the very edge of civilization. Evidently fresh out of law school, or perhaps just having finished an apprenticeship, he was an obvious tenderfoot, carrying law books but no weapon.

Suddenly, a masked man stepped into the road, his gun pointed at the stage driver. "Stand and deliver," he shouted. It was a holdup. The driver reined in the horses as six robbers emerged from the shadows. The frightened passengers were forced to surrender their valuables. One of the thieves noticed the jewelry of an older woman, roughly grabbing at it with his soiled fingers. "Please don't take it," she tearfully begged, "my dead husband gave it to me." The outlaw just laughed. "I'll take it anyway," he said, as he reached for the brooch. The driver and the male passengers watched in horror, too frightened to make a move.

With one exception. Ransome Stoddard stepped forward, shoving the outlaw aside. "What sort of man are you?" he asked, in both shock and dismay. "Take your hands off her."

Stoddard paid dearly for his valor. The leader of the bandits struck him hard across the face, knocking him to the ground. "Now, what kind of man are you, dude?" he smirked.

"I am an attorney at law. And you may have us in your guns now, but I'll see you in jail for this."

"Lawyer? Hah! I'll teach you law, western law."

Using his trademark silver-handled quirt, the outlaw stood over the fallen Stoddard, whipping him savagely until restrained by his own men. Leaving his victim for dead, he tore up one of Stoddard's law books for a synecdoche of good measure.

Ransome's life was saved by Tom Doniphan, a local rancher—played by the ever-sturdy John Wayne—who fortunately discovered him lying unconscious on the road.[4] Tom brought the bruised and delirious Ransome into town, delivering him for nursing care to a young woman named Hallie (a decision Tom would soon regret). Hallie, a waitress at Anderson's restaurant and boarding-house, was Tom's fiancée-apparent. No words had been spoken, but everyone in Shinbone assumed they were destined for each other. This aspect of the plot was bound to thicken, but not until Ransome recovered from his ordeal and began his fatal *pas de deux* with Liberty Valance.

Regaining consciousness, if not local sensibility, Ransome learned the name of his tormentor and began to speak loudly of bringing him to justice. Seeking out the town marshal (played to perfection by the artfully ineffectual Andy "Jingles" Devine), Ransome demanded Valance's arrest. Of course, such an attempt would have been suicide for the bumbling marshal, who quickly begged off. The stage robbery had occurred outside the town limits, conveniently allowing the marshal to disavow jurisdiction.

The fainthearted ploy was evident to everyone but Ransome Stoddard, whose naive faith in the law compelled him to take the marshal's abstention at face value. Everyone else realized that Liberty Valance was simply above the law. The whole town was intimidated; no one would willingly cross him. Except, that is, for Tom Doniphan, who was tough enough to handle Valance but too dispassionate to take him on.

Ransome Stoddard, on the other hand, was not easily deterred. Consulting his law books, he located a territorial statute that did indeed give the town marshal jurisdiction over stage robberies. "Aha," he shouted. "Now we've got Liberty Valance just where we want him!" Of course, no one agreed. They all wanted Liberty Valance as far away from town as possible. Most of all, the marshal wanted no part of him. It was then that Stoddard realized just how thoroughly browbeaten a community he had joined. You could see the steely resolve flash across Ranse Stoddard's face. There would have to be a reckoning; the law demanded it.

But first there would be some symbolic, low-key violence. Finding no immediate demand for a law practice, Stoddard had taken a job waiting tables at Anderson's rooming house. One Saturday night Valance and his henchmen rode into town for dinner. Amused at the sight of a man in an apron, Valance knocked Stoddard to the floor, daring him to get up. Though no physical match for Valance, Stoddard was both principled and unafraid. When Tom Doniphan intervened, apparently ready to shoot it out with Valance over a ruined meal, Stoddard would have none of it. He was willing to accept humiliation rather than be the cause of needless gunplay.

Inescapably, the unsophisticated, beautiful Hallie (played by Vera Miles with spirited grace) was drawn to the well-spoken, nonviolent newcomer. How could it be that the sole unarmed man in town was the only one with sufficient nerve to resist the gunslinger? What was it that gave Ransome the courage that others lacked? It had to be his education, his awareness that the ideals of civilization would ultimately triumph over raw brutality. And though Hallie herself was illiterate, she understood what it would take to cast her lot with Ransome and the forces that were changing the west. She asked him to teach her to read—and then to open a school, for children and adults, where the good people of the town could study the ABCs and citizenship as well.

Hallie and Ranse avoided the realization, but of course they were falling in love. Tom Doniphan may have been the first to notice, but by then it was too late. Hallie would never be his, though he silently vowed to protect her happiness. Which in turn made him the reluctant guardian of Ransome Stoddard. Tom was bitter, though not hateful, over the loss of Hallie. More, he realized that Ransome Stoddard's law would end the frontier way of life on which Doniphan thrived. Nonetheless, he would do everything in his power to keep Ransome alive for Hallie's sake.

Ranse had no way of knowing that he had gained a defender, but he was smart enough to recognize that law and order would not arrive in Shinbone quickly enough to do anything about Liberty Valance. So the lawyer acquired a gun and set out to learn how to use it, heading out to the open range for secret target practice in his spare time. The effort was futile. There was no way he could adequately prepare himself for the inevitable confrontation with Liberty Valance.

With Ransome Stoddard representing reasoned civilization and Liberty Valance standing for loutish anarchy, the eventual showdown came over the issue of admission to the Union.[5] The territory, it seems, was divided on that question, and residents living "south of the Picketwire" were entitled to elect two representatives to a convention that would decide whether or not to seek statehood. As Ransome Stoddard explained it, statehood would mean security, schools, and opportunity for the region's decent, hardworking, church going townsfolk and farmers. It was opposed, needless to say, by the nefarious "cattle interests," who wanted to continue their undemocratic control of the territory.

A town meeting was called to elect the Shinbone delegates. Two pro-statehood nominees were quickly proposed, Ransome Stoddard and Dutton Peabody, the alcoholic-but-incorruptible publisher of the *Shinbone Star*. And then Liberty Valance invaded the meeting hall, accompanied by his thuggish sidekicks (Strother Martin and Lee Van Cleef, one coarse and the other sleek—both appropriately evil). Liberty, obviously in the employ of the sinister cattle barons, announced that *he* would be the Shinbone delegate. He pulled out his six-gun, daring the sodbusters to vote against him.

Steeled by the resolve of Stoddard, Peabody, and Tom Doniphan, however, the assembled citizens screwed their courage to the sticking point and voted for statehood and against the open range. Stoddard and Peabody were duly installed amid ecstatic cheers. Valance left the meeting vowing revenge.

Later that night, a somewhat tipsy Peabody repaired to his office in order to lay out the next morning's edition of the *Star*. Suddenly, Valance and his toughs broke into the print shop. They destroyed the press, smashed the furniture, and scattered the type. Peabody tried to stop them, but even sober he would have been easily overcome by the outlaws. As it was, the enraged Valance used his silver-handled quirt to beat the helpless editor to within an inch of his life.

Word of what happened spread quickly. Valance had nearly killed Dutton Peabody and was boasting that Ransome Stoddard would be next. For the time being, however, Valance and his men were holding forth in a saloon, allowing Ransome time to escape. Hallie begged him to leave town. Tom Doniphan offered to help, putting his wagon and hired hand at Ransome's disposal.

But Ranse stood his ground. He might save his life by fleeing, but that would betray all he stood for. He could not abandon Shinbone to the likes of Valance, even for Hallie's love. He would have to face him down.

Alone and afraid, she prayed that he'd return that night. That night,
When nothing she said could keep her man from going out to fight.
From the moment a girl gets to be full grown, the very first thing she
   learns—
When two men go out to face each other, only one returns.

Gun in hand, Ransome Stoddard headed for the saloon. "Valance," he shouted, "I'm calling you out." Smiling a drunken smile, Liberty Valance stepped into the street. Knowing that Ransome had no chance against him, he decided to toy with his prey. Valance's first shot shattered a gaslight, sending shards of glass down over Ransome's head. Stoddard was no coward, but he was no gunfighter either. He stood transfixed, unable to shoot, unwilling to run, waiting for Valance to make the next move.

Liberty's second shot hit Ranse in the right shoulder, causing him to drop his gun. "Go ahead, pick it up," Liberty taunted. The wounded Ransome retrieved his weapon with his left hand and turned again toward Valance. "The next one goes right between the eyes," the outlaw sneered as he raised his pistol. Knowing this was the end, Stoddard raised his own firearm with his trembling left hand.

Two shots were fired but only one man was hit. Incredibly, it was Liberty Valance who fell dead. Ransome Stoddard—wounded, disoriented, firing with his left hand—had somehow managed to do the impossible. Bloodied but still standing, shocked with disbelief, he was a hero, soon to lead the territory into the comforts and advantages of statehood. Valance's henchmen shouted murder, but Tom Doniphan shut them up in short order. Nobody was about to prosecute the man who shot Liberty Valance.

In the jubilant town of Shinbone, only one man had second thoughts about the death of Liberty Valance. Ransome Stoddard, lawyer and peacemaker, took no pride and little fulfillment in having killed a man. Even less was he willing to trade on his new reputation as a gunman, as much as others might admire him. He confided in Tom Doniphan that he planned to resign his position as territorial delegate.

And then Tom explained what really happened. When Ransome refused to leave town, Tom followed him on the way to the saloon. Standing in the shadows, Tom watched the confrontation while Liberty Valance fired his first two tormenting shots. When Valance announced that the next one would go "right between the eyes," Tom raised his own rifle, firing before Liberty had a chance to shoot.

"It was cold-blooded murder," said Tom, "but I ain't ashamed." He'd done it for Hallie, of course, as Ranse well understood but could not acknowledge.

Ransome married Hallie and went on to a distinguished political career far from Shinbone. First governor of the state, then senator, ambassador to England, and then back to the U. S. Senate, always with Hallie (who presumably had learned to read) at his side.

Many years later he returned to Shinbone for Tom Doniphan's funeral. It was great news that Senator Stoddard had arrived in the town where his legend began. A young reporter and the new editor of the *Shinbone Star* persuaded him to give an interview about the old days, and Ransome surprised everyone by telling the true—but until then unknown—story of the shoot-out.

It was an incredible scoop, but the editor killed the story. It would never be published. "When truth becomes legend," he said, "print the legend."

But what was legend and what was the truth? And what might have happened if an independent prosecutor had looked more closely into the death of Liberty Valance?

Everyone in Shinbone believed they knew the facts. Enraged over the delegate election, Valance had mercilessly beaten Dutton Peabody and threatened Ransome Stoddard's life. Ransome had no choice but to arm himself for the confrontation. In the street, Valance's third bullet would have killed him for sure, but for the lawyer's surprisingly charmed aim. It was a clear case of self-defense, for which Ransome Stoddard deserved well to be praised.

Self-defense is a matter of interpretation, not observation. The only "true fact" was that Liberty Valance lay dead; everything else was a matter of detail and inference. Who was the aggressor? Who had an opportunity or duty to retreat? What was Ransome's actual intent? Was he doing "what a man has to do," or was he out for vigilante vengeance? The answers to these questions—articulated in a trial lawyer's theory and theme—can determine the difference between heroism and guilt.

A successful murder prosecution of Ransome Stoddard would depend on the construction of a viable theory of the case. The best theory would evoke the theme of revenge. Stoddard, once badly beaten and repeatedly humiliated by Liberty Valance, had vowed retaliation. Arming himself for the task, he snuck out of town to practice gunplay in preparation for a shoot-out. The battering of Dutton Peabody provided the excuse. Although Stoddard had every chance to leave Shinbone without a confrontation, he sought out Liberty—who was playing cards in the saloon, not stalking the streets—and insisted on a duel. The theme of the trial, of course, would be "taking the law into his own hands." No one liked Liberty Valance, who was a bully and a brute, but that was not lawful cause to gun him down.

But theory is one thing and proof is another. The case would yet have to be supported by the accumulation of persuasive details. The prosecution would begin, no doubt, with the stagecoach robbery.

Liberty Valance had beaten Ransome Stoddard and torn up his treasured law books. Unable to fight back or even begin to defend himself, Stoddard must have been tormented by his own weakness. Believing that lawyering would bring him power over men like Valance, he found out that he was at their mercy. He must have raged at the thought.

Ransome's anger could only have increased when he discovered that his law degree meant nothing in Shinbone. He drew amazed laughter when he suggested the arrest and prosecution of Valance, even when he succeeded in locating an applicable statute. Finding no work for lawyers, he was reduced to donning an apron and washing dishes. And when he ventured into the dining room—there was Liberty Valance mocking him again. Valance knocked Stoddard to the floor, causing him to endure the raucous laughter of dozens of customers. Worse, it happened in front of Hallie, who rushed to protect him from further harm—making Ransome the one man in Shinbone to hide behind a woman's skirts.

Of course, this account exposes Liberty Valance as a bully and thug, making Ransome Stoddard's theorized angry reaction seem all the more human, and perhaps unavoidable. But that is precisely where trial theory plays its most important role. It is often said among trial lawyers that "every fact has two faces." Here, the advocate's challenge is to take the fact of Valance's bullying—which would ordinarily seem to work in Stoddard's favor—and turn it into evidence for the prosecution.

First, the prosecution would have to openly acknowledge Valance's cruelty. Any attempt to soft-pedal or sanitize Valance would only engender sympathy for Stoddard. On the other hand, recognition of Valance's ruthlessness could be used to develop the theme of Stoddard's bitter frustration. The worse Valance appears, the more reason Ransome had for challenging him. In other words, the prosecution will need to develop the idea that Ransome was motivated by personal animosity rather than enforcement of the law.

The catch, then, will be to demonstrate that Ransome's life was never in danger. So long as Valance can be portrayed as "merely" sadistic, Ransome cannot be excused for killing him. If Valance was murderous, Ransome could make his own case for self-defense.

Until the final showdown, however, we never see Liberty Valance use a firearm. In the stage robbery he battered Stoddard with his silver-handled quirt, a tactic he repeated on Dutton Peabody when he destroyed the office of the *Shinbone Star*. At one point it is rumored that "Valance and his men murdered two sodbusters up near the Picketwire," but that claim is never repeated or substantiated. For all we know, for all Ranse Stoddard knew, Liberty Valance like to threaten and pummel people, but he never shot them.

Stoddard, of course, was no match for Valance with his fists; he needed an equalizer. That is why he armed himself, sneaking alone out of town to work on gunplay. What reason did he have for taking target practice other than preparing to shoot Liberty Valance? On the night of the election, Valance had done his dirty work by hand, never drawing his gun. When he threatened that Ransome would be next (a threat, by the way, that he took no immediate steps to carry out), the reference must have been to a beating.

To be sure, Ransome was under no obligation to accept a whipping from Valance and his men, but neither was he entitled to use deadly force to prevent it, especially since he had every opportunity to avoid the confrontation and keep the peace. He could have left town, with or without Hallie. He could have hidden. He could have surrounded himself with other citizens, on the theory that even Valance wouldn't attack him in front of a crowd. He could even have locked himself in the marshal's jail until his tormentor left town. Instead, he deliberately chose the single course of action that was certain to lead to violence. He went gunning for Liberty Valance.

Valance, on the other hand, had taken no steps to pursue Stoddard. He seemed content to enjoy himself in the saloon—perhaps biding his time, or perhaps having decided that he had exacted sufficient revenge on Peabody. In any event, he was not given the chance to menace Stoddard because Stoddard acted first.

In fact, Ransome approached the saloon gun in hand, demanding that Valance come out and fight. Liberty emerged with his pistol holstered, facing a man with his weapon already drawn. Was Stoddard a victim or an aggressor? Was Valance ready or reluctant to fight?

Encountering Stoddard at gunpoint, Valance was surely entitled by the "law of the west" to accept the challenge. In fact, he probably could have killed the lawyer immediately in the name of self-defense. Instead, however, his first two shots were intentionally wide of the mark, giving Ransome two opportunities to back down.

Here again we see that every fact has two faces. Valance was actually warning Stoddard, not toying with him. At any moment, Liberty could have dispatched his adversary with ease. Instead, he fired a warning shot above his head, hoping to make him flee. But Ransome stood there, gun at the ready. But again Valance did not shoot to kill, aiming instead at Stoddard's shoulder in order to forestall the fight. Undeterred, Ransome retrieved his weapon, leaving Valance little choice. Said Liberty, "the next shot goes right between the eyes," but still he didn't fire while he had the chance. Valance waited, giving Ransome Stoddard one final opportunity to call the whole thing off.

And that hesitation, arrogantly merciful if not entirely generous, cost Liberty Valance his life and made Ransome Stoddard a murderer. The outlaw attempted to avoid the fight, and the lawyer shot him down.

Indicted and brought to trial, Ransome Stoddard would not be without defenses. The shooting of Liberty Valance, as everyone in Shinbone seemed to believe at the time, was a case of justifiable homicide. The man was a brute and a killer, dangerous to everyone who got in his way. He had used his whip and gun to intimidate the entire town, including the marshal. In the end, only Ransome Stoddard stood between Liberty Valance and continued mayhem.

At the territorial election, Valance had threatened everybody who refused to vote for him. After the ballot he left the hall vowing quick retribution. And it was no empty promise, as Dutton Peabody quickly learned. Valance's own men had to pull him off the luckless editor, beaten into unconsciousness and perhaps to the brink of death. Liberty announced that Stoddard would be the next victim, and nobody doubted his word.

Thus, the trial strategy for the defense would no doubt be some variation on the theme of "duty and courage." Ransome Stoddard had the moral duty to defy Liberty Valance and the courage to do it.

True, Stoddard could have fled town to avoid the fight, but that would have left Shinbone at Valance's mercy. And certainly the duly elected territorial delegate had a public responsibility to stay and represent his constituency. With Dutton Peabody bludgeoned and Ransome Stoddard gone, Valance could have subverted the process of democracy itself by insisting that he become Shinbone's new representative. And while the citizenry had mustered the nerve to resist him once, could they do it again after he had trampled (literally) his opponents?

Besides, with Valance loose and angry it was only a matter of time until he tracked down Ranse Stoddard. Why let Valance pick the time and place of the inevitable confrontation? Why should the lawyer risk being ambushed or shot in the back? Liberty Valance had never shown any respect for fair play. It was far safer for Ransome to choose the venue, so to speak, giving him what little chance he might have of surviving the showdown. By calling Valance out of the saloon, for all the town to see, at least Ransome would be protected against a bushwhacking.

And, as defense counsel would be certain to remind the jury, Ranse Stoddard had approached the showdown with no illusions about winning the fight. He believed, along with everyone else, that he was heading into nearly certain death, or at least grave harm. It was honor and sacrifice that Ransome had on his mind, not murder.

But would that be enough to establish self-defense? Murder for honor is murder nonetheless, and the fact remains that it was Ransome who called out Liberty Valance.

To be sure, Stoddard's best defense would be the absolute truth. He had not killed Valance at all, the fatal shot having been fired from the shadows by Tom Doniphan. Would Ransome share this secret with his own lawyer? And if he did, would he then allow his attorney to make the argument in court?

Tom Doniphan saved Ransome's life, not out of friendship but rather for the sake of the woman they both loved. How would Ransome now see his obligation to his rival? He could reveal Tom's involvement, which would save his own skin and thereby ensure the happiness of Hallie, which was Tom's intention in the first place. Or he could keep his mouth shut, risking trial and pinning his hopes on his counsel's powers of persuasion in the name of self-defense. Each course of action could be morally justified, one in the name of honesty and the other for the sake of loyalty.

A more challenging question arises when we consider the participation of counsel. Imagine that Stoddard told his attorney all about Doniphan's deadly role. The lawyer, being primed always to win if possible, would obviously jump at the chance of blaming the crime on someone else, no matter what the cost to decent Tom. And of course it would be ethical to do so. No matter how despicable the motivation—and some people would find the betrayal of Tom to be contemptible indeed—it could hardly be improper for a lawyer to tell the truth.

But what if Ransome Stoddard—perhaps out of gratitude, perhaps to keep Hallie's love and respect—insisted that Tom Doniphan be protected? Could his lawyer go along? And if so, how would that affect the conduct of the defense?

In modern terms, a lawyer is required to "abide by a client's decisions concerning the objectives of representation . . . and [to] consult with the client as to the means by which they are to be pursued."[6] We do not know what formal rules might have applied in pre-statehood Shinbone, since we do not even know the name of the territory, but it is a safe assumption that the profession would have followed some variation on the objectives-means division of authority. In Ransome Stoddard's case, the client's unquestionable objective would be acquittal or exoneration, unless he decided to plead guilty instead. But once the client makes that decision concerning his objective, do all other decisions fall to the lawyer—subject to "consultation"—in the name of selecting the "means" of the defense? In other words, could counsel virtually compel Ransome to betray Tom Doniphan: "You can plead guilty if you want to, Ranse, but if this case goes to trial I'm afraid you cannot stop me from calling Doniphan to the stand."

For good or ill, the contemporary rules allow for more client autonomy than that. The Comments to the American Bar Association Model
Rules of Professional Conduct provide that "the lawyer should assume
responsibility for technical and legal tactical issues, but should defer to
the client regarding such questions as . . . concern for third persons who
might be adversely affected."[7]

In other words, Ransome Stoddard could order his lawyer to keep
Tom's name out of it, suffering the consequences if that decision resulted
in conviction.[8] A more subtle question, however, cannot be quite so easily resolved. How would—indeed, how could—a competent, ethical
lawyer conduct a defense under such a constraint?

The prosecution always goes first. Unsuspecting of Tom Doniphan's
handiwork from the shadows, and unaware of the issues confronting the
hobbled counselor for the defense, the prosecutor would call his witnesses as planned, based on the theory that Stoddard had instigated the
fight and murdered Valance with an admittedly lucky shot.

Defense counsel would likewise proceed to claim self-defense, cross-
examining witnesses to establish Valance's history of threats and brutality. Though well-informed that Stoddard had not killed Valance at all,
much less in self-defense, the lawyer would nonetheless seek to draw out
all the reasons that Ranse had to fear for his life: Didn't Liberty Valance
attempt to intimidate the entire town into electing him territorial delegate? Hadn't he immediately threatened revenge when the vote went to
Peabody and Stoddard? Wasn't he a notorious criminal with a reputation for having killed "two sodbusters up near the Picketwire"? Hadn't
he already attacked Dutton Peabody, leaving him for dead? If he wanted
to save his own life, what choice did Ranse Stoddard have but to shoot
Liberty Valance?

Except, of course, that Stoddard didn't shoot him. In other words, the
cross-examinations would all be designed to hide the truth, to create the
false impression that Ransome had acted in self-defense—all the while
concealing the fatal involvement of Tom Doniphan.

In criminal cases especially, we accept the idea that cross-examination
may be used to suggest hypothetical scenarios that deflect attention
from the defendant's culpability. While some chafe at what they see as

the facile obfuscations of defense counsel, most understand that the concept of "proof beyond a reasonable doubt" permits the defense to propose "reasonable hypotheses inconsistent with guilt."[9] Stated otherwise, a criminal defendant is entitled to demand that the prosecution prove his guilt to a moral certainty, which can mean the exclusion of other reasonable explanations for the crime. Short of such protection, the presumption of innocence could well be eroded.

Moreover, there is a meaningful ethical limitation on what can be done in the course of insinuating reasonable doubt. Most important, cross-examination questions may not "allude to any matter . . . that will not be supported by admissible evidence."[10] This principle, sometimes also referred to as the "good faith basis" rule, provides that lawyers must build their cases on a foundation of truth. They are free to use their questions to intimate all manner of guilt-negating possibilities, but only on the basis of truthful answers.

The most familiar pedagogic example is the truthful, nearsighted eyewitness. Knowing full well that the identification was accurate, defense counsel may nonetheless challenge the witness's ability to observe: Isn't it true that you suffer from myopia? Don't you need corrective lenses in order to drive? In fact, that is a condition on your driver's license? Wasn't the crime committed late at night? Isn't it true that you weren't wearing your glasses? Or your contact lenses? And you only observed the criminal from a distance of at least twenty feet? These questions are legitimate so long as the witness truly is myopic and truly does need glasses in order to drive. They are impermissible, however, if the lawyer is simply trying to create a smoke screen without any basis in fact.

Applying that standard, Ranse Stoddard's counsel would have license to develop the theory of self-defense, so long as the supporting facts could be elicited through truthful testimony. Thus, it would be entirely aboveboard to ask questions about Valance's cruel demeanor, evil reputation, and repeated threats.

But wait. Let's take another look at the reason for allowing attorneys to develop alternate, if misleading, scenarios. There is only one justification for such sanctioned obfuscation—the presumption of innocence. Cloaked in that presumption, a defendant is entitled to make it hard—exceptionally hard!—for the government to obtain a conviction. Thus, the rights of the innocent are protected, since wrongful convictions would surely result if successful prosecution became too easy. So it is logical, even imperative, to allow Ransome Stoddard's lawyer to protect his client by raising a not-really-true claim of self-defense. Ransome is in jeopardy and his rights must be protected.

So far, so good—except that the self-defense claim is not really being put forward on Ransome's behalf. Remember, Stoddard has an even better defense. It was Tom Doniphan who fired the fatal shot. These facts are being withheld because Ransome has decided to shield his friend from arrest. Consequently, we must wonder whether the attorney's warrant to obfuscate in Stoddard's defense must be extended to allow the same tactic solely for Doniphan's benefit.

As might be expected, the formal rules do not address this situation (as must also have been the situation in the late nineteenth century), requiring only an admissible "factual basis" for cross-examination questions, without regard to their ultimate motive or beneficiary. Perhaps the underlying rationale for wide-ranging latitude might be understood to exclude noble sacrifices for the sake of worthy confederates (or, as would more often be the case, ignoble sacrifices for the sake of nasty co-conspirators), but there would be no way to police such an exaction. After all, the questions themselves would sound the same—and the answers would be equally truthful—in either case.

We can say with some assurance that no frontier trial lawyer would give a hoot about—or even notice—the nice distinction between defending (exclusively) Ranse Stoddard and safeguarding (incidentally) Tom Doniphan. With unencumbered conscience, the advocate would simply use his cross-examinations to develop the theme of self-defense, wishing perhaps that he could blame the whole thing on Tom, but acquiescing in his client's insistence that he shoulder the burden alone.

The ultimate claim of self-defense would be a bit of a sham, of course, but it would be an honest sham.

Cross-examination allows defense counsel tremendous leeway. So long as the questions are asked in good faith and the answers are truthful, the lawyer is relatively free to stack inference upon innuendo in order to construct a story that can lead to acquittal. But sooner or later the prosecution will rest and the defense will have to stop cross-examining and begin to present its own case. The ethical considerations now become trickier.

If there is one bedrock principle, it is that a lawyer may not "counsel or assist a witness to testify falsely."[11] On cross-examination, the attorney may skirt that requirement by eliciting sincerely truthful, if unwittingly misleading, answers. But direct examination, especially of the defendant, presents a different problem. The defendant is not unwitting. Complicit in any deception, he knows where the examination is headed and why it is being conducted. Perhaps sincerity is not an absolute condition of "technical truth,"[12] but a purposeful contrivance, once begun, may set in motion an ethically dangerous chain of events—as becomes immediately evident in the case of Ransome Stoddard.

Ransome Stoddard knows more than any jury will ever find out, perhaps more than he could even explain to his own attorney. Most important, of course, only Ransome could know—depending on how deeply he was willing to search his soul—whether he truly acted out of fear for his life or whether he was wildly spurred by hatred and revenge.

But putting aside the ineffable secrets of the human heart, the more immediate point is that Ransome knows, even without introspection, all about Tom Doniphan's role in the killing. Concealing that fact during direct examination will require some serious collusion between lawyer and client. Imagine their final, pretrial meeting:

Counsel: Ranse, this is your last chance to tell the whole truth about Tom's involvement. It could keep you from hanging.

Stoddard: Tom saved my life. There is no way I will betray him now. I'm willing to take the responsibility, no matter how it turns out. After all, I would have shot Valance in self-defense, if I'd been fast enough.

Counsel: Then I guess there's nothing I can do to stop you. But there's still a limit on what I can do. When you testify, Ranse, you have to tell the truth. That means that you can never say that you killed Valance. You can describe how you felt and why you called him out, but you can't say that you killed him.

Stoddard: So I can explain about Valance's threats and the way that he nearly killed Dutton Peabody.

Counsel: Absolutely.

Stoddard: And I can tell the jury why I thought that Valance would track me down and shoot me in the back, even if I tried running away.

Counsel: Yes, you can.

Stoddard: Can I tell them that I had my gun in my hand, pointed at Valance?

Counsel: If that's true.

Stoddard: Can I tell them that I had my finger on the trigger?

Counsel: Yes, if that is what happened.

Stoddard: And I was sure I was going to die if Valance had a chance to fire another round?

Counsel: Yes.

Stoddard: Can I say that everyone heard two shots ring out—one shot made Liberty fall?

Counsel: You can, Ranse. But don't push it.

And then what? Ransome can truthfully set the scene for self-defense, but eventually he will have to confront the actual shooting—at which point his attorney cannot allow him to lie. Perhaps they will try yet more artful evasion, confining the examination to the night of the shooting when Ransome had not yet learned of Tom Doniphan's intervention.

Counsel: Ranse, how did you feel at that moment when you saw Liberty Valance lying dead in the street?

Stoddard: I couldn't believe it. I was stunned at the thought that I had killed a man. I wanted to cry at what had happened. I did not feel any happiness, only bitter relief. I wished there could have been some other way.

Counsel: Ranse, as you stood there that night, was there any doubt in your mind that Valance intended to kill you?

Stoddard: No. He'd made himself all too clear.

Counsel: Did you have any doubt that it was impossible to run or hide?

Stoddard: None.

Counsel: Did you have any choice but to confront him that night?

Stoddard: No. He would have shot me down for sure.

The lawyer has done his job well. The story fits the facts, and Tom Doniphan's name was never mentioned. The testimony is all true, or rather, none of it is untrue, and it covers all of the necessary elements of self-defense.

But is it all too facile, too crafty, too slick? Does counsel truly avoid "assisting a witness to testify falsely" by asking Ransome about the necessity of "confronting" Liberty Valance rather than "killing" him? How much sleight of hand are we willing to tolerate in the name of vigorous advocacy or the presumption of innocence?

The answer does not come easily. Clearly, the lawyer and client have engaged in a practice that we might call "evasive recharacterization," intentionally telling an essentially false story through the wily arrangement of tidbits of truth. Many would consider that simply a skillful form of lying, all the more dishonorable, and dangerous, because it is hard to detect.

On the other hand, we continue to place a high value on requiring rigorous proof from the prosecution. For example, suppose that the prosecution in a burglary case accidentally assigned the wrong date to the crime, thinking it had happened a day later than was really the case. The only eyewitness mistakenly testified that the defendant was seen fleeing the crime scene on a certain Thursday afternoon, when it had really happened the previous day. Now assume that the defendant happened to have an ironclad, truthful alibi for Thursday. Wouldn't the defendant be entitled to testify—truthfully—that she was in a hospital emergency room that Thursday afternoon, offering x-rays and medical records to back her up? Certainly the Fifth Amendment would protect her from having to volunteer the fact that she actually robbed the place on Wednesday. And keeping her off the stand entirely seems like a harsh consequence, imposed on the defendant because of the prosecutor's error.

Most important, there is an extremely strong social interest in requiring prosecutors to prove crimes for the correct day. Laxity in that regard would be extraordinarily dangerous to the innocent, since prosecutors could just as easily end up assigning crimes (negligently or otherwise) to dates on which the defendant had no alibi. Thus, it may turn out to be socially useful to allow the guilty defendant to testify truthfully that "I was nowhere near the crime scene on *Thursday* afternoon—I was in the hospital emergency room." It keeps the prosecution honest.

Moreover, there is a strong corrective within the system itself. Cross-examination.

Let's return to Shinbone and the trial of Ransome Stoddard, who has just testified on direct examination. Defense counsel nimbly steered the examination through the narrows of deception, avoiding outright lies while allowing Ransome to convey adroitly, if ever so indirectly, the claim that he shot Liberty Valance in self-defense.

Now comes cross-examination. Even an unsuspecting prosecutor, without so much as an inkling of Tom Doniphan's involvement, would at some point confront the defendant about the killing.

Prosecutor: Mr. Stoddard, you heard about the beating of Dutton Peabody, correct?
Stoddard: I did.
Prosecutor: You decided to head for the saloon, didn't you?
Stoddard: I feared for my life.
Prosecutor: So you went to find Liberty Valance, right?
Stoddard: I didn't think I had a choice.
Prosecutor: You had a gun in your hand?
Stoddard: Right.
Prosecutor: You called him out of the saloon, didn't you?
Stoddard: Yes.
Prosecutor: Isn't it true, Mr. Stoddard, that you shot him dead on the streets of Shinbone?

Ranse Stoddard is now on his own. He cannot turn to his lawyer for help constructing a sly answer to the direct question (although they may have discussed his options in advance). Perhaps he can dodge once:

Stoddard: Valance fired at me first.

But not indefinitely:

Prosecutor: Well, you're the man who called him out, right?
Stoddard: Yes.
Prosecutor: You're the man who went to the saloon, gun in hand, right?
Stoddard: Yes.
Prosecutor: And you're the man who shot Liberty Valance, aren't you?

The line is drawn. Ransome must decide whether to tell the truth or lie. If he tells the truth, the game is up and Tom Doniphan will be exposed. That doesn't get Ransome off the hook, however. The jury might well mistrust his sudden implication of Doniphan, who was never named during direct examination. They might consider it a desperate ploy to shift the blame, and convict Ransome nonetheless.

Realizing this, would Stoddard—a lawyer himself, after all—decide to go for broke?

Stoddard: Yes, I am the man who shot Liberty Valance.

That would be a lie. Well-intentioned, perhaps even noble, but a lie nonetheless. What will defense counsel do?

The prevailing modern rule requires the defense lawyer to inform the court of the truth. "A lawyer shall not knowingly . . . fail to disclose a material fact to a tribunal when disclosure is necessary to avoid assisting a criminal or fraudulent act by the client," even if that requires disclosure of client confidences.[13]

So Ransome Stoddard probably could not get away with protecting Tom Doniphan. He would almost certainly be caught if he brazened it out; he would either be tripped up on cross-examination or his own attorney would be compelled to reveal the truth. And the jury would probably penalize him for misleading them even if—once exposed on cross-examination—he retreated to the flimsy refuge of insisting that he had given "legally accurate" testimony on direct.

A capable attorney would quickly realize that Ransome's well-intentioned efforts to protect Tom Doniphan would most likely lead to disaster for all involved. Tom's role would probably come to light in the course of investigation and trial, though Ransome might still be convicted of either perjury or even murder—if the jury rejected his profession of self-defense along with a belated, and therefore seemingly contrived, claim that Tom Doniphan had fired the killing shot. The lawyer would have to worry about his own exposure as well, since the line between an accurate-though-misleading trial strategy (which may be permissible) and outright assistance in a perjurious cover-up (which is not) is at best indistinct and undeterminable. One misstep and the lawyer could find himself facing discipline or indictment.

While Ransome Stoddard might be inclined to take a grave risk in order to shield Tom Doniphan, his lawyer would surely balk. After all, Tom never saved counsel's life. "Ranse," the lawyer would likely say, "I can defend you with the truth, or you can refuse to testify at all, but you'll have to find yourself another lawyer if you insist on sticking with self-defense."

And then Ransome Stoddard would be faced with a bitter choice. The only certain way to protect his friend and benefactor would be to plead guilty; perhaps he could cut a plea bargain for voluntary manslaughter.[14] But even Ransome would be unlikely to go that far in the name of friendship and obligation. He would have to share the blame and credit with Tom Doniphan, letting the chips fall where they may. Tom, of course, would have his own defenses. He could plead necessity, or defense of another, or he could stake his hopes on jury nullification (always a possibility in the Old West). But that's another story.

The Murder Trial of the Man Who Shot Liberty Valance would be a fascinating movie in its own right. Would Ransome Stoddard take the fall? Would his lawyer agree to deceive the jury? Would the prosecutor buy into the implication of Tom Doniphan, or would he proceed against Ransome nonetheless? Would Tom calmly accept indictment, or would he go after Ransome with guns blazing? How would Hallie react to Ranse's silence, or betrayal?

However the story might turn out, and whatever strategies the characters might follow, for our purposes it is most interesting to consider the ways in which the structure of the adversary system pushes the participants toward justice.

First, the general acclaim for the killer of Liberty Valance would not preclude an objective examination of the facts by an able prosecutor. Trained to understand that "every fact has two faces," the prosecutor would recognize that even bullies can be murdered. The concept of a trial theory is not merely a device that enables an advocate to win a case. It is also a tool that allows an attorney to reinvestigate facts, looking at them from multiple angles, in order to analyze events from all possible perspectives.

A prosecution for homicide would force Ransome Stoddard to test the extent of his own readiness to protect his friend. If he were indeed willing to endure a trial rather than implicate Tom Doniphan, his lawyer would have to caution him against the deception, if not outright deceit, necessarily implicit in that decision. Ransome could order his attorney to keep Tom's secret, but the lawyer could not assist him in shaping a defense that relied directly on a lie. Ransome's efforts to present a fabricated story, even one with many elements of truth, would face impediments at every turn.

Eventually Stoddard would have to confront a harsh reality. The more he tried to extricate Tom Doniphan, the more likely he would be to face conviction for a crime he did not commit. Even Tom would not want him to go that far. (Recall that Tom saved Ranse's life for Hallie's sake, and she would be no less heartbroken to see her beloved hanged by the sheriff rather than gunned down by Liberty Valance.)

But where is the justice in virtually compelling Ransome to betray Tom Doniphan? Ransome, after all, believed that he had shot Liberty Valance, until Tom confided the truth. And indeed, Ransome certainly would have shot Liberty Valance—he had the nerve and the will, lacking only the dexterity. Wouldn't justice be equally served by allowing Ranse to argue self-defense, presenting the facts as he intended them to have occurred? Couldn't a calculated elision in the defense of Ransome actually serve a greater, more holistic truth—that the gunfight was a moral necessity, lest Liberty Valance continue to terrorize the helpless town of Shinbone?

In fact, the answer is negative. Ransome Stoddard's willingness to suffer conviction might be heroic, but it would not be justice. The social role of the prosecutor is not to accuse just anybody, but to charge the right person with an offense and thereafter determine whether a crime in fact was committed. The prosecution does not win, and neither does society (even frontier society), by trying the wrong man, no matter whether the defendant voluntarily undertakes the risk.

And, of course, Ransome Stoddard—confronting Valance openly in the street, facing almost certain death for the sake of decency in Shinbone—would be a tough defendant to convict, likely as he would be to enjoy a jury's sympathy if not outright admiration and support. Tom Doniphan, in contrast, stood with his rifle safely in the shadows, unwilling to face Valance and never giving him a chance. Perhaps it was murder, perhaps not, but justice would seem to require a definitive answer. And it was not for Ransome Stoddard to decide who would be the one to face trial, to take the credit or carry the blame.

There are some questions—legal, moral—that can only be answered by the Man Who Shot Liberty Valance.

NOTES

1. Words and music by Burt Bachrach and Hal David. Gene Pitney began work on "The Man Who Shot Liberty Valance" for Musicor Records in 1962 while the John Ford western was still in production by the Paramount Studio. Interestingly, the film was released somewhat ahead of schedule, before the song was finished. Consequently, one of the most recognizable of all western movie theme songs was not actually included in the film.

2. Dorothy Johnson, "The Man Who Shot Liberty Valance," in COSMOPOLITAN, July 1949; reprinted in James C. Work, GUNFIGHT 38 (1996).

3. The facts that follow are from the movie (screenplay by James Bellah and Willis Godbeck), not the short story from which it was adapted with a good deal of cinematic license.

4. It was never explained why the stage driver and passengers abandoned Stoddard following the robbery. Even if they believed he was dead, one would hope they would have brought the body in to town for burial. Perhaps they were afflicted by the same cowardice that kept all of Shinbone in thrall to Valance and his men.

5. The film seems to take place in the 1870s (before the railroad reached towns like Shinbone) and appears to be set in Arizona, but that would make the statehood issue an anachronism—Arizona having been admitted to the Union in 1912. Dorothy Johnson, whose short story formed the basis of the movie, was a Montana writer. Montana became a state in 1889, which almost fits into the time frame of stage coaches and gunslingers, though the topography does not match the scenery in the film. An alternative possibility is Colorado, admitted to the Union in 1876, with enough desert landscape to satisfy John Ford.

6. Rule 1.2(a), American Bar Association, MODEL RULES OF PROFESSIONAL CONDUCT.

7. Rule 1.2 Comment, American Bar Association, MODEL RULES OF PROFESSIONAL CONDUCT. The former Model Code of Professional Conduct was even more explicit, stating that "[I]n the final analysis, however, the . . . decision whether to forego legally available objectives or methods because of nonlegal factors is ultimately for the client." EC 7–8.

8. Another question is whether the attorney, thus hobbled, would be entitled to withdraw as counsel on the ground that the "representation . . . has been rendered unreasonably difficult by the client." Rule 1.16(b)(5), MODEL RULES OF PROFESSIONAL CONDUCT. We will assume that Ranse Stoddard's lawyer has chosen to stick with him.

9. This does not mean that the prosecution must always preclude "every reasonable hypothesis inconsistent with guilt in order to sustain a conviction," but only that the defense is free to suggest, based on the evidence, other possible scenarios. See, e.g. *United States v. Reeder*, 170 F.3d 93, 102 (1st Cir. 1999).

10. Rule 3.4(e), MODEL RULES OF PROFESSIONAL CONDUCT.

11. The predominant modern iteration is found in Rule 3.4(b) of the MODEL RULES OF PROFESSIONAL CONDUCT.

12. Bill Clinton's memorable trope was "legally accurate."

13. Rules 3.3(a)(2) and 3.3(b), MODEL RULES OF PROFESSIONAL CONDUCT. For a minority position, see MONROE FREEDMAN, UNDERSTANDING LAWYERS ETHICS 109–142 (1990) (arguing that a lawyer's duties of loyalty and confidentiality require actively presenting a criminal defendant's perjured testimony). Under any approach, a lawyer who knows in advance of intended perjury, as Stoddard's attorney would at least have to suspect, must attempt to dissuade the client from offering false testimony.

14. Ironically, the appellate cases are clear that one does not need to *actually be guilty* in order to *plead guilty*. Due process is satisfied if the defendant rationally determines that he does not want to undertake the risk of trial, so long as he knowingly and intelligently waives his rights. Moreover, there is no apparent ethical bar against a defense attorney's involvement in such circumstances.

CHAPTER SIX

ATTICUS FINCH
Race, Class, Gender, and Truth

Atticus Finch. No real-life lawyer has done more for the self-image or public perception of the legal profession than the hero of Harper Lee's novel, To Kill a Mockingbird. *For nearly four decades, the name of Atticus Finch has been invoked to defend and inspire lawyers, to rebut lawyer jokes, and to justify (and fine-tune) the adversary system. Lawyers are liars. What about Atticus Finch? Attorneys only serve the rich. Not Atticus Finch. Professionalism is a lost ideal. Remember Atticus Finch.*

So Atticus Finch saves us by providing a moral archetype, by reflecting nobility upon us, by having the courage to meet the standards that we set for ourselves but can seldom attain. And even though he is fictional, perhaps because he is fictional, Atticus serves as the ultimate lawyer. His potential justifies all our failings and imperfections. Be not too hard on lawyers, for when we are at our best we can give you an Atticus Finch.

But what if Atticus is not an icon? What if he were more a man of his time and place than we thought? What if he were not a beacon of enlightenment, but just another working lawyer playing out his narrow, determined role—telling a story not for its truth, but only because it might work?

The following chapter considers the possibility that Atticus Finch was not quite the heroic defender of an innocent man wrongly accused. What if Mayella Ewell was telling the truth? What if she really was raped (or nearly raped) by Tom Robinson? What do we think then of Atticus Finch? Is he still the lawyers' paragon? Were his defense tactics nonetheless acceptable? Does his virtue depend at all on Tom's innocence, or is it just as noble to use one's narrative skills in aid of the guilty?

～

In the unreconstructed Maycomb, Alabama, of the 1930s, Atticus Finch was willing to risk his social standing, professional reputation, and even his physical safety in order to defend a poor, black laborer falsely accused of raping a white woman. Serving for no fee, Atticus heard the call of justice. His defense was doomed to failure by the very nature of southern life, but Atticus nonetheless succeeded in demonstrating both the innocence of his client and the peculiar sickness of Jim Crow society. Through his deft, courtly, and persistent cross-examination, Atticus made it apparent to everyone that Tom Robinson was being scapegoated for a crime that had not even occurred. He even made Tom's innocence apparent to the all-white jury, which deliberated for an unprecedented several hours even though the judgment of conviction was a foregone conclusion.

The text of *To Kill a Mockingbird* contains three distinct narratives of the Atticus Finch story.[1] Two of these stories, as told by Scout, Atticus's daughter, and Tom Robinson, his client, provide the time-honored saga of the virtuous lawyer. The third, barely audible, narrative is that of Mayella Ewell, Tom's accuser.

Mayella's story, put simply, is that she was violently raped. As conveyed to us through Scout's eyes, it is told only to be discredited. Though she is pitied as much as censured, the ultimate lesson about Mayella is, above all else, that she is not to be trusted. An entirely different story emerges, however, if we consider the possibility that Mayella is telling the truth.

Jean Louise Finch, known to everyone as Scout, is Atticus Finch's seven-year-old daughter. We learn of Atticus's exploits only through the child's narration; indeed, Scout is our only source of knowledge of Maycomb, Alabama. Although others witnessed the key events, including Scout's brother, Jem, and their friend Dill, it is Scout alone who tells the story. She is our witness to Atticus as he explains his initial reservations about being appointed to represent Tom Robinson. She sees him, and ultimately helps him, face down a lynch mob outside Tom's jail cell. Most significantly, Scout chronicles the trial of Tom Robinson, providing her own assessment of the credibility of the witnesses.

Scout's narrative has been characterized, by none other than Harper Lee herself, as "a love story, pure and simple." And that is what it is. Atticus can do no wrong. His choices are all brave and noble, which is why the community of Maycomb ultimately puts its faith in him. Whether saving the town from a rabid dog, representing the county in the state legislature, or exposing the people to their own juridic hypocrisy, Atticus, at least in Scout's eyes, can be counted on to do the right thing.

Thus, Scout's story of the trial is elegant and simple. Mayella and her father, Robert E. Lee Ewell, are simply lying about the rape. Mayella is lying out of shame, and to protect herself from scorn and humiliation, after having been caught aggressively embracing a black man. Bob, as the elder Ewell is known, is lying out of anger and race hatred. In Bob's worldview, no white woman could possibly consent to sexual contact with a black man. So when he saw his daughter kissing Tom, the only explanation had to be rape.

To Atticus, as Scout explains, Mayella and Bob "were absolute trash." In fact, Scout lets us know, she "never heard Atticus talk about folks the way he talked about the Ewells." Their lying nature was compounded by their general distastefulness. They were dirty, no-account, brutal, prolific, shiftless, diseased, and untrustworthy. Not at all the sort of "decent folks" whom Scout was reared to respect and honor.

And make no mistake, Scout had no respect at all for any of the Ewells, who lived behind the town garbage dump, competing with the "varmints" for refuse. In Scout's words,

[e]very town the size of Maycomb had families like the Ewells. No economic fluctuations changed their status—people like the Ewells lived as guests of the county in prosperity as well as in the depths of a depression. No truant officers could keep their numerous offspring in school; no public health officer could free them from congenital defects, various worms, and the diseases indigenous to filthy surroundings.

Bob Ewell's face was "as red as his neck," and only "if scrubbed with lye soap in very hot water" would his skin be white.

Scout's assessment of Mayella is slightly more sympathetic, but not much. "A thick bodied girl accustomed to strenuous labor," she managed to "look as if she tried to keep clean." She was intimidated and in tears from the moment she took the witness stand, but to Scout it was all a ploy, in aid of her soon-to-be-told false testimony—"She's got enough sense to get the judge sorry for her." All in all, "there was something stealthy about her, like a steady-eyed cat."

Mayella was a complete stranger to refinement or even manners. Said Scout, "I wondered if anybody had ever called her 'ma'am' or 'Miss Mayella' in her life; probably not, as she took offense to routine courtesy. What on earth was her life like?"

Scout soon found out the answer to that question, as Mayella's home life quickly became a theme in Atticus's cross-examination. Mayella, the oldest of eight children (whom Scout derisively called "specimens"), had gone to school only two or three years. Her family lacked money, and almost all other necessities:

> [T]he weather was seldom cold enough to require shoes, but when it was, you could make dandy ones from strips of old tires; the family hauled its water in buckets from a spring that ran out at one end of the dump—they kept the surrounding area clear of trash—and it was everybody for himself as far as keeping clean went: if you wanted to wash you hauled your own water; the younger children had perpetual colds and suffered from chronic ground-itch; there was a lady who came around sometimes and asked Mayella why she didn't stay in school—she wrote down the answer; with two members of the family reading and writing, there was no need for the rest of them to learn.

Perhaps worst of all, Mayella had no friends. To Scout, she seemed like "the loneliest person in the world." She seemed "puzzled" at the very concept. "You makin' fun o'me agin?" she asked, when Atticus pressed her on the subject. At the end of her testimony, Mayella "burst into real tears," and would not continue answering questions. Scout interpreted this as contempt on the part of the "poor and ignorant" witness.

~

Tom Robinson worked for Mr. Link Deas, which caused him to pass the Ewell shack every day on his way to and from the field. According to Tom, Mayella often called him to come "inside the fence" so that he could help her with chores. Tom refused payment, which caused Scout to think that he was "probably the only person who was ever decent to her." Tom echoed that thought: "I felt right sorry for her. . . . She didn't have nobody to help her."

Tom said that he never once "set foot on the Ewell property without an express invitation." On the day in question, Tom was returning from work when Mayella called him into the yard, and then asked him to do some work in the house. After Mayella herself shut the door, it occurred to Tom that the house was awfully quiet. He asked Mayella where the other children were: "She says—she was laughin' sort of—she says they all gone to town to get ice creams. She says, 'Took me a slap year to save seb'm nickels, but I done it. They all gone to town.'"

Tom started to leave, but Mayella asked him to take a box down from a high chifforobe. He reached for it, and the next thing he knew "she'd grabbed me round the legs, grabbed me round th' legs." Then she "sorta jumped" on Tom, hugging him around the waist. Tom found it difficult to testify to the next part, but he swallowed hard and continued:

> She reached up an' kissed me 'side of th' face. She says she never kissed a grown man before an' she might as well kiss a nigger. She says what her papa do to her don't count. She says, "Kiss me back, nigger." I say Miss Mayella lemme outa here an' tried to run but she got her back to the door an' I'da had to push her. I didn't wanta harm her, Mr. Finch, an' I say lemme pass, but just when I say it Mr. Ewell yonder hollered through th' window.

Charging into the room, Bob Ewell shouted, "[Y]ou goddamn whore, I'll kill ya." Seizing the opportunity, Tom ran, not out of guilt, he explained, but because he was scared and had no choice.

Tom did not claim that Mayella was lying, but only that she was "mistaken in her mind." He never had his eye on her, never harmed her, and certainly never raped her. It was Tom who resisted Mayella's advances.

~

Mayella, of course, tells a completely different story, but no one really believes her. Not Atticus, certainly not Scout. Not Judge Taylor, not Sheriff Heck Tate, and not even Mr. Gilmer, the county attorney whom Scout observes to have been "prosecuting almost reluctantly." Nor does it seem that the jury believed Mayella, since it took them a full two hours to bring the trial to its foreordained conclusion.

That, of course, is the point of the book. Mayella is a sexually frustrated, love-starved aggressor, who lies her way out of a dilemma and participates in a judicial lynching in order to avoid revealing the truth.

But that is not the way Mayella sees it. She says she was raped. She says that she just offered Tom Robinson a nickel to "bust up" a piece of furniture. She went into the house for the money and "'Fore I knew it he was on me. Just run up behind me, he did. He got me round the neck, cussin' me an' sayin' dirt—I fought 'n' hollered, but he had me round the neck. He hit me agin an' agin."

Mayella hollered for all she was worth, and she fought tooth and nail, but she failed: "I don't remember too good, but next thing I knew Papa was in the room a'standin' over me hollerin' who done it, who done it? Then I sorta fainted an' the next thing I knew Mr. Tate was pullin' me up offa the floor and leadin' me to the water bucket."

She was positive that Tom had taken "full advantage" of her. "He done what he was after."

Mayella sparred with Atticus on cross-examination. She denied his assertion that the beating was administered by her father. She denied that she had been the one to approach Tom. She insisted that she had never before asked Tom inside the fence. As to Atticus's main theory, that Tom's crippled left arm made him incapable of the crime she'd described, Mayella raged, "I don't know how he done it, but he done it—I said it all happened so fast I-"

> I got somethin's to say an' then I ain't gonna say no more. That nigger yonder took advantage of me an' if you fine fancy gentlemen don't wanta do nothin' about it then you're all yellow stinkin' cowards, stinkin' cowards, the lot of you. Your fancy airs don't come to nothin'—your ma'amin' and Miss Mayellerin' don't come to nothin', Mr. Finch.

Whatever the truth of the rape charge, Mayella clearly understood that everyone else in the courtroom considered her trash, hardly worth protecting. Throughout her testimony, as though she herself were on trial, she was nervous and jumpy, she cried repeatedly, she reacted with "terror and fury." That is also part of her story.

The purpose of a trial is to resolve competing factual narratives. Mayella (and her father) claimed that she had been raped by Tom Robinson. Tom denied the crime. Atticus was assigned to represent Tom. The stage was set for Atticus to employ his theory, theme, and frame.

In the mid-1930s (when the events took place) as in the early 1960s (when the book was published), one standard response to a rape charge was to plead consent. It is no surprise, then, that Atticus Finch defended Tom Robinson on that very theory; that is how rape prosecutions were defeated in those days.

Of course, Atticus did not merely raise "consent." Rather, he used a specific form of the defense that can be particularly offensive, in both senses of the word. Let's call it the "She wanted it" defense. Mayella didn't merely agree to a little romance with Tom, she was the intense aggressor. She schemed and plotted for "a slap year" to get the children out of the house on an opportune day, she jumped on Tom, she wrapped her arms around him, she demanded that he kiss her, and she blocked the door with her body when he tried to leave.

So Atticus Finch advanced a trial theory that was demeaning and stereotyped. True, he did it in a courteous and courtly manner, but Mayella easily realized what was being done to her, that she and her family and her way of life were being placed on trial, that she was being accused of a crime that could (and did) lead to a man's death. Did Atticus Finch have the right, or perhaps the duty, to treat Mayella in that fashion?

As a starting point, our evaluation of Atticus's conduct rests on an appraisal of Tom Robinson's guilt. There are three possibilities. Perhaps Tom Robinson was telling the truth. Perhaps Tom Robinson was lying. And perhaps Atticus did not know and did not care about the truth of Tom Robinson's story.

Generations of readers (and moviegoers) have accepted Tom Robinson's account of how he befriended Mayella and was then betrayed by her. Given what we know of then-contemporary southern mores and justice, his narrative is credible and compelling. And should there be any doubt, the physical evidence supports his innocence.

First, there was no medical examination of Mayella, and therefore no physical evidence that a rape had occurred. Atticus refers to this as "lack of corroboration." More important, Mayella's blackened right eye, bruises, and other injuries were inconsistent with Tom's crippled left arm.

All this gives credence to Tom's story. If Tom was truthful, then Atticus simply had no choice but to attack Mayella as he did. Advocacy means nothing if it doesn't mean bringing out the truth, no matter how painful, on behalf of the innocent.

To Atticus's credit, he was generally polite to a young woman who was clearly despised by virtually everyone else in the courtroom. But politeness can be intimidating in its own way, as it was to Mayella. And Atticus left no doubt that he intended to do his job. "Miss Mayella," he began his cross-examination, "I won't try to scare you for a while, not yet."

So here we have Atticus Finch, seasoned courtroom warrior, marshaling all his considerable skills and talents on behalf of his innocent client. This is the Atticus Finch of legend, beyond reproach or even criticism.

The story becomes substantially more confusing if we consider the possibility that Tom Robinson may have been lying about some or all of his contact with Mayella Ewell. To be sure, the narrator makes it clear that she believes Tom and that we should believe him too. Nor do I mean to suggest that I reject his innocence.

On the other hand, Scout merely told the story and Harper Lee merely wrote the book. Neither one can control our interpretation of the finished text, so we may surely consider the possibility that Scout, worshipfully devoted to her father, might have misapprehended either the facts or the credibility of the witnesses. And, as it turns out, there is much in the text that supports Mayella's story.

The primary evidence against Tom came from Mayella and Bob

Ewell. The father and daughter were reasonably consistent in their ac-counts of the alleged rape, and neither one could be made to retract any-thing on cross-examination. They were steadfast; Mayella's "eye was blacked and she was mighty beat up."

Atticus's effective cross-examinations established that Mayella's right eye was injured and that her father, Bob, was left-handed, while Tom had no use of his left arm. This is meant to prove that Tom could not have administered the beating, since it must have come from the left side. But it does not strain credulity to conclude that he could have used his right hand to hit her right eye—either as her head was turned or perhaps with a backward slapping motion. Tom was a phys-ical laborer, a powerful man who admitted that even with his dam-aged arm he was "strong enough to choke the breath out of a woman and sling her to the floor." For Mayella, the shock of being attacked might make it difficult for her to fight back effectively, or to remem-ber the precise timing of the blows.[2]

There are other gaps in Tom's defense as well. He claimed that Mayella set out to seduce him, saving seven nickels so that she could send her sib-lings into town for ice cream. That story has its problems. It has Mayella lying in wait for an entire year, and then sending the children into town without even knowing whether Tom would show up on that particular day. Though Tom had to pass the Ewell cabin on his way to work for Link Deas, the attack occurred in November, when there was no cotton to be picked. Tom still worked "pretty steady" for Deas in the fall and winter-time, but apparently not every day.

Tom's narrative, then, requires us to believe that Mayella was cunning and predatory enough to hatch her plan, but she then doled out her year-long hoard of nickels without even knowing whether Tom would pass by that day. If Mayella were truly as desperate as she is painted by Tom (and Scout), wouldn't she have made certain that her nickels would really be put to their intended use?

Rape is often described as a crime of opportunism. A counternarra-tive, then, would be that Mayella had saved her nickels for no other rea-son than to give her siblings an otherwise unobtainable treat. Tom, as Mayella describes it, was in fact asked to help with some chores in the yard. Learning of the children's absence, he attacked her.[3]

Let me be clear that I do not sponsor this version; I am not arguing that Tom Robinson was a rapist. My point, however, is that Mayella's story is also coherent and supported by the facts adduced at trial. Atticus Finch undermined her credibility, but he did not, Scout's prejudices aside, prove Mayella to be a liar. As a simple matter of narrative interpretation, it is *possible* that Mayella was basically telling the truth.

Once we consider the possibility of Tom's guilt, and that Atticus might have known about it, we have to take a very different view of the cross-examination of Mayella Ewell. Was it ethical, could it still be admirable, for Atticus to treat Mayella as he did?

Atticus's story was harmful to Mayella. He held her up as a sexual aggressor at a time when such conduct was absolutely dishonorable and disgraceful. Atticus ensured that Mayella, already a near outcast, could have no hope whatsoever of any role in "polite" society.

The "She wanted it" defense in this case was particularly harsh. Here is what it said about Mayella. She was so starved for sex that she spent an entire year scheming for a way to make it happen. She was desperate for a man, any man. She repeatedly grabbed at Tom and wouldn't let him go, barring the door when he respectfully tried to disentangle himself. And in case Mayella had any dignity left after all that, it had to be insinuated that she had sex with her father.[4]

In short, the defense of Tom Robinson employed most, if not all, of the well-worn negative conventions historically used to debase and discourage rape victims. One writer calls these "the most insulting stereotypes of women victims," amounting to a judicial "requirement of humiliation."[5]

Does our view of Atticus change if it turns out that he used his trial skills to drag Mayella through the mud for the sole purpose of freeing the guilty?

The third possibility, in reality perhaps the most likely one, is that Atticus did not care about the relative truth of the charge and defense. He was appointed by the court to defend Tom Robinson, an obligation that he could not ethically decline or shirk. Atticus Finch was neither a firebrand nor a reformer. He'd spent his career hoping to avoid a case like Tom's, but having been given one, he was determined to do his best for his client. Not every Maycomb lawyer would have done as much.

In the classic formulation, every person accused of a crime is entitled to a vigorous defense. Guilt or innocence do not figure into the equation; that is for the jury to decide, not the attorney. It is not uncommon for lawyers to avoid learning, or forming strong convictions, about their clients' guilt, since zealous advocacy is required in either case.[6]

Agnostic lawyers take their clients as they find them, assigning to themselves the task of assembling the most persuasive possible defense supported by the facts of the case. Their goal is to create a reasonable doubt in the mind of at least one juror, not to "prove" the innocence of the client. Innocence is irrelevant. Doubt is all that matters.

Doubt, in turn, may be found only in the mind of the beholder. A case is not tried in the abstract, but rather to a very specific audience. It is the lawyer's job—the advocate's duty—to identify and address the sensibilities, predispositions, insecurities, and thought patterns of the jury. Following this model, Atticus Finch defended Tom Robinson neither in the name of truth nor in disregard of it. He defended Tom Robinson in a way that he hoped might work.[7]

Modern feminist writers have shed much light on the "classic" trial of rape cases, exposing the manner in which accepted defenses were built on layers of myth, prejudice, and oppression of women. In the once venerated but now much discredited words of English Chief Justice Lord Matthew Hale, rape was considered a charge "[E]asily to be made and hard to be proved, and harder to be defended by the party accused, tho' never so innocent."[8]

The general suspicion of rape victims was at times so great as to cause Dean John Henry Wigmore, the great expositor of the common law of evidence, to call for mandatory psychiatric evaluation before a complainant's testimony could be heard by a jury: "[Rape complainants'] psychic complexes are multifarious, distorted partly by inherent defects, partly by diseased derangements or abnormal instincts, partly by bad social environment, partly by temporary physiological or emotional conditions."[9]

There seems little doubt that Atticus Finch shared this mistrust of women, or at least those who claimed to have been sexually assaulted. He adopted it as his trial theme. Atticus twice told the jury that Mayella's testimony was uncorroborated. Later, after the verdict, he told his children that he had "deep misgivings when the state asked for and the jury gave a death penalty on purely circumstantial evidence," adding that there should have been "one or two eyewitnesses." Of course, Mayella's testimony was corroborated and there were two eyewitnesses. But in Atticus Finch's account, Mayella and Bob Ewell were not simply inadequate witnesses, they apparently did not count at all.

As to the jury, Atticus understood that "people have a way of carrying their resentments right into a jury box." He had a low opinion of the veniremen, who "all come from out in the woods." He knew that the case had to be pitched to their prejudices, understanding that "we generally get the jury we deserve." Perhaps Atticus thought he was speaking only of race, but can there be any doubt that the all-male jury was prejudiced against women as well? Atticus could not help smiling when he explained to Scout why Alabama prohibited women from serving on juries: "I guess it's to protect our frail ladies from sordid cases like Tom's. Besides, . . . I doubt if we'd ever get a complete case tried—the ladies'd be interrupting to ask questions."

It was against this backdrop wariness and condescension that Atticus Finch, rightly or wrongly, designed his defense to exploit a thematic catalog of misconceptions and fallacies about rape—each one calculated to heighten mistrust of the female complainant.

Fantasy. It appears to be an age-old male fantasy that women dream about rape. According to the defense, Mayella obsessed over Tom for a "slap year," saving scarce money and contriving to have her siblings away so that she could lure him into an assignation. With no provocation or encouragement, she seems to have deluded herself into believing that he might reciprocate her passion. Perhaps she even succeeded in bringing herself to believe that she had been raped.

Spite. Another sad stereotype is that of the spurned woman who cries rape in revenge. Tom, though kind to Mayella when she needed help around the house, resisted her sexual advances and refused to fulfill her physical needs. In return, she branded him a rapist and "she looked at him as if he were dirt beneath her feet."

Shame. It seems hardly to need saying that women lie out of shame.

Atticus told the jury that Mayella lied "in an effort to get rid of her own guilt, ... because it was guilt that motivated her. ... She must destroy the evidence of her offense." This is a theme that is played over and over in the literature on rape.

Sexuality. In the lexicon of rape defense, sexuality is closely related to shame, and no less likely to cause a woman to lie about being the victim of a crime. Since women can barely control, and sometimes cannot even understand, their desires, they proceed to victimize the men whom they ensnared. As Atticus explained it, "She knew full well the enormity of her offense, but because her desires were stronger than the code she was breaking, she persisted in breaking it. ... She was white, and she tempted a Negro. ... No code mattered to her before she broke it, but it came crashing down on her afterwards."

Confusion. Women may be so confused about sex that they do not even understand what they themselves have done. Mayella, who lived among pigs, whose family was unwashed and illiterate, was pitiable in her "cruel poverty and ignorance." And so the cross-examination proceeded to show her dazed unreliability. She couldn't keep her story straight, she couldn't provide a blow-by-blow description: "You're suddenly becoming clear on this point. A while ago you couldn't remember too well, could you? Why don't you tell the truth, child?"

The advocate's job is to provide the jury with reasons for acquittal. Atticus Finch gave his jury at least five separate justifications for disbelieving Mayella. His theory was that Mayella had entrapped Tom, his theme was that "she wanted it," and his frame was to transform the story from one about race into one about gender. Thus, Mayella lied, Atticus told the jury, perhaps in fantasy, or out of spite, or in shame, or as a result of sexual frustration, or maybe just because she was confused.

To Kill a Mockingbird was intended, above all, to be a story about race and racial oppression. In the America of 1960, the topic was daring and the points were probably best driven home through the use of didactic characters, almost stick figures. Atticus is good and noble, Tom guiltless and pure of heart, Mayella low-born and conniving. We know, of course, what Harper Lee intended, and the flaws in Tom's defense are really just weaknesses in the author's storytelling. But the flaws go unnoticed because the readers, earnestly complicit in the story, are anxious for Tom's vindication.

If Atticus Finch accurately gauged the jury that he faced, so too did Harper Lee understand hers. For Tom to be the most believable, Mayella must be the most disgraceful. We can no doubt all agree that in the fight against racism, a little class and gender bias can be an effective literary device. In formula fiction, the job of means is to bring us steadily to the end.

But how does that work in real life? When would a real Atticus Finch be justified in eviscerating a real Mayella Ewell in order to defend a real Tom Robinson? Always? Never? It depends? The absolute positions have their adherents, and the arguments are compelling on both sides. But this is not the place to rehearse at length the considerable literature criticizing and defending the adversary system.

Suffice it to say that adversary system purists cannot allow themselves to care about the defendant's innocence or guilt, insisting instead on counsel's utmost efforts to obtain an acquittal in either circumstance. We have all heard it said that

> an advocate, in the discharge of his duty, knows but one person in all the world, and that person is his client. To save that client by all means and expedients, and at all hazards and costs to other persons . . . is his first and only duty; and in performing this duty he must not regard the alarm, the torments, the destruction which he may bring upon others.[10]

Other writers—perhaps we should call them communitarians or relationalists—are more distressed by the dangers that the adversary system poses to "human or emotional equities."[11] In this regard, they are concerned that full-bore advocacy, for either party, may do irreparable harm to all involved.

For the traditionalists, then, the "She wanted it" defense would always be permissible (and perhaps even required), so long as one could raise it using nothing but the truth. Among postmodernists, or certain of them, the defense would always be suspect, since it relies on a theme and frame that assault human dignity.

Most lawyers (and most observers of lawyers) would probably try to steer a middle course, giving restrained approval for such a defense when counsel was convinced of its truth, yet denouncing it if used simply as a ploy.

Consider another cross-examination from another famous rape trial. On March 25, 1931, nine young African American men were arrested in Paint Rock, Alabama, and charged with the forcible rape of two white women. The alleged crime was said to have occurred on a moving train; it was brought to the attention of the authorities by a number of white youths who had been thrown off that same train by several of the eventual defendants. The matter was shortly brought to trial in Scottsboro, Alabama, and it therefore became known as the Scottsboro case.

The initial trial of the case was held only twelve days after the arrests. The entire county bar was appointed to represent the defendants, which, predictably, amounted to no defense at all. Eight of the nine defendants were found guilty and sentenced to death.[12] This outrage soon made the Scottsboro case a national cause célèbre, bringing the entire issue of lynch law and racial justice into the international spotlight.[13] One thing was clear. The Scottsboro Boys, as they were then called, were plainly innocent, the targets of a racially motivated frame-up.[14]

Once the original convictions were vacated by the U. S. Supreme Court,[15] Samuel Leibowitz, one of the foremost trial lawyers in America, arrived from New York to lead the defense. His position was simple. There had been no rape. The two women brought the false charges in order to cover up their own misconduct on the train.[16]

But the defense did not stop there. The alleged victims, Victoria Price and Ruby Bates, were portrayed as the last sort of people to be believed—promiscuous tramps at best, more likely prostitutes. Following the first convictions, affidavits were filed in court reporting that the two women were "notorious prostitutes and one of them . . . was arrested in a disorderly house in *flagrante delicto* with a colored man." Another source claimed that "it made no difference whether she slept with a white man or a negro to her and they would both get drunk and they danced with and embraced colored men, and would hug them and kiss them." One of the women was said to have asked to "meet and have intercourse with three men [on one] afternoon." The other was described as "dressed in a lewd and almost nude fashion" and "drunk and in a fight with another woman and she had her clothes up around her body . . . and exposed her private parts [in] a drunken, disgraceful spectacle in the presence of a number of colored people."[17]

At the first retrial, Victoria Price had to endure Samuel Leibowitz's ferocious cross-examination, which was described by one reporter as "the shredding of her life with a patient scalpel." Price had committed adultery and prostitution; she "treated" with black men; she traded sex for liquor, favors, money, food, companionship, and love. Following that tour de force, one headline read, "Leibowitz Impales Price Girl as Prostitute."

The assault on Victoria Price was made all the more brutal by the fact that it was designed solely to degrade her, and not to develop any evidence actually relevant to the case.[18] The defense, after all, was that the alleged intercourse had never occurred. There was no claim of consent, much less prostitution. Thus, the women's purported proclivities to have sex for hire and to "treat" with "negroes" had scant factual bearing on the case as it was tried.

The Scottsboro case sets the "advocacy" issue in severe relief. The cause was unquestionably just, yet the tactics were absolutely ruthless. Was it right or wrong to humiliate Victoria Price? Did Samuel Leibowitz have any choice, with the lives of his innocent clients on the line? But can any rule of legal ethics depend on the lawyer's faith in the particular client, who, after all, must by law be presumed innocent in every case?

The answer, I believe, is at once both stark and subtle. Advocates will use the tools they have. The adversary system all but ensures that every *available* argument will be employed.[19] Until prohibited or restricted or discredited or declared out of bounds, every line of defense *will be exploited.* Facts, character, bias, innuendo—it is counsel's job to locate the fault lines in the prosecution case. Faced with the alternative of a client's imprisonment or worse, the defense lawyer will fasten on vulnerability just as predictably as manure draws flies.

For proof of this proposition, we need only return to Atticus Finch.

As Scout's "love story" to her father makes plain, Atticus was a man of decency, honor, compassion, and courage. If he embraced the "She wanted it" defense, what ordinary lawyer could resist?[20] Atticus was able to recognize and rise above the race prejudices of his time, but he was not able to comprehend the class and gender prejudices that suffused his work. As he understood his obligations to his client, he was compelled to treat Mayella Ewell as he did. His disregard of even the slightest possibility that she might have been telling the truth evidences perhaps a moral or social failing, but not a professional one. In Atticus Finch, whose compensating virtues are universally respected, it is a failing that generations of admiring readers have readily forgiven or overlooked.

Atticus Finch, a pillar of the Maycomb establishment, told the jury to suspect Mayella Ewell and believe Tom Robinson. He asked them to reject the conventional story frame of racial subjugation, in favor of one premised on mistrusting women. In the Alabama of 1935, or even 1960, that was no small achievement. The "code" of his time and place required that a white woman's word always be accepted, and that a black man was never to be trusted. Atticus was not a civil rights crusader, but he was able to look past race in structuring his defense. He was even optimistic that the jurors might see the light and agree with him. Surely there had been other racial injustices in Maycomb, but we have no hint that any prior incident had ever stirred Atticus to action. He was, if anything, indulgent of the tendency to prejudice, and almost amused by the Ku Klux Klan.[21] What was special about the prosecution of Tom Robinson? What was it that enabled Atticus Finch to take his worthy stand?

Perhaps the time was right. Perhaps, upon appointment by the court, he simply felt that his duty was clear. And perhaps the social structure of Maycomb actually depended on the humiliation of Mayella Ewell, even while it required the conviction of Tom Robinson.

Bob and Mayella, after all, were a disappointment to their race, and that allowed the story to be reconstructed as a struggle between chaos and order. Social outcasts, the Ewells were drunk, illiterate, filthy, welfare-dependent, and worse. Tom Robinson, on the other hand, was a "respectable Negro," polite, hardworking, and not a troublemaker. Did Tom ever once set foot on the Ewell property without an "express invitation from one of them?" "No suh, Mr. Finch, I never did. I wouldn't do that, suh."

Scout believed Tom, because he fulfilled his assigned part in the social framework, as she well understood: "He seemed to be a respectable Negro, and a respectable Negro would never go up into somebody's yard of his own volition." Tom was so respectable that he did not even attempt to shoulder his way past Mayella, desperate as he was to escape from his awful dilemma: "Mr. Finch, I tried. I tried 'thout bein' ugly to her. I didn't wanta be ugly, I didn't wanta push her or nothin'."

Tom's propriety was so well regarded in Maycomb that Mr. Deas, his employer, interrupted the trial to shout from the spectators' gallery: "I just want the whole lot of you to know one thing right now. That boy's worked for me eight years an' I ain't had a speck o'trouble outa him. Not a speck."

In other words, Tom knew his place. He played his prescribed part, fitting into Maycomb society, presenting no challenge and no affront. He was the sort of "quiet, respectable, humble Negro" who would stand aside deferentially as white people passed.

Mayella and her father, though, were just the opposite. They broke the mold, insulted the norms, violated the rules and the culture. They were the very contradiction of everything that the "fine folks" of Maycomb stood for. If Tom Robinson never caused a "speck o'trouble," the Ewells were pure trouble.

Can there be any doubt that this unexpected role reversal, the proper Negro versus the offensive whites, allowed Atticus Finch, and to a lesser extent even the sheriff (and perhaps even the judge and the prosecutor), to see class, perhaps for the first time, as a more salient characteristic than race?

Of course, in the Alabama of 1935, race could not be dismissed. Innocent or guilty, Tom Robinson had to pay the price for allowing himself into an unforgivable predicament. But neither could class or gender be overlooked. As surely as Tom had to be convicted, Mayella Ewell, again, innocent or guilty, had to be disgraced.

Where does this leave us and what do we think now of Atticus Finch? At the very least we must renew our respect for his skill as an advocate. It is a great accomplishment, of course, to compel a bigoted Alabama jury to hesitate before convicting an innocent black man. But it would take a monumental performance indeed to accomplish that same feat for a guilty defendant. On a purely technical level, then, it is safe to say that Atticus remains an icon, if not an idol.

The deeper problem is more difficult, if not intractable. Whether Tom was innocent or guilty, Atticus no doubt fulfilled his obligations under the standard conception of professional ethics. But that only brings us directly to the hardest question of all. Is Atticus still a hero? Does his standing depend on Tom's innocence, or can we still idealize him if it turns out that Tom committed the crime? If Atticus knew, or ignored the possibility, of Tom's guilt, does that reduce him in our eyes to a talented but morally neutral actor?

For lawyers, the resolution lies not in guilt or innocence, but in truth. Atticus would betray his oath if he connived with Tom to make up lies about Mayella's character and actions. Short of concocting a dishonest story, however, Atticus had great latitude to conduct the trial as he did. The first challenge in Maycomb, perhaps even the most daunting one, was to obtain a fair trial for a black man charged with raping a white woman. In a culture that denies fair trials on the basis of race, no minority is safe. After all, the presumption that every black defendant will be convicted weighs most heavily on the innocent. By standing in the way of a racially motivated prosecution—even if Tom was in fact guilty as charged—Atticus was indeed doing everything he could to protect the blameless.

Atticus's own contribution to the defense was developed in his lawyer-created cross-examinations. And they were all based palpably on truth. Mayella was bruised about her right eye, Tom's left arm was crippled, and Bob was left-handed; there had been no medical examination and there was no physical evidence of rape; the younger Ewell children were uncharacteristically and mysteriously absent that day; Tom was a respectable, hardworking, married man. Under any concept of procedural fairness and burden of proof, the defendant would have to be allowed to make these points to the jury. A system could not achieve proof "beyond a reasonable doubt" if the jury is left unaware of facts that favor the defense.

Which brings us to Tom Robinson's testimony in his own behalf. As was Mayella, Tom was either lying or telling the truth about the events that November afternoon. There is no middle ground. And with only Scout's partisan account to inform us, we cannot fully resolve the discrepancies. That is a task that confronts every jury, bringing order to the turmoil of competing, self-interested, unreconcilable narratives. Lawyers are widely thought to impede this process by throwing up barriers to clarity and trust, but Atticus Finch ultimately demonstrates the moral value of advocacy. Whatever the whole story, he did all he could to exact a fair trial for Tom Robinson, using nothing but the truth.

NOTES

1. HARPER LEE, TO KILL A MOCKINGBIRD (1960).

2. There is yet another explanation for Mayella's injuries, one that shows the Ewells to be hiding something but that does not absolve Tom Robinson. Isn't it possible that Tom indeed raped Mayella, and that Bob Ewell beat up his daughter after discovering the rape? It is well known for rape victims to be blamed for what happened to them. It is easily imaginable that Bob Ewell, living in Maycomb, Alabama, in the 1930s, might have taken out his anger on the victim of the crime. So the fact that Mayella protected her father does not mean that she lied about being raped.

3. Tom denied having sex with Mayella, but recall that Tom testified to Bob Ewell's words upon entering the cabin: "[Y]ou goddamn whore, I'll kill ya." What would cause Bob to react that way if all he had seen was Tom trying to push his way past Mayella? Wouldn't the scene, as Tom depicted it, be more likely to cause Bob Ewell to be enraged at the intruder? On the other hand, if Bob really did see Tom "ruttin' on my Mayella," he could easily have reacted with anger and fury at his daughter.

And we must also ask why Mayella would go so far as to claim having been raped? Given the events as Tom gave them, a charge of attempted rape would obviously have served her purposes just as well, and without imposing upon her the stigma of a rape victim. Why would Mayella increase the import of her lie, when the only result would be to make herself even more of a pariah in Maycomb?

4. "She says she never kissed a grown man before an' she might as well kiss a nigger. She says what her papa do to her don't count." In Mayella's case, the explosive charge of incest seemed to evoke no outrage. Contrast the case of Richard Allen Davis, convicted in 1996 for the kidnapping, rape, and murder of a twelve-year-old girl. At his sentencing, in an effort to save himself from execution, Davis testified that he had refrained from raping the child because she begged him, "Just don't do me like my Dad." His slander of the victim and her family did not succeed. Judge

Thomas C. Hastings said that Davis's defiant statement made it "very easy" to sentence him to death.

5. SUSAN ESTRICH, REAL RAPE 56, 53 (1987).

6. Many lawyers and advocacy teachers, myself included, take the view that a lawyer *should* insist that clients tell counsel all about the events of the charged crime. Full disclosure is necessary to an adequate defense.

7. Atticus no doubt was aware that his southern, Christian, Bible-reading jurors would be familiar with the basis for his defense. It parallels the biblical tale of Potiphar's wife. As the jurors surely knew, she attempted to seduce Joseph, who refused her advances. She spitefully accused him of rape, which led to his imprisonment by Pharaoh. Genesis 39:7–20.

8. MATTHEW HALE, THE HISTORY OF THE PLEAS OF THE CROWN *635 (1778), *quoted in* Ronet Bachman and Raymond Paternoster, *A Contemporary Look at the Effects of Rape Law Reform: How Far Have We Really Come*, 84 J. CRIM. L. & CRIMINOLOGY 554 (1993).

9. JOHN HENRY WIGMORE, EVIDENCE IN TRIALS AT COMMON LAW, (James H. Chadbourn ed., rev. ed. 1970)(originally published in 1904), *quoted in* ESTRICH, *supra* note 5, at 48.

10. Trial of Queen Caroline 8 (1821), reported in MONROE FREEDMAN, UNDERSTANDING LAWYERS ETHICS 65–66.

11. Carrie Menkel-Meadow, *The Trouble with the Adversary System in a Postmodern, Multicultural World*, 38 WM & MARY L. REV. 5, 6 (1996).

12. The procedural history of the case is complex, involving seven separate retrials and two important decisions by the U. S. Supreme Court.

13. The NAACP and the International Labor Defense (a Communist Party affiliate) vied over control of the defense of the case, in which they were supported by the great weight of public opinion, at least in the North.

14. One of the alleged victims, Ruby Bates, subsequently recanted the charges. She testified for the defense at several of the retrials and toured the country, raising support and funds, for the defendants. Though it took over forty years, even the state of Alabama eventually acknowledged the innocence of the Scottsboro defendants when Clarence Norris, the last survivor among them, was pardoned in 1976 on the basis of "innocence." That decree, signed by Governor George Wallace, marked the first time in its history that Alabama conferred a pardon on the basis of innocence rather than forgiveness. William Rashbaum, *Funeral Held for Last "Scottsboro Boy,"* UNITED PRESS INTERNATIONAL, Jan. 31, 1989.

15. Powell v. Alabama, 287 U.S. 49 (1932).

16. The likelihood of a false rape charge was taken for granted at the time. Supporters of the Scottsboro defendants pointed out that this was "a common experience in the pathology of women," and that "nine out of ten charges of rape are false and are due to a peculiar psychological condition of the woman." These "rape fantasies" often misled even the most experienced judges, leading to the conviction of

"innocent men accused of rape by hysterical women." JAMES GOODMAN, STORIES OF SCOTTSBORO 168–71 (1994), and sources cited therein.

17. *Id.* at 186–88, and sources cited therein. Unless noted, all subsequent quotations concerning the Scottsboro case are taken from Goodman's exceptional book.

18. By the time Leibowitz entered the case, Ruby Bates had become a defense witness.

19. Samuel Leibowitz no doubt saw himself as doing no more than fighting fire with fire. He had to endure the anti-Semitic taunts of the prosecution and the constant reference to the defendants as "niggers." When Leibowitz objected, one prosecutor replied, "I ain't said nothin' wrong. Your Honor knows I always make the same speech in every nigger rape case." The defense objection was not sustained. Eric Sundquist, *Blues for Atticus Finch, in* THE SOUTH AS AN AMERICAN PROBLEM 181, 199 (Larry J. Griffen & Don H. Doyle eds., 1995).

20. Nor could Atticus resist indulging in some creative exaggeration when he argued to the jury. During the cross-examinations of Bob Ewell, Sheriff Tate, and Mayella Ewell, Atticus had taken pains to imply that Mayella's blackened right eye was injured by a left-handed blow. There was no evidence about the angle of impact that might have caused her other bruises. By final argument, however, Atticus had it that "Mayella Ewell was beaten savagely by someone who led almost exclusively with his left." Apparently, even the most honest lawyers can fall prey to the temptation of embellishment.

21. Monroe Freedman, *Atticus Finch—Right and Wrong*, 45 ALA. L. REV. 475–76 (1994) (observing that Atticus referred to the Klan as a "political" organization, Professor Freedman asks, "David Duke, can you use a campaign manager who looks like Gregory Peck?").

CHAPTER SEVEN

SHEILA McGOUGH
The Impossibility of the Whole Truth

Anyone who has ever been to law school—and anyone who has ever seen a movie about it—will probably recognize the drill. On the first day of the first class of the first year in law school, one unfortunate student is called on and asked to recount the facts of the first case. Nervously paging through the casebook, the beleaguered soul generally manages to locate and read from the initial few paragraphs of the appellate opinion in question. The professor then begins the Socratic dialogue, aimed at demonstrating the flexibility of law, or perhaps (depending on the professor) its utter indeterminacy.

Whatever the professor's approach, however, it is nearly certain that she will regard the facts of the case as given. In most law school classes, and virtually all those in the formative first year, "the facts of the case" are viewed as the rote preamble to the truly interesting discussion of the law. Facts are static, confined, inert, stationary, passive, inanimate. Of course, we need to know "what happened" in order to apply (or manipulate) the doctrine, but only in the sense that an opera must have a plot in order to proceed from overture to finale. Just as opera-goers do not expect to be surprised by the story, law professors breeze quickly past the facts.

And if facts are trivial, well, you can pretty much forget about trials. Judging solely by the material in most first-year casebooks, one might easily conclude that appellate opinions—concerning torts, contracts, crimes, property—spring fully formed from some jurist's brow. There is hardly a suggestion that hardworking lawyers spent months or years investigating, assembling, managing, and finally presenting the facts of each case. As most classes are taught, the facts of a case are easily determined while the law is always subject to interpretation.

Real lawyers know better. Law school has it exactly backwards. In ac-tual litigation, the law is most often relatively clear while the facts are in-evitably obscure and equivocal. It is the rare case that presents a truly difficult issue of law, but almost every case involves endless variations of fact. Of course, by the time a matter gets to the U. S. Supreme Court the facts have been more or less washed out of it—filtered and purged through the appellate process so that the stark legal issues may be ad-dressed without complication. But even then the law choices are rela-tively few, often no more than two.

In contrast, there will be scores—maybe hundreds—of factual disputes in even the simplest of trials. Add to that the various shadings, inferences, combinations, and permutations, and a picture begins to emerge of the in-finite complexity of trials (a picture that is treated as little more than a palimpsest in most appellate opinions).

Why are trials so little appreciated by both appellate judges and law pro-fessors? Perhaps it is because of the common and understandable misap-prehension that there is such a thing as readily discernible truth, which needs merely to be related accurately in order for a trial to work. In this con-ception—of both trial and reality—events occur in linear fashion and may be perceived and recalled with reliable precision, in order to be understood and acted on by the trier of fact. Trial lawyers, in this model, would ideally act as facilitators, seeking out the necessary witnesses and producing them to tell their stories. Discrepancies, when presented, are explainable as either errors, misrepresentations, outright lies, or failures of memory. The job of the judge or jury, then, is to harmonize any inconsistencies or, failing that, to "look the witnesses in the eye" and decide who is telling the truth.[1]

One need not be a devout relativist or mad semiotician to realize that this bipolar view of justice is too neat to be real. Of course there is such a thing as objective reality and of course witnesses sometimes lie to achieve their own ends. But often, perhaps most often, all the witnesses are sin-cere and honest, no one is intentionally deceptive, the facts are truly am-biguous, and the varying accounts cannot be reconciled. In these circum-stances, the best the jury can do is to choose the "best" or most likely in-terpretation of events.

That is where lawyers come in. It is counsel's job to "make the case" by promoting the version of events most favorable to her client. This process is often touted by attorneys as the best possible way to discover the truth, but that is not quite right. It would be more accurate to say that adversarial storytelling is an inevitable feature of testimonial trials, where the stakes are high, the outcome uncertain, the fact finder neutral, and the "truth" ineffable. It is naive to think that anyone—in any conceivable system—would do anything but put the best available spin on the facts. The challenge, then, is to determine just how to accommodate—harness, control, regulate—the irrepressible impulse to advocacy.

One alternative would be to suppress advocacy by requiring lawyers to take objective positions, rather than argue the client's subjective case. Under this approach, for example, counsel could not "defend the guilty," but could only argue for mitigation. No rule of ethics or procedure, however, could force "the guilty" themselves to respect the same restraints as their attorneys. No doubt they would quickly learn to refrain from telling the complete story to their lawyers, resulting in trials filled with more falsehoods rather than fewer. Consequently, our current regime allows the lawyer to mount a vigorous defense while drawing the line at perjured testimony or malicious cross-examination. Yes, we still have plenty of perjury and too many belligerent and intimidating cross-examinations—but that is a flaw in execution, not concept.

The story of Sheila McGough, as told by the journalist Janet Malcolm, provides the perfect conclusion for our examination of trial lawyers' connection to the truth. Malcolm believes that Sheila McGough was wrongly convicted and sentenced to prison because the adversary legal system could not accommodate her insistence on telling "the whole truth." The defendant could not (or would not) cut and fit her defense to the needs of a linear trial, and she therefore fell victim to the prosecutor's superior talent at "purposive storytelling." Thus, as Malcolm relates it, the Sheila McGough case illustrates with great precision the conflict between "the whole truth" and "nothing but the truth." While Malcolm's observations are acute, her moral and social judgments are less compelling, as this final chapter explains.

Perhaps better than any other contemporary journalist, Janet Malcolm understands the highly nuanced art of trial advocacy, which she explores in fine detail in *The Crime of Sheila McGough*.[2] She is able to convey, in surprisingly few words, the complex and sometimes paradoxical relationship between veracity and truth, reality and proof. She appreciates the subtle complexity and inherent unruliness of facts.

The plot of a trial, as Malcolm sees it, revolves around two struggles:

> One struggle is between two competing narratives for the prize of the jury's vote. The other is the struggle of narrative itself against the constraints of the rules of evidence, which seek to arrest its flow and blunt its force. . . . The story that can best withstand the attrition of the rules of evidence is the story that wins.

In other words, a trial lawyer must bring order to chaos. As Malcolm explains, "truth is messy, incoherent, aimless, boring, absurd. The truth does not make a good story, that's why we have art." The full onslaught of untempered truth—the unmediated description of everything that happened and everything that was perceived—would overwhelm and confuse even the most attentive jury. Thus, counsel must pick and choose, reporting some facts while omitting others, emphasizing the most favorable events and sliding right past the inconvenient ones. To Malcolm this is the "work of narration—of transforming messy actuality into an orderly story."

And then the trial is won by the most elegant story, the one that accounts for the facts in the most meaningful way, the one with the most explanatory power, the one that speaks best to the jury in the most familiar terms: "Trials are won by attorneys whose stories fit, and lost by those whose stories are like the shapeless housecoat that truth, in her disdain for appearances, has chosen as her uniform." It is the advocate's task to weave together an intelligible narrative, not simply to produce an unending line of disjointed factlets. Truth, or at least the variety of truth that we achieve through trials, turns out to be a highly qualitative concept, requiring far more evaluation than the simple addition of its component parts.

And, in any event, the "whole truth," though demanded of witnesses by the customary oath, is impossible to achieve. "It runs counter to the law of language, which proscribes unregulated truth-telling and requires that our utterances tell coherent, and thus never merely true, stories." Even in the absence of the lawyers' craft, it turns out that "[m]emory functions as a ruthless editor of God's long-winded truth. It cuts through tedious, insignificant detail."

Bravo, then, for Malcolm the journalist, or even for Malcolm the anthropologist. Her powers of observation are acute and her description of the trial process is almost perfectly accurate. She knows what lawyers do for their clients and why they do it. She understands what works, how it works, and where the traps lie for the unwary.

But fewer cheers, or perhaps none at all, for Malcolm the social critic, as she has thoroughly misapprehended the moral value of adversary justice. Recognizing that effective trial narratives cannot be "merely true," Malcolm ultimately concludes that they are not true at all—indeed, that "truth is a nuisance in trial work."

> Law stories are empty stories. They take the reader to a world entirely constructed of tendentious argument, and utterly devoid of the truth of the real world, where things are allowed to fall as they may. Trial law shares a vocabulary with science—"fact," "evidence," "proof"—but its method is the opposite of scientific method, the experiment is always fixed. The method of adversarial law is to pit two trained palterers against each other. The jury is asked to guess not which side is telling the truth—it knows that neither is—but which side is being untruthful in aid of the truth.

She is wrong about law (and indeed, about science—more on that later). Trials are, in the final analysis, concerned with truth. Facts matter and lawyers are not free agents, licensed to embellish and dissemble at will. Though Malcolm asserts otherwise, trials ultimately rest on reality. While the process is imperfect it is not debased, or at least not so debased as Malcolm suggests.

All of which brings us to the crime of Sheila McGough and Janet Malcolm's heartfelt brief on the defendant's behalf.

Sheila McGough, a lawyer in solo practice, was convicted in 1990 of fourteen felonies and sentenced to three years in a federal penitentiary. McGough's crimes all involved assisting a client—a multiply convicted con man named Bob Bailes—in his ongoing financial frauds. Central among these was an "escrow scam" in which, according to the prosecution, McGough allowed her trust account to be used as a siphon by which her client relieved his victims of their funds.

The transactions were all documented, so McGough could not deny that she had acted as the conduit by which the money disappeared. But she disclaimed criminal intent. The use of her trust account had merely been an "accommodation" to Bailes, whom she believed to have been engaged in a legitimate business transaction. This is the classic stuff of trials. One big fact was uncontroverted—McGough had helped Bailes get his hands on the money—but all of the nuances were in doubt. What did Sheila McGough really think, know, intend, or believe about Bob Bailes's schemes? Was she a naive dupe or a willing accomplice? What did she actually say during a crucial telephone call, when one of the victims agreed to transfer $75,000 to her trust account? Did she promise to hold the money for safekeeping, as the prosecution contended? Or was it understood that the funds would be disbursed immediately, as she herself later claimed? Far from interstitial details, those were the questions that the jury had to answered in order to distinguish innocence from guilt.

Janet Malcolm first took an interest in Sheila McGough in 1996, about a year after her release from prison. In a letter to Malcolm, McGough insisted that federal prosecutors had "made up some crimes for me and found people to support them with false testimony." Intrigued, Malcolm spent a year "poking and peering" at the case, and eventually coming to the conclusion that McGough had been wrongly and unfairly convicted.

But why? Malcolm does not fully accept McGough's own contention that she was "framed" because she had "irritated some federal judges and federal prosecutors." Oh, Sheila was irritating all right, and that contributed to her downfall, but Malcolm avoids the conclusion that the prosecution was malicious or contrived. Instead, Malcolm believes that McGough was done in, ironically, by her own "preternatural honesty and decency." McGough was so honest, so committed to the "bigger game of imparting a great number of wholly accurate and numbingly boring facts," that she simply could not deliver a "plausible and persuasive and interesting" account of her own innocence. She was so decent that she could not bring herself to testify in her own behalf, lest she damage the client with whom she was accused of conspiring. Consequently, she disabled her lawyers from presenting a viable story that could counteract the "elegant" case constructed by the prosecution.

In other words, Sheila McGough fell prey to the epistemology of trials. Recall Malcolm's view that the case is won by the attorney who best overcomes the nuisance of truth, the lawyer who devises a story that "fits." Sheila could not make her story fit because she refused to cooperate with her own lawyers. She was so lacking in guile, so incapable of distinguishing and arranging the helpful facts, that she placed herself "beyond rescue by narrative." She was, it turns out, too truthful to be believed, too honest for her own good.

The prosecution, however, faced no such impediment. The story of McGough's guilt was well-managed and coherent, without a trace of the numbing disorder that plagued the defense. As explained by the lead prosecutor in his opening statement to the jury:

> Now the government doesn't contend that there was anything wrong with Sheila McGough representing Bob Bailes on criminal charges. It's what criminal defense attorneys do. But the evidence will show, ladies and gentlemen, that what led to her downfall and what led to these proceedings today is that instead of remaining at arms' distance from Bob Bailes, and remaining Bob Bailes' criminal lawyer, Sheila McGough came too close to Bob Bailes, and began to handle his business affairs, and as the business affairs of a con man like Bob Bailes involve conning people, so too did the defendant, Sheila McGough, become involved in the con schemes.

Malcolm calls this a "devastating opening address," and it built strength as it continued:

> Now the defendant worked closely with Bob Bailes in this scheme. Her role was to tell potential investors, people who were looking into the possibility of buying one of these insurance companies, victims . . . that if they sent to her account, her attorney trust account, a refundable deposit to hold one of those insurance companies, she would retain the deposit in her attorney trust account, in her escrow account. . . . Sheila McGough would tell the investors that she would hold the money in [her] account

and then having induced the investors to turn over the money to her, she would disburse it [to Bailes].

And, of course, there had to be a motive. In this case it was an alleged "romantic attachment" between Sheila and Bobby, supported by errant details such as receipts for roses from a local flower shop.

Janet Malcolm has little doubt that there has been a miscarriage of justice. Sheila McGough did not participate in any schemes, she did not deceive any investors, and she did not promise to hold anyone's money for safekeeping. Most certainly, she was not romantically involved with Bob Bailes, but only tried to protect his interests as her client. The conviction came, Malcolm believes, only because the prosecution was able to construct the best narrative, thus illustrating the inevitable triumph of "the forces of purposive storytelling against those of aimless truth-seeking."

That is Janet Malcolm's critique of the criminal justice system. It is dominated by the lawyers' search for a "story that fits" rather than one that is true. A preternaturally honest defendant such as Sheila McGough has no chance, since she is unwilling to cut and paste her account until it fits neatly into a powerful counter-story, a narrative of acquittal. "In a sense," says Malcolm, "everyone who is brought to trial, criminal or civil, is framed," because it is the framing of the story—the purposive arrangement of its facts by the prosecutor—that will eventually determine guilt. Or, as Malcolm also put it, "truth is a nuisance in trial work," and, as she might as well have said, the innocent get screwed.[3]

Or maybe not. Malcolm's premise of injustice rests on two assumptions: first, that Sheila McGough was innocent in fact; and second, that the criminal justice system was unable to accommodate, or even express interest in, her "devotion to the truth." As to the first point, we have only Janet Malcolm's less than totally definitive word. As to the second point, we will shortly see that Malcolm is entirely wrong.

Janet Malcolm believes Sheila McGough because, well, because she believes Sheila McGough. Having spent a year in close company with her—meeting Sheila's parents, joining her family for dinner and at church—Malcolm developed great faith in her subject: "Veracity was her defining characteristic, like the color of an orange. Her behavior may have been odd, deviant, maddening, but her devotion to the truth—almost like a disease in its helpless literalness—was an inspiring given."

To Malcolm's credit, she acknowledges the stubborn shortcomings inherent in such strongly held personal opinions: "We maintain a loyalty to our opinions that is like our loyalty to our friends; to change our minds seems a kind of betrayal. As nothing will now shake my faith in Sheila." But if nothing will shake her faith in Sheila, what is the point of reviewing the evidence?

It is a sad fact that we are all susceptible to deception, professional journalists included. It is possible that Sheila McGough ran a con on Janet Malcolm, just as McGough herself claims to have been duped by Robert Bailes. Another possibility, well known to trial lawyers, is that Sheila has convinced herself that she is innocent, though the facts are objectively otherwise. It could well be that Sheila McGough was "accommodating" Bob Bailes by allowing him to use her trust account and that she also had sufficient knowledge of his scheme to render her an accomplice. Once indicted, McGough would, of course, tend to remember and emphasize the legitimate aspects of her representation of Bailes, while suppressing (some might say conveniently forgetting) all the corner cutting. We have already seen Malcolm's description of memory as "a ruthless editor of God's long-winded truth. It cuts through tedious, insignificant detail." In much the same way, memory also may cut through nagging, worrisome detail, to allow us to believe in our own innocence. Sheila the naif might thus be innocent in her own eyes but guilty in the eyes of the law.

And she might be guiltier than that. She was, after all, convicted by a jury and the conviction was upheld on appeal. In a scathing review of Malcolm's book, Judge Richard Posner examined the actual trial record in the case *United States v. Sheila McGough.* Posner concludes that Malcolm's "use of the record is selective and misleading" and that "the case against Sheila McGough was much stronger than Janet Malcolm lets on."[4] He tersely proceeds to detail much compelling evidence of guilt that went unreported by Malcolm, including a witness named Blazzard who testified (unimpeached and uncontradicted) that McGough told him an outright lie about the disposition of the money in the trust account.

Our purpose here, however, is not to resolve the guilt or innocence of McGough. In any event, Malcolm concedes her "unwillingness to change my mind about Sheila," and Posner rests his case firmly on the immutable verdicts of two federal courts. No further analysis here would bring a clearer resolution. But it must be pointed out that Malcolm has engaged in the very same selective narration that she found so objectionable on the part of the prosecution. She elaborates on the facts that "fit" while minimizing or omitting much that is inconvenient, including the very existence of the above-mentioned Blazzard.

But even assuming that Malcolm is right and Posner wrong (along with the original judge, jury, and appellate court), that does not mean an injustice was done, much less that the judicial system is irretrievably flawed by virtue of its inability to appreciate "the whole truth." Because, as it turns out, Sheila McGough contributed to her own conviction in a way that could not be remedied by any lawyer or court.

If Sheila McGough is so inspiringly honest, why didn't the jury believe her? Were they bamboozled by the slick prosecution and its well-crafted narrative? Is it so, as Malcolm claims, that real truth is so shapeless as to be unrecognizable at trial and that innocent defendants are at a terrible narrative disadvantage? Well, not exactly. In fact, probably not at all.

As it turns out, Sheila McGough was not done in by her unwillingness to play the game, or even by her inability to match the prosecutor's polished storytelling. She did not refuse to allow truth to be "laboriously transformed into a kind of travesty of itself." Rather, she declined to testify at all. Whatever her story might have been, she chose not to share it with the jury, thus depriving them of the opportunity to test and compare her version of events with that of the prosecution. That could amount to a system-damning injustice only if McGough had somehow been gagged or unfairly prevented from testifying. But that was not the case.

Malcolm repeatedly attempts to cloak McGough's decision in the mantle of heroism. Though she might have saved herself by testifying, duty to client required that Sheila keep her silence. Says Malcolm,

[T]he decision not to testify was made not by her lawyers but by Sheila herself, out of protectiveness for her client. If she had testified in her own behalf, she would have been cross-examined and inevitably forced to answer questions about Bailes, and her answers might have been harmful to Bailes. To save herself at her client's expense was unthinkable.

When she finally spoke to the court at sentencing, McGough described her "deep feeling of duty—not affection—to my client," continuing that

> I felt that I could not ethically and properly take the stand and refute the lies that I heard as I listened to the government's case.... [I]t was not possible for me to put myself in the position of being interrogated under oath by the very prosecutors who had sent a target letter to my client, who had identified him in the indictment against me as a co-conspirator, someone having committed, himself, according to them, very serious crimes, and subject myself to interrogation under oath about matters dealing with that client.

Malcolm finds this explanation credible. "When you stop and think about what a lawyer's obligations to his client are, you realize that Sheila is simply fulfilling them to the letter: Lawyers are not supposed to bad-mouth their clients." And so Sheila's determination to protect her client at all costs led "magnificently and disastrously" to her conviction and imprisonment.

There is one slight problem with this account. Notwithstanding McGough's protestations and Malcolm's esteem, there was simply no ethical requirement that Sheila McGough refrain from testifying. It is true, of course, that lawyers are required to keep confidences and protect the interests of their clients. But there is an exception when the lawyer herself has been implicated in the client's crime:

> A lawyer may reveal [confidential] information to the extent the lawyer reasonably believes necessary . . . to establish a defense to a criminal charge or civil claim against the lawyer based upon conduct in which the

client was involved, or to respond to allegations in any proceeding concerning the lawyer's representation of the client.[5]

The purpose of this provision is precisely to allow lawyers to defend themselves in circumstances such as McGough's. In fact, the official commentary to the rule specifically contemplates a situation where a "person claim[s] to have been defrauded by the lawyer and client acting together."[6] By the time McGough faced trial, she owed no duty of either loyalty or silence to Bailes, nor would any judge or lawyer have expected her to maintain silence on Bailes's account.[7]

Of course, the formal rules of professional conduct are not the only bases for moral decision making. Perhaps Sheila McGough is all the more virtuous for having eschewed the self-defense exception in order to protect Robert Bailes. Literature and folklore both extol the nobility of such a selfless gesture, as in the case of the "Long Black Veil,"

Ten years ago on a cold dark night
Someone was killed beneath the town hall light.
There were few at the scene but they all agreed
That the man who ran looked a lot like me.
The judge said son what is your alibi?
If you were somewhere else you don't have to die.
I spoke not a word although it meant my life.
I had been in the arms of my best friend's wife.[8]

But if Sheila McGough was willing to sacrifice herself for the sake of Robert Bailes—out of affection, misplaced sense of duty, or even irrational devotion—that was her choice alone. The judicial system assumes that defendants will act autonomously in their own best interest; no one is compelled to testify, even in the name of truth. Sheila McGough was surely counseled that she risked conviction if she stayed off the witness stand; indeed, her lawyers complained to Malcolm that Sheila had "tied our hands."

It could have been a grave injustice if McGough had actually been prevented from testifying in her own behalf, if her story had been suppressed by some inviolable obligation. But that is not what happened.

No system can provide safeguards sufficient to protect a defendant bent on unnecessary self-destruction. Should the court have forced McGough to testify against her will? Should her own lawyers have violated her instructions or disclosed her confidences? Where would be the justice in that?

Responding to Richard Posner in the pages of the *New Republic,* Janet Malcolm summarizes one of her themes as "the paucity in law, as in life, of indisputable facts."[9] She explains further that "[i]t is the beauty and the problem of our system of advocacy law that doubt hovers and lingers over almost every case that comes to trial. No member of any jury—even in the apparently 'open and shut' cases—can ever know for sure what happened or who is lying and who is telling the truth."

Well, sure. We weren't there so we can't know what happened; even Richard Posner would not argue with that proposition. Therefore—with Posner's (more or less) approval, and to Malcolm's (periodic) chagrin— we have to rely on lawyers' reconstructions in order to make sufficient sense of a crime or accident, or even a breach of contract.

Malcolm recognizes the challenge of this endeavor, and she describes its essence better than most: "History is a story chafing against the bonds of documentary fact. Trial lawyers are a species of historian who work in a more charged atmosphere and for higher stakes than do regular, clientless historians, but who are part of the same guild of hobbled narrators. (Biographers and journalists are other members.)"

She is alert to the ambiguity and imprecision of "facts" in a way that seems to have escaped Richard Posner almost entirely. While Malcolm tries to speak of truth, Posner resorts to the trial record. When Malcolm says that McGough committed no crime, Posner replies that the evidence was sufficient to support the conviction. They talk past each other, using different languages. That is understandable, more than understandable, given that Posner went directly from law school teaching to the appellate bench. Returning to our opening theme, both law professors and appellate judges tend to regard facts as neatly given, recoiling from the idea that they might be messy and indeterminate. Show me the record, says the appellate judge, and I will tell you whether the conviction should stand. Or, as Malcolm puts it, "[a]s an agent of the desire for closure, Posner is naturally impervious to the doubts my book casts on the narrative he so confidently presents as if it had been written by God rather than by a capable government lawyer."

While Janet Malcolm shows great understanding and appreciation for trial lawyers' art, she has much less respect for their values. To her, structured stories lawyers tell are tendentious and misleading, loosely tethered (if at all) to anything real or authentic. In Malcolm's memorable phrase, "Trials are won by attorneys whose stories fit, and lost by those whose stories are like the shapeless housecoat that truth, in her disdain for appearances, has chosen as her uniform."

Alas, Janet Malcolm has confused the notions of truth and reality. Reality—the idea of what happened—is indeed as shapeless and disorganized as Malcolm declares. It is careless, unsettled, confused. The more one attempts to describe it, the harder it becomes to separate meaningful information from the hopeless welter of random details. It might well be, as Malcolm posits, that Sheila McGough's downfall was due to her "maddeningly tiresome and stubborn" inability to refrain from "imparting a great number of wholly accurate and numbingly boring facts." In other words, she could not—or would not—winnow inexhaustible reality into a more refined measure of "nothing but the truth."

Legal truth, it turns out, represents the conscious organization of reality, when facts are culled and arranged in such a way as to allow conclusions, decisions, agreements. Truth is necessary to answer a question or support a proposition, and is consequently deliberate in nature. Malcolm is wrong, therefore, when she contrasts "the forces of purposive storytelling against those of aimless truth-seeking." Indeed, "aimless truth seeking" is nearly an oxymoron, and certainly not a task that any judicial system can perform.

Even in science—Malcolm's paradigm of truth seeking—no investigator attempts to accumulate, much less comprehend, the full shapeless expanse of reality. No less an authority than Richard Feynman, Nobel laureate in physics, cautioned against admonitions to pay attention to all available data: "You can't look at everything. When you look at everything, you can't see the pattern." Rather, Feynman emphasized the importance of "the imagination and the judgment of what to record and what to omit," even when seeking scientific truth.[10]

Gerald Holton, a historian of physics, explained that "all readings are not data. Sometimes you have to have the feeling in the tips of your fingers to understand what the difference is," adding that Albert Einstein used the word *Fingerspitzengefühl* to describe this process.[11] In science, noted the physical chemist David Eisenberg, "[t]he facts never speak for themselves. They're always interpreted."[12]

Niels Bohr, the great Danish physicist, might well have been speaking of trials when, in 1927, he announced the quantum principle of "complementarity." According to Bohr, for every measurable quantity there exists a complementary quantity: the more accurately one measures the first, the more difficult it becomes to measure its complement. At his first lecture devoted to this observation, Bohr was immediately asked a challenging question: "What, then, is complementary to truth?" Without hesitation, Bohr replied, "Clarity."[13] That is a lesson, of course, for trial lawyers. More facts produce less clarity.

In the case of Sheila McGough, as in almost all litigation, there was little doubt about the applicable law. The intentional diversion of funds from her trust account would be a crime; no one even wasted time arguing about that. But was the money actually diverted? Did she lie to the victims of the con? What was the nature of her intent? Those are questions of fact—incredibly intricate and perplexingly profound. Janet Malcolm has done a great service by reminding us that it is scarcely within our resources to resolve such issues definitively, and that uncertainty persists even when appellate judges reduce the facts to a few stiff, final paragraphs.

Trial lawyers also do a great service, underappreciated as they are, by organizing the narratives that extract shape and meaning from the whole truth. There is a moral in that.

NOTES

1. It seems an article of faith that honesty can be discerned through the simple process of "looking the witness in the eye," a mantra that was repeated over and over, for example, in the impeachment trial of President Clinton as the House managers sought permission to bring witnesses to the well of the Senate. "Wouldn't you

want to observe the demeanor of Miss Lewinsky and test her credibility?" urged House manager Ed Bryant. "Look into her eyes." This credulous belief in one's ability to recognize truth or falsehood serves further to demean the work of trial lawyers, who realize that the real burden of establishing facts lies in the painstaking accumulation of corroborating details. Indeed, nearly all studies show that people have only random success at recognizing falsehoods on the basis of demeanor.

2. JANET MALCOLM, THE CRIME OF SHEILA McGOUGH (1999).

3. Here is what she did say: "In the unjust prosecution . . . much of the work of narration—of transforming messy actuality into an orderly story—has already been done. . . . For truth to prevail at trial, it must be laboriously transformed into a kind of travesty of itself."

4. Richard Posner, *In the Fraud Archives*, NEW REPUBLIC, Apr. 19, 1999, at 29.

5. American Bar Association, MODEL RULES OF PROFESSIONAL CONDUCT Rule 1.6(b)(2)(1999). See also American Bar Association, MODEL CODE OF PROFESSIONAL RESPONSIBILITY DR 4–101(C)(4) ("A lawyer may reveal . . . confidences or secrets necessary . . . to defend himself or his employees or associates against an accusation of wrongful conduct").

6. MODEL RULES OF PROFESSIONAL CONDUCT Rule 1.6(b)(2), cmt. ¶18.

7. Nor is the self-defense exception the only ethics rule McGough seems to have overlooked. Even at her sentencing she continued to refer to Bailes as though he were her current client. But her own indictment raised an absolutely unresolvable conflict of interest between McGough and Bailes, which should have caused her immediately to withdraw from his representation. MODEL RULES OF PROFESSIONAL CONDUCT Rule 1.7(b).

8. There are numerous contemporary recordings of this folk song, each making the same point with slightly different lyrics, including thirteen separate renditions by Joan Baez. See, e.g., <http://baez.woz.org/jbdiscSA.html>.

9. Janet Malcolm, *Case Closed*, NEW REPUBLIC, May 31, 1999, at 4.

10. Quoted in DANIEL KEVLES, THE BALTIMORE CASE 263 (1998). Or consider the view of the biologist David Baltimore, another Nobel laureate and now the president of the California Institute of Technology, that a scientist must inevitably make judgments about the usefulness of data. "Deciding when to write up a study is an arbitrary and personal decision. A paper is written when an investigator decides that a story can be told that hangs together [and] makes sense." David Baltimore, Statement, HEARINGS ON SCIENTIFIC FRAUD, May 4, 1989, at 107–9, quoted in KEVLES, *supra*, at 386–87.

11. Quoted in KEVLES, *supra* note 10, at 486.

12. Quoted in id..

13. Lawrence Litt, *One Thing Is Certain: They Mysteries of Physics*, N.Y. TIMES, May 18, 2000, at A30.

INDEX

ABOUT THE AUTHOR

Steven Lubet is Professor of Law at Northwestern University, where he directs the award-winning Program on Advocacy and Professionalism. Professor Lubet is the author of a dozen books including *Modern Trial Advocacy* (2d ed. 1997) and *Judicial Conduct and Ethics* (3d ed. 2000).